A History of the Screenplay

MW00772085

A History of the Screenplay

Steven Price

School of English, Bangor University, UK

palgrave
macmillan

First published 2013 by
PALGRAVE MACMILLAN

Palgrave Macmillan in the UK is an imprint of Macmillan Publishers Limited, registered in England, company number 785998, of Houndmills, Basingstoke, Hampshire RG21 6XS.

Palgrave Macmillan in the US is a division of St Martin's Press LLC, 175 Fifth Avenue, New York, NY 10010.

Palgrave Macmillan is the global academic imprint of the above companies and has companies and representatives throughout the world.

Palgrave® and Macmillan® are registered trademarks in the United States, the United Kingdom, Europe and other countries.

ISBN 978-0-230-29181-2   ISBN 978-1-137-31570-0 (eBook)
DOI 10.1057/9781137315700

A catalogue record for this book is available from the British Library.

A catalog record for this book is available from the Library of Congress.

Contents

Acknowledgements

I am indebted to the British Academy for an award under their Small Research Grant scheme, which in combination with Bangor University's sabbatical arrangements enabled me to conduct some of the primary research and to write up the results. The book has its origins in a few chapters originally proposed as part of a project that became *The Screenplay: Authorship, Theory and Criticism* (Palgrave Macmillan, 2010). I am grateful to the anonymous readers of that proposal for recognising that the material would be better organised as two separate projects; to Christabel Scaife, who acted as editor on the first of them; and to Felicity Plester, whose infectious enthusiasm and commitment to this area of research has been a continuing source of encouragement. It has latterly fallen to Chris Penfold actually to drag the thing out of me; many thanks to both Felicity and Chris, and to Cherline Daniel, for their extreme patience and unfailing courtesy.

The biggest change in the field since I completed the first of the projects has been in the flowering of the Screenwriting Research Network (SRN). While conducting research for that book I was under the impression that I was almost alone in writing about this area; it turns out that several other people were independently working on screenplays, all of us under the same misconception. It has taken the growth of the SRN to put these people in touch with one another. For that and much more, I, like many others, am indebted to the tireless efforts of Ian Macdonald and Kirsi Rinne, and to those who have been instrumental in organising the annual conferences I have been fortunate enough to attend: Kirsi at Helsinki in 2009, Eva Novrup Redvall at Copenhagen in 2010, Ronald Geerts and Hugo Vercauteren at Brussels in 2011 and J. J. Murphy and Kelley Conway at Madison in 2013. Two further, related developments have been the founding of the *Journal of Screenwriting*, under the editorship of Jill Nelmes, and the establishment of the London Screenwriting Research Seminar, co-ordinated by Adam Ganz.

Through these means I have encountered so many people whose comments, advice and scholarship have been helpful that I could not possibly name them all, but I must give warm thanks to Steven Maras, J. J. Murphy and Paul Wells, while Margot Nash saved me from a howler I was certain I hadn't committed, but had. David Bordwell, Ian

Macdonald, Jill Nelmes and Claus Tieber all generously gave me access to some of their research findings. Outside the conference circuit I have been grateful for the discussions, face-to-face and by email, with Joanne Lammers, Patrick Loughney, Tom Stempel and Selina Ukwuoma. What has emerged is a kind of loose-knit research community in which there is no party line, people from a remarkably diverse range of specialisms are welcomed, and while disagreements may sometimes be pointed, they are always good-humoured, generous and free of the aggressive pursuit of self-interest. Who knew?

What has not changed is the unfailing helpfulness and meticulous scholarship of the staff at the many different libraries whose archives I have explored. I must especially thank Barbara Hall and Jenny Romero at the Margaret Herrick Library, Academy of Motion Picture Arts and Sciences, Los Angeles; Karen Pedersen and Joanne Lammers at the Writers Guild Foundation Library, Los Angeles; Patrick Loughney at the Library of Congress, Washington, D.C.; and Jonny Davies at the Reuben Library, British Film Institute, London. On a much earlier visit to the United States I benefited greatly from the assistance of Ned Comstock at the Doheny Library of the University of Southern California, and Charles Silver at the Museum of Modern Art in New York.

Closer to home, I learned a great deal from my doctoral students, Ann Igelström and Chris Pallant, and Chris's post-doctoral work continues to interact productively with my own interests. Julia Knaus's internship at Bangor University in 2013 has been a godsend, and Michelle Harrison has uncomplainingly tidied up several loose ends left behind when I embarked on a period of research leave. I am grateful to Domini Stallings for the cover illustration, and to Russell Hall for assistance with the final design; my thanks to Domini more generally, and to Joey and Abigail, are beyond words.

Some of the material in Chapter 1 considerably expands on arguments I previously presented in 'The First Screenplays? American Mutoscope and Biograph Scenarios Revisited', *Journal of Screenwriting* 2.2 (2011); conversely, the section on the AM&B scenarios in Chapter 2 is considerably condensed from the same article.

Introduction

Among the 'Thirteen Film Scores' that Yoko Ono created in 1968 is 'Film No. 4', entitled 'Bottoms'. Here is the remainder of the text: 'String bottoms together in place of signatures for petition for peace.'[1]

Is this a screenplay? From one perspective the question is quite pointless: the text fulfils whatever function Ono intended it to have, whether that be for herself or for anyone else to develop into a film; it is, perhaps, a piece of conceptual art, or an open invitation, like her 'Six Film Scripts' of 1964, which 'were printed and made available to whoever was interested at the time or thereafter in making their own versions of the films, since these films, by their nature, became a reality only when they were repeated and realised by other film-makers'.[2]

The question does matter, however, if we are interested in the history of the screenplay, because the Ono texts show that quite literally anything could, in theory, function as a scenario. The word 'scenario', which is one of the terms used before the coinage of our word 'screenplay' (and all such terms are problematic), captures very well the sense of a pre-production *idea* for a film; and unless this idea is posited within an industrial context, or at least one that requires a division of labour, that idea can be retained in any textual form whatsoever, or indeed just in the film-maker's head. In the earliest days of cinema many, perhaps most, films would have been made without written planning, while digital technology today means that distinctions between writing, shooting and post-production stages are becoming increasingly unclear. Arguably, both print culture and industrial-scale film-making, both of which would seem to be necessary for screenplays to exist, are in terminal decline, and today this opens up possibilities for radically new ideas of what a screenplay could be.

Conversely, today's published screenplays and screenwriting manuals pose a different problem: seen in their light, a history of the screenplay would not be a piecemeal catalogue of innumerable different kinds of material, but instead would be quite brain-numbingly repetitive. The form appears remarkably consistent, even in terms of length, with the typical script being around 120 pages long, with those for certain genres such as light comedy and, in particular, children's films being somewhat shorter—perhaps 85 to 90 pages. This is usually held to result from a rule of thumb whereby one page equals one minute of screen time, a convention that itself derives from industrial requirements: the length of the script enables an initial estimate to be made of the length of the proposed film. For similar reasons, the contemporary screenplay has a striking regularity of format in such matters as scene headings ('slug lines') and the lineation of the different elements of the text, including the presentation of dialogue and prose descriptions of the action.

On these counts, 'Bottoms' is out, and we might suggest that the terms Ono uses—'score' and 'script'—are quite precise and apposite. Digging a little deeper, we might discover that the word 'screenplay' does not appear as a compound noun until the 1930s, a decade that also saw the now familiar screenplay format emerging, in embryonic form at least, following the introduction of sound. Yet neither the word nor the form materialised out of thin air. The two-word term 'screen play' has a longer history, stretching back at least to 1916, when it referred to the film rather than the script, for which other terms—'scenario' and the just-emerging 'continuity'—were in use.[3] In turn, these had replaced the rough outlines of action that formed the only written planning of many films prior to the introduction of the industrialised Hollywood studio system in 1913. Ono's text is not a 'screenplay', but it has much in common with these earliest forms of screenwriting in functioning as a simple prompt or invitation to the film-maker.

A history of the screenplay, then, needs to explore several interconnected texts and practices. It should be attentive to the relationship between the written documents and their functions, distinguishing between screen*plays* and screen*writing*, the latter of which may encompass both the composition of the texts themselves and other kinds of cinematic 'writing' such as filming or editing. It also needs to examine the historical development of the screenplay as a particular kind of script, its emergence from other kinds of cinematic pre-text such as the scenario and the continuity, and the often confused relationships between these various kinds of text and the terminologies used to define them.

Screenplays and screenwriting

In *FrameWork: A History of Screenwriting in the American Film* (1988), Tom Stempel affirms that following the introduction of sound, 'screenwriters... were smart enough to master the new craft of writing for talking pictures. The new craft, in fact, was not all that different from the old.'[4] Although Stempel writes this in the context of an account of screenwriters as storytellers, there is perhaps an implication that mastering this 'craft' required the mastery of a particular textual *form*, which would tend to support the view that this form acquired its shape during the silent period, with relatively straightforward alterations due to the introduction of sound.

Marc Norman, whose general survey *What Happens Next: A History of American Screenwriting* was first published in 2007, is more explicit:

> By the end of the 1910s the screenplay had acquired its definitive format, a text divided into individual, numbered scenes, each new scene beginning with a capitalized slug line that usually included the names of the characters in the scene and an indication of whether the shot was day or night, and then a paragraph, perhaps as little as a sentence, of scene description. The scene's dialogue then cascaded down the center of the page, interrupted by more scene description when necessary. This format, still the industry standard, evolved from multiple sources but mostly from Thomas Ince.[5]

This view is not necessarily either right or wrong; it is instead a matter of perspective. If we are content to know simply that some elements of today's screenplays can be found in those of the silent era, and perform similar functions, then Norman's thumbnail sketch may be sufficient. We are then left with a screenplay that has changed little over time. If, however, we concentrate on the implications of his assumption that this essentially unchanging text remains an 'industry standard', then we might begin to focus attention on the relationships between industrial and formal change. For example, clearly there must have been some significant changes between the silent and the sound eras in the representation of dialogue. We might then begin to look for evidence of how the written text responded over time to the demands of differing modes of industrial production. At this greater level of detail, we could begin to think that what Norman might regard as rather trivial changes in form are in fact crucial in identifying significant changes in industrial practice.

Beyond this, neither Norman nor Stempel (in *FrameWork*, at least) are especially interested in the relationship between textual form and industrial function. As the titles of their books suggest, their focus is on screen*writing* as an activity, rather than screen*plays* as material texts. To the extent that this distinction can be made, a consideration of screenwriting (at least in these two books) engages such matters as the working lives and careers of a large number of individual writers at different studios, their recurrent themes or story ideas and so on. Equally important within this approach are matters of broader concern such as censorship, the role of screenwriters' unions, the complexities surrounding writing credit, the work of blacklisted Hollywood writers in the 1950s[6] or the position of women screenwriters within the industry.[7] What emerges is a kind of shadow history of Hollywood from the writer's point of view, a little like Richard Corliss's 1974 'pantheon' of writers that shadows Andrew Sarris' 1968 pantheon of directors.[8] None of these critics, however, is particularly interested in a screenwriter's *style*; instead, they are examining Hollywood film as a storytelling medium, much as, in a different way, does the recent work of both David Bordwell and Kristin Thompson.[9]

In his 2009 study *Screenwriting: History, Theory and Practice*, Steven Maras approaches screenwriting from a very different angle. Again, he does not engage in any detail with screenplay texts themselves, but whereas Stempel and Norman are interested in the working lives of the writers, Maras explores the 'discourses surrounding screenwriting'—the construction of ideas *about* screenplays. Equally importantly, he follows the lead of many practitioners and earlier commentators in extending the meaning of the term 'screen writing' to include 'writing not *for* the screen, but *with* or *on* the screen. It can refer to a kind of "filmic" or "cinematic" or audiovisual writing'. Maras promotes the term 'scripting' to accommodate these practices, and in part his book is an effort to examine the causes and consequences of what he sees as the damaging attention to the written document at the expense of these other forms of scripting.[10] Maras's book is also exceptionally helpful in historicising both the term 'screenplay' and the emergence of the kind of text to which it properly refers, and he notes the confusions that can arise from using the word as an umbrella term to accommodate earlier, different forms such as the scenario and the continuity.

Although each of these studies is very different from the others, what connects them is that, aside from a very small number of quotations here and there, the written texts themselves—scenarios, shooting scripts, screenplays—are almost entirely absent. The present book, by contrast, makes these texts the centre of attention, and for this reason, among others, it does not aim to reproduce the storytelling drive of Stempel or Norman. Instead, while being organised in an approximately chronological fashion, it pauses regularly to examine matters of textual interest and signs of historical change in the writing of cinematic pre-texts. It is not especially interested in any particular writer's recurrent narrative or thematic concerns, as Corliss is; and it engages only infrequently with the idea that the screenplay can function as a mode of personal expression, although there are important exceptions, as in the work of Carl Mayer and Ingmar Bergman. Instead, it aims to show how prevailing relationships between screen writing and film industries brought certain modes of writing into being at certain times, how and why those relationships changed, and what the scripts resulting from these changes typically look like.

An industrial history of the screenplay

Any commentary on screenwriting is bound to observe that it is tied to a particular industry in ways that the novel, poem or even theatrical play is not. These industrial contexts impose some limitations on the properties of the text. As with other modes of writing, it makes sense to examine screenplay form in relation to function, except that in this case the focus is likely to be less on the expressive qualities of the text than on the ways in which it engages the concerns of the other members of a team working on the production of a film. This is certainly one of the reasons why the most extensive studies of screenwriting have been in relation to Hollywood cinema. Not only has Hollywood been the world's dominant film economy since the end of the First World War, but it also took the lead in organising and dividing film labour into discrete practices—producing, directing, shooting, editing and so on—and adapting the film script to address these readerships. Consequently, significant changes to the organisation of labour are likely to bring about changes in screenwriting itself.

   This is the approach taken in what is undoubtedly the most influential account of the American screenplay, by Janet Staiger in her contributions to *The Classical Hollywood Cinema*, co-written with Bordwell and Thompson, and published in 1985. Like Stempel and Norman, Staiger analyses few scripts in any great detail. Unlike these other writers, however, she is concerned to show that changes in the mode of industrial production necessitated changes in the forms that screenplays and their precursors took. Working at this more particular level of generalisation enables Staiger to establish certain norms within which screenwriting functions. There are exceptions to the rules—for example, when a powerful producer or director was permitted to develop a particular project in relative freedom—and certain parameters within them, but during any given period film scripts would be presented in ways that enabled them to fulfil their necessary industrial functions within the mode of production that was dominant at that time.

Because all subsequent studies of screenplay history need to take account of Staiger's work as a starting point, it is worth outlining here the six major relevant stages in Hollywood screenwriting history that she identifies in her contributions to *The Classical Hollywood Cinema* and in her important essay 'Blueprints for Feature Films: Hollywood's Continuity Scripts'.[11] Each of these stages was dominated by a particular mode of production that led, where necessary, to the creation of a particular form of written pre-text to accomplish its objectives.

1. During the 'cameraman system', essentially a one-person mode of production that prevailed from 1896 to 1907, a script was not necessary, other than perhaps as an aide-mémoire or memo to self.
2. 1907 to 1909 saw the emergence of the 'director system', which introduced a rudimentary division of labour between a director, whose role was akin to that of the theatrical stage director, and a photographer. With more than one person having to work on a project, the 'outline script', perhaps no more than a few words to indicate the content of each scene and their sequence, often became necessary.
3. Between 1909 and 1914 the increasing size of companies and the need to increase supply brought with them a more complex and hierarchical structure. This was the 'director-unit system', in which a company would utilise several directors, each working more or less autonomously with a particular production team or unit. This saw the introduction of the 'scenario' script, which developed the outline into a properly narrative form, initially tailored to meet the desire for a logical, continuous story within the 1000-foot length that had become the standard unit for films manufactured for the distribution exchanges and exhibited in nickelodeons.
4. The period between 1914 and the late 1920s saw the consolidation of the Hollywood studio system and the rise of the producer. Bookended by the establishment of the silent feature film at its beginning and the emergence of talking pictures at its end, this period was characterised by a 'central producer system' in which the managerial control of budgets by a powerful producer necessitated a more

complex form of 'continuity' script, which performed the function of an industrial blueprint designed to monitor quality and to facilitate more reliable projections of the financial costs of a given project.

5. The new industrial demands of the sound movie, in addition to other burdens, made it almost impossible for a single producer to oversee the whole of a studio's output. Around 1930, then, the 'producer-unit system' emerged. In a fashion analogous to the earlier director-unit system, an individual producer—possibly specialising in a particular genre—would now take control of a smaller number of pictures. Meanwhile, the introduction of sound had created a temporary rupture in the smooth organisation of scriptwriting, with the improvisation of different ways of incorporating dialogue within the script. Towards the end of 1932 the studios therefore attempted to homogenise the formatting of scripts, leading to the establishment of the 'master-scene' screenplay that, with some modifications, remains in place today.

6. Staiger ends her analysis of screenplay texts themselves with *Juarez* (1938), but the structure of *The Classical Hollywood Cinema* leads to the inference that the end of vertical integration and, by the late 1950s, the emergence of the 'package-unit system' we are familiar with today, in which less rigidly organised teams would come together to work on individual projects, would have some effect on screenwriting: logically, to less formulaic methods, with the particular form of a script being a matter for discussion between individuals, especially the writer, producer and director.

This analysis has been overwhelmingly influential, not only in relation to Hollywood but in several significant studies of European screenwriting, including Alexander Schwarz's meticulous account of German and Russian screenplays in the silent era,[12] Colin Crisp's monumental study of the French film industry between 1930 and 1960,[13] and Thompson's invaluable essay on silent screenwriting in all three of these countries.[14] All of these scholars help to establish that a proper understanding of screenwriting requires a recognition of the relationship between industrial function and textual form.

Staiger's account could be challenged or qualified in several ways, and, importantly, she notes that there will be exceptions to and variations within the norms she identifies. For example, higher-budget, prestige pictures created by established figures might allow for a greater degree of what we might term authorial input from a particular producer, who might have personal preferences about how the script should be developed. For this reason, the films that have achieved the highest acclaim and become prominent in attempts to establish Hollywood as a cinema of 'auteurs' might be highly inappropriate examples if we want to understand Hollywood as an industrial system that functioned according to particular kinds of economic and creative practice.

It still follows, however, that the establishment of the norms themselves is exceptionally useful in providing a framework within which to understand historical change in screenplay form, and to some extent the earlier chapters of the present study follow Staiger's distinctions between different kinds of screenwriting in different periods, though paths frequently diverge. The materials examined in chapters 1 and (especially) 2 take forms that go beyond the mere *aides-mémoire* that would have represented the limits of screenwriting competence required under the pre-industrial 'cameraman' system. Chapter 3 discusses the 'outlines' and 'scenarios' of the pre-feature film era to 1914, while illustrating the variety of texts subsumed under these umbrella terms. Conversely, the silent feature 'continuity' provides the strongest evidence for a more or less precise correlation between a particular mode of production and a relatively invariant textual form—the soundest argument, that is, for the screenplay as a 'blueprint'. This is examined in Chapter 4. Chapter 5 draws on Thompson's evidence that in the 1920s the American continuity became an important influence on the organisation of screenwriting labour in France, Germany and Russia, while also examining a variety of texts that were created in these countries in the silent era.

Thereafter, Staiger's periodisation becomes less significant as a model for the present book, Chapter 6 of which details some of the ways in which Hollywood attempted to adapt the continuity script to meet the requirements of sound. *The Classical Hollywood Cinema* proposes, slightly ambiguously and elliptically, that in the 1930s Hollywood then effected a change from the numbered continuity to the 'master-scene' script that is the default screenplay format of today. However, both the screenplay in the classical Hollywood sound era and the transition to the master-scene script more generally are messy affairs. Chapters 7, 8 and 9 each tackle this transition from a different perspective. Chapter 7 aims to show that prior to the Paramount case of 1948 there is less consistency in screenwriting than might be expected: the screenplay is something of a hybrid of master scenes and shots, and there are many inconsistencies and variant approaches both between studios and within individual scripts. Chapter 8 turns to Europe to examine the rise of the cinematic 'auteur' in the 1950s. Screenplays for films associated with this development are often closer in form to the prose treatment than to the shooting script, partly because this facilitated a greater degree of improvisation in filming. This in turn became an influence on the 'New Hollywood' film-makers of the 1960s and 1970s, while the emergence of the 'master scene' screenplay within America in the 1950s was also important as a marker of the increasing independence of the writer after the closure of the studios' writing departments. These developments are examined in Chapter 9. Chapter 10 traces the rise to ascendancy of today's master-scene screenplay as a standardised form, partly in connection with the rise of the contemporary screenwriting manual, with Chapter 11 looking at other kinds of recent film writing.

The Classical Hollywood Cinema is, as it were, methodologically in sympathy with the managerial practices it describes: that is, it organises a huge body of disparate materials and procedures within a structural system that assigns an appropriate place to each. To accomplish this, it draws on what we might think of as two master narratives. The first is derived from contemporary trade papers and screenwriting manuals. Like the manuals of today, these purport to describe accurately the screenwriting forms prescribed by the American film industry and tend to support Staiger's own meta-narrative about Hollywood as a particular kind of industrial system. These narratives also contribute to a certain view of what a screenplay and its functions are. The second is the analysis of industry associated most prominently with Frederick Winslow Taylor (1856–1915), who proposed a division of labour between the 'conception' and 'execution' stages of manufacture. Staiger applies this to Hollywood cinema: screenwriting belongs to the 'conception' stage, and the shooting of the film to the 'execution' stage.

Each of these master narratives, however, is open to challenge. Staiger herself notes problems in placing too great an emphasis on representations of the early Hollywood film industry within the pages of trade papers such as *Motography*, *Motion Picture World* and *Nickelodeon*, the reliability of which is open to question, since while they may or may not indicate the nature of screenwriting at the time, they certainly 'do not indicate what was actually occurring in the films'.[15] A more fundamental challenge is to the argument that the Taylorite model effected the separation of conception and execution—writing and filming—as fully as the 'blueprint' metaphor suggests. Maras, for example, suggests that this confidence in the 'sovereign' script is dubious at best, that any idea that screenplays are 'shot as written' is fraught with difficulty, and that their provisional status would be more clearly apparent if we were to reposition them in the context of the other kinds of re-writing, or scripting, that take place continuously throughout the process of making a film.[16] Such questions will recur throughout the present study.

Furthermore, although Staiger's analysis of the screenplay in relation to an industrial system is indispensable, as is her methodology in charting the relationship between different kinds of screenplay and different modes of production, it can only tell us so much about the nature of any given script that was produced within that system: it begins with the principle that the screenplay is an industrial document and proceeds to assign individual features of particular screenplays to their appropriate place within that framework. From other perspectives, however, we might be interested in other potentialities within the written text (e.g. as a form of expressive literature or creative labour), and want to examine those aspects of the screenplay that exceed a purely industrial function.

Perhaps the most helpful methodology for analysing screenplays in these ways is provided by Claudia Sternberg, who distinguishes the 'dialogue text' from the remaining prose elements within a screenplay that comprise the 'scene text'.[17] It is not difficult to think of screenwriters— Harold Pinter, David Mamet and Quentin Tarantino are latter-day examples who immediately come to mind—whose dialogue is instantly recognisable. Even within the scene text, however, there is still widespread variation. Sternberg breaks the scene text down into three 'modes': description (of set, characters and so on), 'report' (the presentation of the series of actions, usually human) and 'comment'. The comment mode is routinely thought to be prohibited in screenwriting because it breaks the convention that the scene text should contain only what can be seen on the screen. Sternberg disputes this, holding that 'screenwriters rarely miss the opportunity to use the mode of comment. It is in this mode of presentation that ever newer forms and designs of screenwriting shall be revealed.'[18]

This provides opportunities for the analysis of an individual writer's style, but of wider significance is the relationship between the mode of production and the nature of the screenplay text. The most obvious example is that the transition to sound required the writing of dialogue, but more interesting are variations within the scene text, for example, in the exploitation of the prose narrative or 'treatment' form by 'auteur' directors such as Ingmar Bergman (Chapter 8).

A terminological history of the screenplay

As this discussion shows, writing for film encompasses a large number of different kinds of text. However, the history of these writings does not simply see one form replaced by another in a straightforward chronological sequence. Similarly, the words used to refer to these documents do not reveal any clear pattern of terminological change, with an older word falling into disuse and being replaced by a newer alternative. One kind of text may be referred to by two different terms; conversely, a single word like 'scenario' or 'continuity' may be used to refer to more than one kind of text, which can cause still greater uncertainty when, as is usually the case, a given film project generates more than one kind of document. Therefore, it may be helpful at this point to give an account of the historical usage of some of the more common terms we shall encounter in this book.

1. *Photoplay*. In 1912 the United States Copyright Office created two new classifications for feature films, of which fictional films (as opposed to non-fiction or animation) were designated 'photoplays'. However, just as a screenwriter today might be said to be 'writing a film', so too the term 'photoplay' quickly came to be applied to written texts also. In the same year of 1912, Epes Winthop Sargent's oft-cited column in *Moving Picture World* changed its name from 'The Scenario Writer' to 'The Photoplaywright', remaining under that title until 1918. Sargent also figured prominently in *The Photoplay Author: A Journal for All Who Produce Photoplays*, with the caption 'Who Can Produce Photoplays?' appearing on the cover of the June–July 1913 issue.[19] The terminology can therefore contribute to confusion about the relationships between writing and film in this period.

2. *Synopsis*. Maras's summary of accounts of the synopsis in the silent era suggests that the term was being applied to prose narratives of anywhere between 300 and 8000 words in length.[20] Clearly, the same word is being used to describe many different kinds of script, with varying functions; moreover, a single narrative telling of a story can have different kinds of utility. For example, in the silent feature era the synopsis was routinely integrated into the continuity: as a separate item accompanied by other documents, including the script, or as a preface to the script itself. In its shorter forms, it can function as a capsule condensation for purposes of pitching a story, assessing its commercial potential, or summarising the narrative for executives who may be disinclined to read a screenplay or continuity in full. A somewhat longer form of prose narrative, of perhaps five pages in length, was used as the 'scenario' for many of the shorter films of the 1910s, and could in this form serve the function of a shooting script. This could even be the case with longer narratives, under certain conditions, as for example in its deployment by many European 'auteur' directors in the 1950s, especially when

augmented by dialogue in the form of a treatment (see below). As we shall see, the dividing lines between a synopsis, a prose fiction form of scenario and a treatment are relatively unscientific, and often a matter for judgement.

3. *Scenario.* One form of scenario invites immediate comparison to (but, therefore, confusion with) the synopsis: scenarists John Emerson and Anita Loos, writing in 1920, define it as 'a detailed synopsis of the plot in ordinary short story form'.[21] Most such synopses are not entirely ordinary, however, in being composed in the present tense. Moreover, it was quite common for such scenarios to take a more paratactic form, anticipating shot sequences by separating individual moments of action within a scene by the use of dashes within the running text. For example, the first scene of *The New Stenographer*, a comedy by J. Stuart Blackton (Vitagraph, 1911), begins as follows: 'Enter Cutey—goes to his desk—picks up morning paper—begins to read. Enter Mr. Brown, goes over to Cutey who puts paper down and asks him where the new stenographer is. Brown goes to stenographer's desk in center—moves the chair—looks at watch—goes back to Cutey.'[22] This begins to move the scenario a little closer to the later 'continuity', in which shot type would be specified (see below).

A dictionary definition of the scenario as 'A sketch or outline of the plot of a play, ballet, novel, opera, story, etc., giving particulars of the scenes, situations, etc.' (*OED*) may carry the suggestion that the material should be divided into scenes: a 'scene-ario'. The division of the prose narrative into scenes is quite typical of the scenarios of the 1910s that we shall encounter in Chapter 3, but Patrick Loughney has also retrospectively applied the term to texts written between 1904 and 1905 for the American Mutoscope and Biograph company (Chapter 2), which directly imitate the format of the theatrical play. Defining the scenario in terms of its formal properties is becoming problematic, which is hardly surprising given the range of media to which the *OED*'s description refers, or the imprecision of its alternate definition of a scenario as simply 'A sketch, outline, or description of an imagined situation or sequence of events'.

Each of these definitions may carry the implication that a scenario functions as a kind of rough draft or outline of action that will be further developed in some later iteration. Yet *OED* also cites an 1884 piece in the *Pall Mall Gazette*, which refers to the writing of 'an elaborate scenario...minutely setting down, not only the scenes as they follow, the action of the personages engaged, the sense of all they have to say, but even the "stage business"'. This is similar to the *OED*'s cognate, film-specific definition: 'A film script with all the details of scenes, appearances of characters, stage-directions, etc., necessary for shooting the film', its earliest citation being 1911. A 'scenario', then, can be either a rough sketch or a minutely detailed script, leading to potential confusion with the 'continuity'.

The distracting use of the same word to refer to both kinds of text could be explained as resulting from a lag in recognising that one textual form had been superseded by another, or simply from a contemporary failure to develop a consistent terminological distinction that would have been helpful to future historians. If so, the confusion persisted for a remarkably long time, as Maras's many revealing illustrations suggest.[23] In 1921, Frances Taylor Patterson was describing as a 'scenario' the composite document (containing a list of characters, plot synopsis, breakdown of scenes and the 'plot of action' or script itself) that is usually referred to as the 'continuity'. In 1924, Frederick Palmer also mentions this possible meaning of the term 'scenario', alongside several others, in describing the great 'difference of opinion' over the usage of the word. The situation becomes no clearer following the introduction of sound: Tamar Lane suggested in 1936 that 'scenario' could refer to 'anything from an original story to a continuity'. The following year the prolific Hollywood screenwriter Frances Marion, in the glossary to her book *How to Write and Sell Film Stories*, defines 'scenario' as 'A continuity; a story with action, sound and all directions for photographing; a shooting script'.[24]

Taking all of these inconsistencies into account, perhaps the easiest way to understand the scenario is, nevertheless, by contrasting it with the continuity. Formally, the scenario breaks the action down into scenes; the continuity is a more detailed breakdown that subdivides the material into specific shots. This also assigns a place for each within film production: the scenario renders the story in ways that are appropriate for cinema by identifying discrete scenes, and the continuity is a later iteration that transforms this material into a shooting script. The matter is complicated in any number of ways, partly because of confusions in the terminology, and partly because these definitions carry with them the assumption that film production, including the writing, proceeds in an essentially linear series of distinct stages.

4. *Continuity*. OED's definition of the continuity as a 'detailed scenario for a cinema film; also, the maintenance of consistency or a continuous flow of action in successive shots or scenes of a cinema or television film' immediately repeats the terminological confusion with 'scenario'. More useful is the citation of G. F. Buckle's *Mind and Film*

(1926): 'continuity...is the correct name for the working script', if by 'working script' we mean what would now be called the shooting script.

Staiger implies that the word 'continuity' was not in widespread usage in the early 1910s, since—referring to the producer who has most widely been credited with bringing both industrial production generally, and the continuity script specifically, to new levels of sophistication— '[Thomas] Ince's scenarios had, by 1913, become what are *now* labeled continuity scripts'.[25] By 1916, C. Gardner Sullivan, the best-known of Ince's writers, was explaining that '[e]ach scene in our continuity is practically a short story in itself they are so fully described',[26] and by the end of the decade foreign visitors were reporting the conventional usage of the term in American studios and suggesting its adoption as a method of introducing greater efficiency to European film industries, as we shall see in Chapter 5.

Nevertheless, as with 'scenario', there is significant slippage in the use of the word both in the Hollywood of the time and in later critical and historical studies. 'Continuity' may designate

(i)   the dramatic text or plot of action, usually still termed the 'scenario' in the Hollywood of the time, written by a 'creative' writer;

(ii) a later modification of the scenario, which recasts it into shots and/or contains additional technical detail supplied by specialist studio workers if not by the 'creative' writer; or

(iii) the compilation of 'breakdown' documents of which the scenario, together with the list of characters, plot synopsis, breakdown of scenes and, usually, a post-production report, forms a part.

If the 'scenario' properly belongs to stage (i), and 'continuity' refers to composite document (iii), this leaves a highly troublesome terminological confusion surrounding stage (ii). The word 'continuity' appears to be generally, although not consistently, applied to both (ii) and (iii). Essentially, the difficulty concerns whether or not, in a given film project, a stage (ii) document represents a re-write of a scenario stage (i), or whether instead the writer(s) proceeded immediately to the fairly technical stage (ii) document without creating a 'scenario' first. This can obscure certain aspects of creative labour: the widespread assumption is that stage (ii) would ordinarily be compiled by technical experts, but there is no particular reason why an experienced scenario writer would be incapable of also developing the 'continuity' text (ii), or proceeding directly to it. The scale of the problem can be judged by a comment in the introduction to the anthology *What Women Wrote: Scenarios, 1912–1929*, compiled by Ann Martin and Virginia M. Clark:

> Although continuities reflect the scenario, they necessarily include directorial intervention, and [...] cannot be proved to stem from the original author of the scenario. In fact, the recordkeeping of the time did not always distinguish between credit for the original story versus credit for scenario; thus definitive attribution can be problematic.[27]

A yet further complication—only slightly tangential to the present problem—is that the term 'continuity' is often widely used to refer to

(iv) the editing sheet used by a studio editor to compile the shot sequence; or
(v) what is now usually termed the 'cutting continuity', which is a post-production document created by the studio for technical and legal reasons to provide a written record precisely corresponding to the release print of the film.

5. *Treatment.* This is defined in the *OED* as 'A preparatory version of a screenplay, including descriptions of sets and of the camerawork required', with a citation from 1928 describing it as 'a sort of synopsis'. In 1937, Marion identified the treatment as 'an intermediate step between the film story and the continuity'.[28] Staiger indicates that this had become a standard stage in the pre-production process in the 1920s, whereby the original material was translated into 'lengthy prose form prior to the more technically complex writing process of the next stage'.[29] As noted above, as a prose narrative the treatment has connections to both the synopsis and the short story form of scenario. Maras helpfully draws attention to this spectrum in referring to 'the extended synopsis/treatment/scenario', noting the possibility that 'contrary to a linear hypothesis the scenario does not merely "evolve" into the continuity script, or part of it, but informs the still-emerging notion of the "treatment"'.[30]

This question of the relationships between forms is crucial. With the addition of dialogue, the treatment can be developed into a kind of screenplay, and in this form became a distinct stage of pre-production in France in the years following the Second World War. Treatments also allow directors who prefer more improvisational methods to work directly from it, without an intervening screenplay or shooting script (see Chapter 8). All of these possibilities suggest that an understanding of the various forms of cinematic pre-text needs to take account of ideas of production other than those that imply a strictly linear progression from one iteration to another.

6. *Screenplay.* Very roughly, we can say that the screenplay is to the shooting script what the scenario was to the continuity in the silent era (always bearing in mind the instability of all of these terms): that is, the screenplay casts a story into scenes, without further segmentation into defined shots. Arguably, the current understanding of the screenplay as a document with very precise formal requirements derives not from industrial practice but from the effect of screenwriting manuals, beginning with those written in the late 1970s. As we shall see in Chapter 10, these argue for a separation of the screenplay both from any later shooting script (by proscribing the specification of shot) and from any preceding treatment stage (by prohibiting authorial narration within the prose text).

As noted, Maras has traced the term 'screen play', as two separate words, to 1916, when it was used to refer to the film, not the script.[31] By the 1920s, 'screen play' can frequently be found on title pages and other materials pertaining to the written text itself, when it often appears to be synonymous with either the scenario or, in particular, the continuity; the precise meaning of the phrase at this date remains fluid. *Broadway* (Universal, 1929) had a 'Screen Play and Dialogue Arrangement by Edward T. Lowe, Jr.', which may imply that the 'screen play' is a continuity modified to accommodate the 'dialogue arrangement'.[32] However, the same year, on a Warner Brothers' script for *The Gold Diggers of Broadway*, Avery Hopwood is credited with the 'final continuity', but the 'Screen Play' is by Robert Lord. Here, 'screen play' indicates something like the older 'scenario', or the more recent 'treatment' or 'screen story'.[33]

Maras suggests that the compound word 'screenplay' did not come into usage until around 1940, in the Academy Awards categories,[34] and notes that significant confusion has been occasioned by the retrospective use of 'screenplay' as a single word in describing texts written before that date, as for example in the Library of Congress's 1951 *Catalog of Copyright Entries: Cumulative Series, 1912–20*, which ascribes an anachronistic 'screenplay by' credit to writers on many films of this period.[35] Maras accordingly considers the screenplay not so much in terms of its formal properties, but as 'underpinning a form of discourse', which emerged in the 1930s and 1940s, 'that articulates a perspective on writing for the screen, a script-centred way of speaking about production, and relations between different crafts'.[36]

On the other hand, the title page of director James Whale's personal copy of the shooting script for *The Bride of Frankenstein* (at this date called *The Return of Frankenstein*), dated 1 December 1934, does bear the credit 'Screenplay [one word] by William Hurlbut and John L. Balderston'.[37] This suggests that we should be cautious in ascribing too much significance to this particular distinction. It is likely that the terminological confusion surrounding the word 'screenplay' is connected to uncertainty in the years following the introduction of sound as to exactly what form this document should take; for example, to what extent, if any, it should differ from a 'shooting script'. It is noticeable that a definitive answer to these questions only took shape in the late 1970s, with the boom in manuals and 'spec' scripts, when the readership for such screenplays had moved decisively away from film-makers and towards other industrial gatekeepers such as script readers (Chapter 10).

7. *Shooting script.* As with the distinction between 'scenario' and 'continuity' above, the 'shooting script' could be defined by its relationship to the screenplay: it constitutes a later iteration of the material, once camera angles, shot specifications and so on have been inserted. During the classical studio era, it is sometimes held to be synonymous with the continuity: 'Under the studio system, a contract writer produced shooting scripts—that is, scripts, whose slug lines, the lines in all caps proceeding (sic) the bodies of description, identified shots rather than scenes.'[38] This is relatively clear, though some complications remain. While the iteration marked 'final' in the Hollywood system is often held to represent the 'shooting script', there are almost invariably significant differences between it and the film, raising the possibility that a director has intervened to produce a later iteration that might itself be designated the shooting script. Moreover, since 'screenplay' becomes prominent as a term and, arguably, as a form during the 1940s, it suggests that at this time 'screenplay' and 'shooting script' could be synonymous. This conflation of terms has become more pronounced over time. Routinely, a master-scene screenplay will form the final iteration of the script prior to shooting, and will therefore be regarded as the 'shooting script' itself, irrespective of whether or not the film-makers will demand rewrites of particular scenes, or intervene themselves to break down some or all of the scenes into shots.

We can think of the relationships between these various forms in several different ways. We could, with Staiger, concentrate on historical change, and see one form giving way to another; or we can think of them as a series of different possible stages within an individual film production. As we have seen, however, in each case this linear way of thinking about the relationships brings with it multiple problems of distinguishing between terms, forms and functions.

Another way of conceiving the relationship, however, is to see these forms as representing a palette of options that a writer or writers may bring together in different combinations. Placing to one side the more experimental kinds of writing, or alternatives to written texts, that we shall encounter in the final chapter, it is clear that most of the obvious methods of writing a story for film—a brief outline of scenes, a prose narrative, a dramatic script—came into use within 10 or 15 years of the invention of cinema in the 1890s, and remain viable options for film writing to the present day. Moreover, one form is often very difficult to distinguish from another, or is an extension of it: the synopsis, short-story scenario and treatment all represent variations on a particular form of prose fiction, the distinction between scenes and shots is not always readily apparent, and many kinds of screenplay, including most of those written in the heyday of classical Hollywood, represent a hybrid of different textual options.

Most of the time, when we encounter a screenplay that looks significantly different from what has come before, in reality it represents an unusual combination of some of these elements, or an extension of their possibilities. Arguably, the master-scene script develops out of the treatment as well as out of the introduction of dialogue-intensive scenes following the introduction of sound, while some writers, such as Paul Schrader in *Taxi Driver* (1976), have created prose-intensive screenplays that resemble a mixture of master-scene dialogue and the treatment (Chapter 9).

A further way of thinking about these texts is to bear in mind the relationships between screenplays and other, less formal textual and verbal communications. Largely missing from Staiger's account, for example, is what we might, in contradistinction to the managerial approach, regard as the micro-narrative of each film project during the classical Hollywood era. While the progress from inception to post-production may have been overseen by a small number of producers, those producers were in regular contact with the production teams tasked with making the films, among whom were the writers. This contact took the form of story conferences and memos, and less formal meetings and discussions, as well as synopses, treatments and screenplay drafts. Focusing on the oral dimension of screenwriting still places attention on the work as an act of communication, but now the act is not so much the issuing of a set of instructions as the development of a conversation.

The scholarship of Claus Tieber is crucial in this, as in other ways, in attempting to shift the perception of classical Hollywood screenwriting away from industrial organisation and rule-governed textual variation, and towards an understanding of it as a set of dialogues and other forms of (frequently oral) communication between interested parties.[39]

These critical reorientations call into question the extent to which written narratives in film industries should be regarded as industrial planning documents: 'blueprints', to use the term that has been applied almost ubiquitously.[40] In practice, screenplay texts during production have usually had a more provisional status. Following the communicational model, we might think of a screenplay as a kind of conversational gambit: an accumulated set of suggestions, usually the product of multiple dialogues between different contributors, which forms a source from which directors, actors, editors and others may diverge on set and in post-production. There is little evidence that these discussions were guided by story templates of the kind we are familiar with from today's screenwriting manuals. Instead, the production of films by discussion and negotiation is a particular illustration of what André Bazin (and, later, Thomas Schatz) calls 'the genius of the system': an accumulated but changeable pool of knowledge on which many people would draw in creating films and, as a part of this process, creating screenplays.

A note on the scope and content of this study: it is only relatively recently that screenwriting research has begun to accumulate any sort of critical mass. Film scholars, with some important exceptions, have naturally focused on films themselves and have tended to regard screenplays as, in effect, industrial waste products: what remains of value after production is the film itself, not the screenplay. It is a view shared even by many screenwriters. Jean-Claude Carrière, who began his career working with Jacques Tati, became a key collaborator of Luis Buñuel and remains perhaps the most eminent of European screenwriters, has remarked that '[e]veryone knows that when shooting is over, screenplays generally end up in studio wastebaskets',[41] while Osip Brik, an important writer and theoretician in the development of early Soviet cinema, similarly suggested that '[t]he script drops into the wastepaper basket and ceases to exist even as an archive document; the rare enthusiasts of the art of script writing are obliged to study from the finished film'.[42] This is an exaggeration—script materials relating to the work of some of the more eminent Soviet directors have survived—but it is symptomatic that a substantial archive of scripts written for that most quintessentially

British of studios, Ealing, survives only because it happened to be retrieved from a skip.[43]

One consequence is that, as the authors of a recent article on early British screenwriting observe,

> [t]he issue of the systematic collection and preservation at a national level of film and TV scripts has never been addressed, either in the United Kingdom or, apparently, elsewhere in the world except in France (for a time), the United States (in part) and some countries like Finland where indigenous film production is small and a source of national pride.[44]

The screenplay archives of the British Film Institute are a hit-and-miss affair, reliant on individual donations, and the situation in many other countries is no better. On the other hand, extensive archives from some former Soviet bloc countries are now becoming accessible, and the burgeoning internationalisation of the Screenwriting Research Network, which was founded only in 2006, combined with the digitisation of materials in archives around the world, holds out the prospect of the dissemination of research into screenwriting in many different countries. At the moment, however, neither the primary nor the secondary materials exist for anything approaching a comprehensive global survey of screenwriting.

Partly for this reason, I have not attempted to engage with screenwriting in countries outside the United States and Europe. One can anticipate that significant studies of writing in other film industries, such as those of India and Japan, will emerge in the near future, but any gesture in this direction in the present study would suffer from inadequate data. In contrast, the Hollywood continuity script was not only a form of screenwriting; it was also a method by which the studios kept a record of the production, and therefore Hollywood studios were creating screenplay archives almost by default, dating in some cases as far back as the 1910s. Some of these, such as those of MGM and Warners, have been made available to scholars in major research centres. Again, this helps to explain why the study of Hollywood screenwriting has to date proved much more fruitful than studies of screenwriting in other film industries. For all of these reasons, in addition to the indisputable economic and cultural dominance of American cinema since at least the end of the First World War, Hollywood remains the necessary point of departure for any attempt to explore the screenplay as a generic form.

On the other hand, the dialogue between Hollywood and European cinemas is long-standing and direct and has significant consequences for the development of the screenplay, in both directions. For example, Kristin Thompson has established that once Hollywood had developed the continuity script for the multi-reel silent film, France, Germany and Russia began to consider it as a model for making their own industries more efficient.[45] In the other direction, the international success of European (and other) 'auteurs' in the 1950s influenced new generations of American film-makers in the 1960s. The emergence of the 'master-scene' script as the default screenplay form around this time owes much to the relative autonomy of different American film workers in this period compared to their positions within the integrated system of the classical era before 1960, and to the availability of European models by which not only directors like Martin Scorsese, but also writers such as Paul Schrader or Robert Towne, could construct an identity as relatively independent artists.

Equally revealing is that the script forms that emerged in the United States before the establishment of the Hollywood system, around 1914, are remarkably similar to those that arose more or less independently in important European film-making countries at the same time. This suggests that particular kinds of script—the 'outline', the pseudo-stage play, the prose short story or the synopsis—were simply the most obvious forms that a pre-production written text might take, regardless of the exact industrial circumstances under which the film itself would be produced. Today, it is possible to speak of 'the screenplay' as possessing a global form—and of more independently minded film-makers as acting more or less purposely in rebellion against it. It is in this dialogue between normative models, alternate forms and independent variation that screenwriting history is written.

1
Prehistory of the Screenplay

There is something quixotic about the pursuit of the 'first screenplay', which as Steven Maras warns 'has proven unhelpful' because 'the search for firsts and origins can have the tendency to "fix" the landscape in particular ways, leading to a reductive view of the development and institutionalisation of screenwriting'.[1] Yet posing the question can nevertheless function as a worthwhile heuristic device, a means of opening up, if not necessarily providing definitive answers to, other, more substantial questions: What *is* a screenplay? In what ways, if any, does it function as a 'planning' document? Does it presuppose the existence of a written text? If so, must that text possess definable formal properties? In what ways is it distinct from other forms of writing? Is it a product and corollary of the division of labour in early studio systems? Is the terminology—scenario, continuity, screen play, screenplay and so on—significant?

The earliest films were made by individuals or very small groups of people who devised and filmed 'actualités': visual records of the movement of trains, waves and wind, for example, that fascinated audiences because such events could not previously have been presented in any other medium. If written texts were required in the preparation of such films, they would have been little more than notes that needed to be comprehensible only to their authors. Similarly, any actual writing involved in the preparation of the story films that appeared before the end of the nineteenth century could have been rudimentary at best. Roy P. McCardell, often credited as the first professional writer for films, began working for Biograph in 1898. As Tom Stempel notes, his stories

> must have been relatively simple, since the films of the period were not much longer than a minute or so. At their least structured, the

films of 1898 were still just photographs of interesting movement of some kind. At their more complex, they consisted of a single action, photographed in a single take, from one angle.[2]

No script from this period has survived, partly because at this date there was no need for anything possessing even the functions, let alone the form, of the modern screenplay. It is a logical inference that it was the introduction of longer and more complex narrative films in the early years of the new century that heralded the beginning of screenwriting. Narrative films have been estimated to comprise just 12 per cent of films made in 1900, but 96 per cent of films in 1908,[3] with actualités outnumbering narrative films until as late as 1906.[4] The length of films increased from the initial limit of 50 feet to 250–400 feet by 1900, and 300–600 feet by 1903. The greater duration entailed the construction of sequences linked into a coherent narrative. The 'seemingly obvious yet strangely elusive' conclusion drawn by Edward Azlant is 'that this vital transition involves the birth of screenwriting, a craft that could be fairly described as the prearrangement of scenes, right up to the present'.[5]

Like the more recent work of Ian W. Macdonald, who prefers the term 'screen idea' to 'screenplay',[6] and Maras, who substitutes 'scripting' for 'writing',[7] Azlant here extends the concept of screenwriting beyond the production of a written text and towards the idea of film writing as a concept or a process, written or otherwise. For Macdonald and Maras, this avoids a recurrent error in the study of screenwriting, whereby the text is conceived as a stable blueprint from which the film is subsequently made. This is rarely the case in actual film production, in which the screenplay is subject to constant revision and creative preparation involves work in media other than writing. In the particular case of early screenwriting, Azlant's argument, that it designates a 'prearrangement of scenes' rather than, necessarily, an actual text, accurately describes what was probably the practice of a large number of early filmmakers, and neatly sidesteps the desire to uncover the chimerical first screenplay.

Indeed, anecdotal evidence for the general *absence* of writing in the early years of film is strong. Gene Gauntier, who began working for the Kalem company as late as 1907, recalls that at that date '[t]here never was a scenario to hand, and Sid [Olcott], after finishing the previous week's work, would hang around the lean-to office waiting for something to turn up'.[8] Such Micawber-like serendipity was widespread. The anonymous writer of 'The Confessions of a Scenario Editor' records a film producer working in New York around 1907 remarking that 'we think up the whole thing as we go along', and crucially noted that at this time 'scenarios' could not even be defined: 'We don't know what a scenario is either—a real scenario [...] it's too early in the game'.[9] The seemingly slapdash approach was not confined to America: British pioneer Cecil Hepworth reports that he thought of stories and then constructed the scenery before filming, but he does not mention any intermediary writing process.[10]

Something was happening, but there is little surviving textual evidence of scenarios prior to 1904. One reason for this is conceptual: pre-production documents of some sort must have existed, but they cannot properly be called scenarios because the conventions that would define them as such were not yet in place. More obviously, to all intents and purposes any such material has disappeared, because of the transitory and provisional nature of the work, the need for early film-makers to practise neither the extensive preparation nor the diligent record-keeping of the later studio system and the simple passage of time. Consequently, the study of early scriptwriting is often a matter of inference and supposition, a working backwards from effect to cause, in pursuit of texts that may never have existed in the first place.

The frustrating lack of material has contributed to three separate but related areas of confusion in this field: the logical difficulties of the argument from design, the confusion between a source and a scenario, and the difficulty of knowing whether a particular document is a pre-production script or a post-production synopsis.

The argument from design: The Lumière films

Stempel's description of a 1902 film directed by Edwin S. Porter advances a familiar argument: 'It is obvious from the lavish production of *Jack and the Beanstalk* that considerable pre-production preparation was done, which suggests the use of a scenario of some kind.'[11] Yet while a complex sequence of events may require careful preparation, it does not follow that the plans will be translated into textual form. Accordingly, most commentators prefer to speak of the design, rather than the scenarios, of early films. For example, the first of the Lumière brothers' pictures, *Sortie d'Usine* (1895), is not simply a documentary record of workers exiting the Lumière factory. It is clearly a staged event: the doors open on cue, and the workers exit the frame in an orderly fashion, indicating rehearsal. The film, then, 'reflects a number of carefully chosen decisions about sequential narrative', and 'its organization reflects an order and direction akin to the movement one associates with traditional plot structure'.[12] This is even more apparent in *L'Arroseur Arrosé* (1895), the Lumière film widely accepted as 'both the first film to tell a story and the first film comedy'.[13] A boy stands on a gardener's hosepipe: when the gardener inspects the nozzle the boy removes his foot, and the gardener is sprayed with water. Louis Lumière recalled in 1948 that 'the idea of the scenario was suggested to me by a farce by my younger brother Edouard'.[14] It is fascinating, if perhaps misleading, that many years after the event Louis would use the term 'scenario' in connection with a film of 1895; 'scenario' here probably implies a mental concept, or the filmic mise-en-scène, *L'Arroseur Arrosé* being 'the prototype of what Méliès called "vues composées" or "artificially arranged scenes"'.[15] There is no need to posit the existence of a written script for such a simple narrative, even though 'the event depicted is not discovered but created, not recorded but acted, the whole a unified design'.[16]

Similarly, Marshall Deutelbaum finds little evidence of organisation in Thomas A. Edison's early Kinetoscope films, which contain much 'dead time and inconclusiveness'.[17] Conversely, of three slightly later Edison films, dating from 1898 to 1899, Kemp R. Niver remarks: 'All show pre-production thinking, either by use of a script or through rehearsal, and are not news events but planned stories'.[18] Both commentators, with appropriate caution, avoid the assumption that design, or lack of it, in such short films in itself provides strong evidence for the presence or absence of a script. A more influential example concerns Porter's early narrative films, but since these conflate the argument from design with the distorting effects of the post-production catalogue description, they are considered below.

The accidental screenwriter

In studies of early screenwriting, there is a widespread confusion between a *source* and a *scenario*. Several films of the late 1890s are demonstrably based on surviving written texts, which arguably performed the function of screenplays. The most commonly cited examples, however, are stage plays and newspaper articles that were not written with films in mind. They therefore provide no evidence of either screenplays or screenwriting practice, although they do reveal early film-makers working methodically from textual adaptation through shooting and perhaps to editing. The temptation to describe such texts as scenarios or screenplays, however tentatively, is a logical error that, repeated sufficiently often, has led to a distorted view of screenwriting activity in the period.

For example, Stempel argues that each of Thomas Edison's films of performing animals and circus acts, dating from 1895, 'was just that: an act that had been created and sometimes actually written (even if not specifically for filming) before it appeared in front of the camera'.[19] If so, the written plans for these circus acts provide some of the earliest examples of what might be termed 'the accidental scenario'. Such texts are surprisingly prominent in the standard histories of screenwriting. In August 1896, the former Edison associate W. K. L. Dickson began preparations for a version of *Rip Van Winkle*, based on a stage adaptation by Joseph Jefferson of Washington Irving's story. Dickson's Mutoscope film, according to Patrick Loughney, 'was the first attempt by an American filmmaker to adapt the complete storyline of a well-known play to cinema'.[20] This certainly makes *Rip Van Winkle* of historical interest and, although it is pushing the claim a little far, one might even accept that Jefferson's play 'survives—if not as a true screenplay—then certainly as an important film-related production text from 1896'. But Jefferson's work was written for the stage; there is no evidence that he intended to translate it to another medium, or that either he or Dickson produced a new, written text from which Dickson worked in creating the film. To describe it as '[t]he "screenplay" on which the film was based'[21] is to accord it an unwarranted status in history.

Loughney follows in a long tradition of film historians who have sought to find evidence of early screenwriting in other genres. The two most frequently cited examples are Sigmund Lubin's restaging of a prize fight of 1897 and an 1898 film of the Oberammergau *Passion Play*, adapted from a stage version written by Salmi Morse. The claim that these films used scenarios was first made in Terry Ramsaye's highly influential *A Million and One Nights: A History of the Motion Picture through 1925*, published in 1926. Ramsaye's method was teleological and evolutionary: he contemplated the cinema around him and looked backwards in an attempt to discover how its magnificent achievement was anticipated in earlier, more rudimentary times. He regards early fight pictures as 'foetal films', belonging to a stage before the medium developed into an art form, yet demonstrating, in Lubin's version of the Corbett-Fitzsimmons fight, an advance through the act of re-creation. Lubin did not have access to the fight itself, and instead engaged two men to re-enact the encounter, their moves prompted by a third man reading aloud from a newspaper report of the fight itself. According to Ramsaye, '[t]his was art,—the re-creation of an event—and the "fight by rounds" column was a scenario, but Lubin did not know it'.[22]

Ramsaye was hoping to find the missing link between such 'foetal films' and art. One sign would be the discovery of a film that made use of processes in script adaptation more closely analogous to those of the golden age of silent cinema in which he was writing. Sure enough, he found it, and in the process made from Salmi Morse the Piltdown Man of screenwriting history. In 1879, Morse had published his adaptation of the *Passion Play*, which was intended for a New York stage production in the 1880–81 season. The proposed performance had been banned on religious grounds, however, and Morse's version had never been staged, a fact which contributed to his eventual suicide. In 1896 it was picked up by Rich G. Hollaman, who used it as the basis for his filmed version of 1898. The script, argues Ramsaye, thereby 'bec[a]me the first motion picture scenario', because the film was 'the first construction of a dramatic event especially for the camera'.[23] Stempel accepts the Lubin and Hollaman films as '[t]he two earliest known intentional uses of written "plans" for films',[24] Loughney describes the *Passion Play* as 'the *Ur*-text in the history of the American movie screenplay',[25] and Azlant memorably suggests that '[t]he current Writers Guild could do worse than mark the spot where Salmi Morse threw himself into New York's North River'.[26]

The note of qualification in these remarks is appropriate, since it is difficult to accept the stronger claims made for any of these texts. They do not provide evidence of screenwriting activity in this period; if anything, they provide evidence of its absence. The Corbett-Fitzsimmons film can be said to have used a 'scenario' only in the sense that Lubin's actors were following precisely a series of actions outlined in a written text, but that text was a newspaper article, and it would be more accurate to say that it was being used as a prompt book. Similarly, Jefferson's *Rip Van Winkle* and Morse's *Passion Play* each provided a *source* from which the directors selected a number of story elements and, in the case of the *Passion Play*, some of the dialogue. However, neither of these texts was a screenplay or a scenario in any sense. They did not occupy an intermediate stage between the sources and the films: they were themselves the sources, and they were never intended for filming or considered by their writers to be in any way related to cinema. Ramsaye concedes that even Lubin himself would not have considered the newspaper report to be a scenario. As for Salmi Morse, his *Passion Play* was published 16 years before the workers at the Lumière factory first walked before a motion picture camera. Morse drowned in the Hudson in 1884; had he been fished out alive in 1898 to be told he was the world's first screenwriter, he would have been the beneficiary of two miracles on the same day.

The catalogue synopsis and early narrative cinema

The brevity of early narrative films means that their storylines are often unintelligible to the modern viewer. Contemporary audiences would have shared our incomprehension, had they not been aided in a number of ways. Among the traits that Noël Burch has identified in 'primitive' cinema is 'nonclosure', whereby the narrative is not self-sufficient but instead depends on the audience's prior knowledge of the events the film purports to narrate, the use of explanatory intertitles, or the presence of a 'lecturer' or on-stage commentator.[27]

The role of this exhibitor has been extensively analysed by Charles Musser. As he points out,

> [t]ravel lectures, Passion Plays and fight films all had recognizable story lines. These earlier films were constructed, however, in such a way that individual scenes, functioning as self-contained units, could be selected and organized at the discretion of the exhibitor. The exhibitor thus maintained a fundamental relationship to the narrative as it was constructed and projected on the screen. [But i]n films like *Jack and the Beanstalk* the exhibitor's role was reduced to one of secondary elaboration.[28]

As film-makers began to experiment with longer and more complex narratives that demanded greater internal coherence, the exhibitor started to become redundant. By 1904 the Kleine Optical Company, citing Porter's *The Great Train Robbery* (1903) as an example, was advising exhibitors that one of the advantages of the 'feature' film was that '[t]he public has been educated to appreciate these long films which tell an interesting story, and need few words of explanation'.[29] It is noteworthy, however, that a comparable role continued to be performed by the Japanese *benshi* throughout the silent era, influenced by the indigenous *kabuki* and *Noh* theatrical traditions.

The existence of the exhibitor has generated a serious difficulty in the history of early screenwriting: it is very easy to misidentify as a pre-production script what is actually a post-production synopsis published in the motion picture catalogues that were in widespread use from as early as 1894. These catalogues were circulated to exhibitors for advertising and promotional purposes, but also contained prose descriptions from which the exhibitors would construct a spoken narrative to connect the disparate sequences of varied films into a relatively coherent programme. Occasionally, but influentially, material from these catalogues has been claimed to represent pre-production scripts prepared by the film-maker, rather than the post-production synopses that most of them undoubtedly are.[30]

When Georges Méliès published details of his films in his 'Star' catalogues, it was with the additional purpose of protecting his copyright in the face of blatant piracy. The catalogues estimate the running times of the kinds of film discussed below at between 15 and 18 minutes, and the length of their footage at between 820 and 850 feet. Providing a synopsis for a film of that length entailed the construction of a short prose narrative, but unlike those of most catalogue descriptions, the synopses of these longer Méliès films often divided the action into numbered scenes. An example is *A Trip to the Moon* (1902). One catalogue printed the following text for what it described as 'An extraordinary and fantastical film in thirty scenes':

Scene 1. The Scientific Congress at the Astronomic Club.
Scene 2. Planning the Trip. Appointing the Explorers and Servants Farewell.
Scene 3. The Workshops: Constructing the Projectile.
Scene 4. The Foundries. The Chimneystacks. The Casting of the Monster Gun.
Scene 5. The Astronomers Enter the Shell.
Scene 6. Loading the Gun.
Scene 7. The Monster Gun. March Past the Gunners. Fire!!! Saluting the Flag.
Scene 8. The Flight Through Space. Approaching the Moon.
Scene 9. Landed Right in the Eye!!!
Scene 10. Flight of the Shell into the Moon. Appearance of the Earth from the Moon.
Scene 11. The Plain of Craters. Volcanic Eruption.
Scene 12. The Dream (the Great Bear, Phoebus, the Twin Stars, Saturn).
Scene 13. The Snow Storm.
Scene 14. 40 Degrees Below Zero. Descending a Lunar Crater.
Scene 15. In the Interior of the Moon. The Giant Mushroom Grotto.
Scene 16. Encounter with the Selenites. Homeric Fight.
Scene 17. Prisoners!!
Scene 18. The Kingdom of the Moon. The Selenite Army.

Scene 19. The Flight.
Scene 20. Wild Pursuit.
Scene 21. The Astronomers find the Shell again. Departure from the Moon.
Scene 22. Vertical Drop into Space.
Scene 23. Splashing into the Open Sea.
Scene 24. At the Bottom of the Ocean.
Scene 25. The rescue. Return to Port.
Scene 26. Great Fete. Triumphal March Past.
Scene 27. Crowning and Decorating the Heroes of the Trip.
Scene 28. Procession of the Marines and the Fire Brigade.
Scene 29. Unveiling a Commemorative Statue by the Mayor and Council.
Scene 30. Public Rejoicings.[31]

Many historians, including Lewis Jacobs, Azlant and Isabelle Raynauld, hold that these catalogue entries reproduce scenarios written by Méliès himself prior to shooting the films. External evidence for this claim is inconclusive. In his introductory comments to the 'Star' catalogue, Méliès's brother Gaston, in arguing that Georges 'is the originator of a class of cinematograph films which are made from artificially arranged scenes', records that he 'conceived the ideas, painted the backgrounds, devised the accessories and acted on the stage', but says nothing about writing.[32] A cameraman recalled that Méliès 'had the *instinct* of how to put together a script. We could never figure out what kind of film we were going to make. He had everything in his head, no written script'.[33] It seems certain, as Elizabeth Ezra argues, that 'most of Méliès's early films did not even use scripts', although she holds that he did indeed write some,[34] and Méliès himself stated that he did, at least on occasion, prepare written scenarios, although he considered that

> the scenario as it was written had no importance, since my only purpose was to use it as a pretext for staging, for illusion, or for scenes with a pleasant effect. [...] Anyone composing fantasy films must be an artist smitten with his art [...] searching above all to make the skeleton of the scenario disappear behind the delicate arabesques within which he envelops them. [...] You might say that the scenario in this case is nothing more than the thread to be used to tie the 'effects' to each other without creating much meaningful relationship between them [...] the scenario is of only secondary importance in this kind of composition.[35]

Clearly the Méliès films indicate considerable pre-production organisation and a more advanced conception of editing than is common in this period, and in light of the statement above it is at least likely that some of his films were prepared in advance on paper. The question is whether the Star catalogues reproduce these plans and, if so, what they tell us about the nature of scenario writing at this time, at least as Méliès conceived of it.

The catalogue entry for *A Trip to the Moon* is sufficiently ambiguous to make it impossible to judge its status on internal evidence alone. One can make only partial sense of scenes 13–18, for example, in the absence of the projected film, and this, along with the condensed note-form in general, would be consistent with regarding the text as a mnemonic device written by Méliès himself prior to staging and shooting. On the other hand, the note form would be equally useful to an exhibitor wishing to be either reminded of the sequence or prompted for appropriate comments to deliver to the audience. Azlant notes that descriptions of Méliès's films were being numbered as early as 1900–01, and suggests that the 'scenario' for *A Trip to the Moon* 'indicates a movement away from a rigid sense of the complete "tableau" as the basic unit', as in scenes 7–10 and 21–24. 'These "scenes"', Azlant suggests, 'display an awareness of the ability to prescribe units shorter than a complete dramatic action, here governed by rapid change in location generated by subject movement, and such abbreviated segmentation of continuous activity would prove one of film's most fertile lines of development.'[36] Even granting that Méliès was at the forefront of such a reconception of the possibilities of film, however, what Azlant here describes are developments in *film*, not scenario writing. They would only demonstrate an advance in scriptwriting if it could be demonstrated that this text of *A Trip to the Moon* really is a scenario.

A 1904 Star catalogue held at the British Film Institute further complicates the issue. *A Trip to the Moon*, film 399–411 in the catalogue, appears in the form reproduced above, except that it is in double columns.[37] Most revealing of its possible status are the supplements appended to the catalogue, which cast an entirely different light on *A Trip to the Moon* and similar 'scenarios'. 'Supplement no. 16', for example, contains two different descriptions of Méliès' *Faust and Marguerite*.[38] On page two of the catalogue is a list of 20 scenes for the film that is formally identical to *A Trip to the Moon*:

1. The laboratory of Dr. Faust.
2. Appearance of Mephistopheles.

3. The Vision of Marguerite.
4. Dr Faust Sells his Soul to Satan.
5. The Kermess.
6. Mephistopheles Seeks a Quarrel with the Students.
7. First Meeting of Faust and Marguerite.
8. Marguerite's Garden.
9. The Temptation.
10. The Gate of the City (Return and Procession of the Soldiers).
11. The Duel.
12. Death of Valentine, Brother of Marguerite.
13. The Church.
14. Mephistopheles Prevents Marguerite from Praying.
15. The Walpurgis Night.
16. The Celebrated Women of Antiquity (Grand Ballet).
17. The Prison.
18. The Death of Marguerite.
19. The Soul of Marguerite Ascends to Heaven.
20. The Kingdom of the Elect—Grand Apotheosis.

Following this is a more detailed prose description of each of the 20 scenes, with accompanying illustrations. In each case, the description of the scene begins with the identical wording to that which appears in the list of scenes, and then expands upon it. For example, '1. The Laboratory of Dr. Faust.—In his laboratory, Dr. Faust, burdened with years, laments that he has become old and can now no longer enjoy the pleasures of youth. He consults his books and invokes Satan.'

The longer version is almost certainly a post-production description of the film as made, because Méliès would have no need to write what amounts to an aide-mémoire at this level of detail. For reasons considered later in this chapter, the more precise the catalogue description, the more likely it is to be a post-production synopsis of the completed film. The relationship of the second catalogue description of *Faust and Marguerite* to the first is, once again, ambiguous. On the one hand, it may suggest that the shorter version preserves Méliès's elliptical pre-production scenario, and the second is a reader-friendly description of the film as shot. That would not explain why the shorter form is more commonly found in the catalogue entries, however, and it is at least possible that the shorter version is actually an abbreviation of a more extensive, but also post-production, prose summary of the film. If so, it means that far from preserving an early form of scenario writing, the version of *A Trip to the Moon* that so excited Jacobs and others is nothing more than a synopsis of a synopsis.

Even if *A Trip to the Moon* really does preserve Méliès's original script, it tells us very little about screenwriting. Méliès had his assistants, but 'he had everything in his head'. Any written texts, therefore, were written in a form that needed to be comprehensible only to himself and a very few others with whom he was in immediate contact at his studio. Film production was little more than a cottage industry, albeit a highly profitable one, and the division of labour that would become essential under the Hollywood studio system was as yet barely visible on the horizon. There was, therefore, no need as yet for the establishment of conventions that would enable several people working on different aspects of the same project to have access to copies of a single text.

The problem was not confined to Méliès, of course. A still more difficult case concerns Edwin S. Porter. Here the stakes are even higher, because Porter has been credited not only as a pioneer of the American narrative film but also as an innovator in the field of intercutting. In *The Rise of the American Film* (1939), Lewis Jacobs printed what he took to be the scenario for Porter's *The Life of an American Fireman* (1902). As he acknowledges, however, the text he reproduces is taken from the Edison Catalogue, and internal evidence alone indicates that it is not a scenario but a synopsis. Had it really been a scenario, it would have gone a long way towards resolving the crucial questions surrounding Porter's editorial practice. As Musser explains,

> [i]t is hard to give a precise narrative account of *Life of an American Fireman*. The Edison Manufacturing Company, for example, offered two quite different descriptions. In the oft-reprinted catalog version, the opening scene shows a fire chief dreaming of his wife and child, whom he subsequently rescues, while another description, offered in the *New York Clipper*, emphasizes the film's documentary qualities over the elements of fictional narrative. Thus it becomes clear that exhibitors could shape the spectators' understanding of the screen narrative along divergent lines through their live narration and advance publicity (newspaper promotions, posters, etc.).[39]

Musser is particularly interested in the role of the exhibitor which, as noted, is influential in the study of early screenwriting because narrative coherence was often as much an effect of the exhibitor's commentary as of the editorial arrangement of the films themselves. Of more immediate interest in the present context, however, is the presence of multiple competing versions of the film. *Life of an American Fireman* presents a fiendishly difficult case because the two different prose descriptions are compounded by the survival of two different edits of the film itself, one of which repeatedly intercuts between events taking place in two different locations, and the other of which does not. If the former represents Porter's intentions, and is not the retrospective work of another, later editor, then the familiar case for Porter as an innovator in the field of cross-cutting could be sustained. The details of this problem in the history of editing need not detain us here.[40] A surviving scenario for the film, of course, would be a material document in the case; but a scenario, despite Jacobs's assumptions, is precisely what we do not have. Marc Norman's account of the authorship of *Fireman* neatly captures the critical ambivalence surrounding textual and other forms of screenwriting: 'Porter wrote it [but] there's no evidence he wrote it down'.[41]

The case for Porter as a pioneer in the history of narrative film rests partly with *Life of an American Fireman*, but even more with *The Great Train Robbery* (1903). There is no particular reason to doubt Ramsaye's claim that in adapting a popular stage play for *The Great Train Robbery*, Porter wrote 'a memorandum of scenes of a simple story of a train hold-up, a pursuit, a dance-hall episode and an escape'.[42] Niver takes the story further, stating that Porter 'began by writing a story in seven scenes to enable him to use previously photographed film which he supplemented by shooting several new scenes'.[43] It is entirely reasonable to suppose that in adapting an existing text written for the theatre into a silent film of perhaps 12 minutes' duration, Porter would have worked directly from the source text, preserving a handful of arresting incidents, and then placing them into a logical sequence—the 'prearrangement of scenes' Azlant associates with the screenwriter. Even if this is the case, however, it hardly constitutes a complicated case of adaptation; there is no need to assume that Porter required a scenario as a mnemonic device to hold such a limited plot together. Still more significantly, if Niver is correct, Porter's written work was, in part, not 'prearrangement' but something more akin to the commentary of the exhibitor, a narrative developed retrospectively to hold together a sequence of scenes that had already been shot.

Although it is universally recognised that the texts in the catalogues are largely post-production synopses, the cases of Méliès and Porter indicate that there is still widespread scope for disagreement about difficult cases. Perhaps more significant than the texts themselves is that the Méliès catalogues came into being partly in an attempt to establish ownership at a time when film piracy was rampant. A more effective method of achieving the same end, however—and one that would go a long way towards establishing the existence of pre-production screenwriting—would be to reverse the practice: instead of countering piracy by publishing a prose narrative of an existing film, the film-maker could register a written text before the film was released. Among other things, this would represent an attempt to copyright both the story idea and the resulting cinematic work. And in New York, in 1904, one company had come up with that very idea.

2
Copyright Law, Theatre and Early Film Writing

The problematic status of the catalogue entries examined in the previous chapter arises, in part, simply because catalogues are one of the few means by which writings connected with early films happen to have been preserved. In a system of production that required the involvement of only a handful of workers in the creation of a film lasting no more than a few minutes, half-a-dozen words to summarise the content of each scene might be sufficient. An 'outline' script of this sort was almost certainly used in the planning of many films before 1904, but for such an ephemeral text to survive it would almost certainly need to have been recycled within a commercial or legal document that had a better chance of being preserved. This chapter examines a second, and more promising, set of archival materials that promises to preserve examples of early screenwriting: the scripts submitted to copyright offices for the purposes of securing legal ownership of films.

Copyright classification and early American cinema

The details of the relationships between early American film scenarios and copyright law are complicated.[1] The first copyright disputes in film revolved around hardware: for example, Edison films could not be played on a Lumière projector, and vice versa. Consequently, each company tended to dupe the prints of the other to create products that could be used on their machines. As Peter Decherney explains, however, around 1903 'patent disputes began to be settled and the technology platforms stabilized', and at this point 'concepts like originality and authenticity in moviemaking registered with producers, who then needed to protect their content as well as their technology'.[2]

This need is bound up with the development of narrative cinema. The 'content' in the earliest films—such as the 'actualités' that exploited the medium's unique capacity to reproduce movement, or rudimentary narratives like those of the Lumières' early experiments—was negligible. From around 1902, however, producers and public were acquiring the taste for longer and more sophisticated narrative films, such as those of Porter or Méliès. This development was accompanied, at least in theory, by ideas of both written pre-planning and the legal protection of a studio's product; and as we saw in the previous chapter, rights to these films as properties were being asserted in the catalogues circulated by the studios to advertise them. Of course, a better and more obvious way of doing this would be to copyright the films themselves; but this was easier said than done.

The legal obstacle to protecting films was that they were not directly accommodated within the classification of formats introduced by the United States Copyright Office between 1900 and 1901, a situation that would not be satisfactorily resolved until a discrete category was created in 1912. In the interim, film producers turned their attention to two classes that seemed promising, though both had their drawbacks. The more technology-appropriate and precise of these categories, class H (for 'Photographs'), was inherently questionable because a film was not a single picture but a sequence of images. The illogicality of attempting to copyright a film under this classification had raised problems as early as 1902.[3] The alternative classification, class D (for 'Dramatic Compositions'), raised the opposite problem: while it satisfactorily accommodated the question of narrative (which a single photograph seemingly could not), it implied publication in print form of a dramatic text. The Edison company attempted to overcome this difficulty by registering their films under both categories.[4] However, the relationship between these two categories is a little more complicated—and this is where it gets interesting for screenwriting.

The problem of copying did not just pertain to outright piracy in the form of film 'duping'; there was also the question of intellectual rights. For example, in 1904 the American Mutoscope and Biograph Company (AM&B), which was the first company 'in the United States, if not the world, to make the decisive shift towards fiction "feature" films— headline attractions that filled at least half of a thousand-foot reel',[5] issued an injunction against Edison, not for duping Biograph's film *Personal*, but for issuing what we might today call an unauthorised 'remake' of it. On 12 November the injunction failed, and it was very shortly after this (on 25 November) that Biograph submitted the first of a series of written texts in support of simultaneous applications for the registration of its films as both 'dramatic compositions' and 'photographs'.[6]

Although the logic is not always transparent, and although Biograph's lawyers did not make the argument explicitly, this appears to be more than a simple assertion that dual registration should comprise a kind of hybrid classification of a narrative film, whereby it is held to be a special kind of dramatic composition (class D) because it is in photographic form (class H). Instead, the film and the scenario were submitted at the same time, but under separate classifications. The chicken-and-egg logic must have been that securing rights on the written scenarios (Class D) would establish a kind of intellectual copyright on the narrative, which would then bolster their rights in the films themselves (Class H); simultaneously, the Class H registration would constitute a form of publication (as a film 'photograph') that would assist in securing the Class D registration for the otherwise unpublished typescript scenario. In short, by means of registering the written text, AM&B was attempting to copyright not just the film, but the narrative idea—in the form of a scenario—itself.

Arguably, the ensuing legal debate about what constituted a 'dramatic composition' brought into being, both conceptually and formally, the very idea of what we would now term the 'screenplay'. Perhaps surprisingly, the Photographic classification proved unproblematic: the Copyright Office was willing to register the sequence of images AM&B deposited in the form of a paper print of the film of *The Suburbanite* as a single 'Photograph'. However, on 1 December 1904 Thorvald Solberg, acting for the Copyright Office, queried the separate attempt to register *The Suburbanite* as a 'dramatic composition' in the form of a written text. The document Biograph submitted in this case was simply a copy of AM&B's entry for the film in their *Bulletin*, which was an advertising vehicle containing descriptions of the company's new releases. The *Bulletin* entry consists of a single-page, present-tense prose description of the action scene-by-scene, and a still more condensed 'synopsis' that restricts the description of each scene to a single sentence. Solberg objected that '[t]he term "dramatic composition" as used in the copyright law has the ordinary meaning of . . . a play consisting of dialogue and action'.[7]

AM&B appealed, arguing 'that a dramatic composition does not necessarily require dialogue', and in the case of *The Suburbanite* '[i]t is the sole purpose of the composition that this narrative or story shall be represented dramatically by action, posture and gesture'.[8] The lawyers cited substantial legal precedent and their appeal was upheld, resulting in *The Suburbanite* receiving the registration number D5895, dated 25 November 1904, when the application was submitted. Nevertheless, AM&B decided to submit in future, not *Bulletin* texts, but what Loughney calls 'actual typescript copies of the original scenarios'.[9] All of these submissions were again successful. As a result, two different kinds of text were now legally classified as 'dramatic compositions': prose narratives (*The Suburbanite*) and the purposely very different documents they submitted thereafter.

The AM&B scenarios, 1904–05

Having encountered legal difficulties with the attempt to register a *Bulletin* entry as a 'dramatic composition', but having also established 'that a dramatic composition does not necessarily require dialogue', AM&B now pursued the logical path and registered five texts under this classification over a period of seven months: *The Chicken Thief* (copyrighted on 17 December 1904), *Tom, Tom, the Piper's Son* (6 March 1905), *The Nihilists* (20 March), *Wanted: A Dog* (12 April) and *The Wedding* (20 May).[10] Precisely why the sequence stopped at this point remains unclear, but in Kemp R. Niver's words 'AM&B applied for a copyright as a "Dramatic Production" for a handful of their films [i.e. for their typescripts], and *The Wedding* was the last of these. From that time on, a copyright was obtained for the motion picture only'.[11]

Each scenario was credited on the title page to Frank J. Marion and Wallace McCutcheon, but copyrighted after the film had been shot. This leaves some room for doubt as to whether the scenarios really were composed prior to shooting, but strong evidence that they were is provided by the corresponding paper print versions of the films submitted to copyright the productions as 'photographs'. For example, in the film version of the sixth scene of *Tom, Tom, the Piper's Son*, Tom unsurprisingly does not 'jump a fence with the pig' in his arms, but instead drags it through a gap in the fence. The climactic scenes of *The Nihilists*, in which a sister and her brothers make two attempts to assassinate a Governor in Czarist Russia, contain a whole series of changes.[12] In general, this kind of disagreement between scenario and film tends to indicate that the scenario was composed prior to shooting, since if it were instead a post-production synopsis the discrepancies would not have arisen.

There is no dialogue in any of the scenarios. They contain instead two other, formally distinct types of material, corresponding to two of the 'modes' identified by Claudia Sternberg in her analysis of screenplay texts.[13] A scene always begins with material in the 'mode of description', namely, 'detailed sections about production design'. This is always underlined, much as cognate material in published theatrical play texts is usually in italics. This is followed by material in the 'report' mode, namely, the temporal sequence of present-tense actions performed, usually by human characters, within the scene; this is never underlined.

The meticulous distinction between these two kinds of material in the AM&B scenarios is illustrated in the aforementioned scene from *Tom, Tom, the Piper's Son*:

Scene 6.

Exterior deserted cottage at left of stage. Across the back, connecting with cottage, so as to clear the way, is a rambling rail fence. At about center, is a space between the rails sufficiently large for the passage of a small boy, but small enough to impede the progress of a grown person.

Tom gets out of the barn in safety and makes for a nearby vacant cottage. He is obliged to jump a fence with the pig, but manages that nicely. Not so with his pursuers. One fat woman gets stuck between the bars and is released only after a great deal of tugging and pushing.

This formal distinction shows clearly the difference between the scenarios and the *Bulletin* versions, since the latter consistently omit the set descriptions and simply repeat the action reports verbatim, sometimes with and sometimes without the scene headings.[14] Consequently, the *Bulletin* texts read as continuous, present-tense narrative prose, whereas the scenarios resemble theatrical play texts shorn of dialogue.

Also absent from most of the *Bulletin* versions are the paratextual materials that accompany the scenarios. These are the title page, a 'cast of characters', indication of time or period and a scene-by-scene breakdown of locations. These pages of paratext help to give the scenarios a degree of physical substance, with the longest piece, *The Chicken Thief*, 'An Original American Comedy in a Prologue and Four Acts. By Frank J. Marion and Wallace McCutcheon', running to a total of 26 sides. Following the paratexts, the 'prologue' occupies page 4 and provides an unusually detailed description of the title character:

As an introductory to this play, a single character is introduced; that of a typical southern colored man. He is dressed in garments peculiar to people of his race living in the south, and he is supposed to typify the plantation negro. His hat is an old crushed felt; his coat a linen duster, and his vest and trousers are considerably too large for him.

The hero, or principal character, as described above, is eating with great gusto a section of fried chicken, having a piece in either hand. As he eats, he grins and gives other evidences of great enjoyment.

The paratexts, and the designation of this shot as a 'prologue', further indicate the ways in which *The Chicken Thief* in particular, but also the remainder of the scenarios, have been constructed to resemble contemporary theatrical play texts. Between the Prologue and the first scene is a single page (p. 5) containing just five words: '*The Chicken Thief* Act I'. Pages 11, 15 and 23 repeat this formulation to complete the division into 'Acts'. The material in the Acts themselves runs to a total of 18 pages. Although Acts 2 and 4 contain a single scene apiece, Act 1 has three scenes and Act 3 no fewer than five. Each scene commences on a new page.

Although each of the scenes could be filmed with a single shot, there is no internal evidence that Marion and McCutcheon are thinking in cinematographic terms. Similarly, each of the total of eight scenes in Acts 1 and 3 commences with the entry of a character or characters and concludes with their departure: this might be regarded either as another theatrical device or as being in keeping with a common mode of transition between scenes in very early cinema. This scene structure varies only in the Prologue (which seems to indicate a single shot of a character who neither enters the frame at the beginning nor exits it at the end: although the word does not appear, the 'discovery' of a character is, again, common to both theatre and film), and in the single-scene Acts 2 and 4. Each of these two scenes shows a group of 'plantation negroes' at dinner, at least some of whom are discovered at the beginning of the scene, with characters remaining on stage at the end and Act 4 closing on a 'tableau'. Action between scenes within an Act is largely, though not entirely, temporally continuous and spatially contiguous: I.ii begins '[v]ery shortly after' I.i ends and in the same location, for example, while at the beginning of III.iii '[c]haracters enter R. U. in the same order that they passed out of the previous scene'. Tellingly, the final direction on the typescript is: 'Curtain'.

The conception of the mise-en-scène as a three-dimensional stage space perceived from a single vantage point, the methods of transition between scenes and the technical terminology all show the scenarios drawing on theatrical practice, but in ways that tended to be replicated by the film technology of the time. Meanwhile, the nature of the correspondences between the scenarios and the films establishes almost beyond doubt that the former were composed prior to filming, and that during the production they served the function of what we would today term a shooting script. Equally, however, it is indisputable that the degree to which the scenarios have been tailored to resemble the theatrical play text, including the paratexts and the separation of the description of the stage set at the beginning of each scene from the action within it, exceeds what would have been required to meet a purely industrial purpose. In Loughney's summary, the AM&B documents 'clearly suggest that early filmmakers relied on some basic types of the theatrical scenario form to give organization to their longer productions'.[15]

French copyright submissions, 1907–12

Similar arguments have been advanced concerning texts composed a few years later, around 1907, in France. As in the United States, the study of early film writing in France has benefited from the practice of depositing textual materials for copyright purposes, while being complicated by a measure of uncertainty about the precise relationship between these texts and the films themselves. Isabelle Raynauld has identified, from scripts now held at the Bibliothèque Nationale in Paris, three distinct stages through which French scenarios in the period from 1907 to 1912 would typically pass. She designates these stages Categories A, B and C:

> The 'A' versions are very much screenplays in the contemporary definition of the term: a text divided into scenes, tableaux or shots, which puts forth a description of the action to be shot, and which is written before the shooting starts.... [T]he 'B' version or 'deposits that conform to the film', are intermediate versions and they clearly make reference to the film. Nowadays this is called the shooting script, the version closest to the film.[16]

Finally, the 'C' version 'is without doubt the summary of a film written after its completion. This is the version that is used to describe the film and is what can be found, directly reproduced, in company catalogues such as Pathé's'.[17]

Raynauld puts the status of the C versions beyond dispute. A film strip is attached as proof that the film has been shot, and the text is labelled 'to the copyist', which Raynauld takes to mean 'for publication' in the company catalogue. The C texts are essentially short summaries of the material found in the B versions. It should be noted that, owing in part to silent film's elimination of the language barrier (other than for intertitles), film distribution in this era was essentially international: the 'Star' catalogues, published by Méliès's brother Gaston in New York, were for films made by Georges in France. Raynauld's research provides additional reasons for regarding most catalogue descriptions as belonging to the C, and not the A, category, and further evidence that the catalogues are unlikely to have reproduced Méliès's own scenarios, though Raynauld believes that they do.

Even more importantly, Raynauld makes a convincing case for the A texts as 'screenplays in the contemporary definition of the term', the anachronism aside. She establishes that the A texts represent an earlier stage than the B versions, and that they indicate a conception of a dramatic action at the conceptual, writing stage, prior to its translation into film. This is clear from her comparison of the A and B versions of *Le Noël du Miséreux* (1908). For example, version A's 'In an attic, three children sit on a pallet' becomes, in version B, 'In an attic, three children sit around a table, which with a bed and two chairs make up the sparse furniture of these poor people'.[18] Raynauld includes as an example of an A version a facsimile of the first page of the four-page text for *Le Bonhomme Noël* (1907). Its designation as a 'Scénario de Scène Cinématographique' precedes the title and list of characters. There follows a detailed description of place and action:

SCENE I—LA PORTE DU CIEL.—Un mur de clôture dans lequel s'ouvre une porte. A droite de la porte une guérite. Devant la guérite un pliant et une petite table. Sur la porte un écriteau; "CIEL" en plusieurs langues. Au premier plan, des nuages qui marchent, limitant le champ en avant.

Un archange monte la garde dans la guérite. Saint-Pierre assis à la petite table lit les journaux. Soudain la porte s'ouvre et le Bonhomme Noël paraît, en livreur, sa hotte de jouets sur le dos.[19]

There is no significant difference between this and a conventional play text written for the stage, but by analogy with the AM&B scenarios, there is no good reason to doubt that Raynauld's 'A' versions of 1907 are indeed among the earliest surviving examples of pre-production writing for film. The search for 'firsts' in screenwriting history is largely pointless; the significance is that within three years, in two different countries, a similar solution appears to have been found for copyrighting films, that this solution involved the deposition of written texts, and that those texts are indebted to the stage play for their form.

The more radical argument pertains to the category B scripts, which, if Raynauld is correct, represent something significantly different from the AM&B scripts because they denote a more cinema-specific mode of writing. As before, however, the issue is whether these are pre-production 'shooting scripts' or post-production documents: not synopses this time, but detailed descriptions or transcripts. Raynauld has only included in this category *screenplays without an accompanying filmstrip and in several versions*, including an A version that is dated earlier than the B version.[20] The B versions are marked by the words 'dépôt conforme à la vue' ('deposit that conforms to the film'). Raynauld draws the following conclusions:

> This notice, 'deposit that conforms to the film', characteristic of 'B' versions, is of great importance because the 'B' versions manifestly contain precise descriptions of actual elements to be found in the film, such as intertitles and *mise-en-scène* directions, which 'conform to the film'. The 'A' version is then the script written prior to the film, and the more elaborate and especially more precise 'B' version is the one that corresponds to the actual film. As well as being what could be called the shooting script and the revised version, the 'B' version also assures copyright protection of both initial subject, and final film.[21]

What is troubling about the B versions, however, is precisely the thing that looks most persuasive: they 'manifestly contain precise descriptions of actual elements to be found in the film'. Owing to the vagaries of the production process, a film is always liable to differ significantly from any pre-production screenplay; the more detailed the script, the more noticeable the differences are likely to be. If the version B scripts 'conform to the film', the obvious question arises as to whether that is because the director has reproduced exactly the elements of the screenplay, or whether someone has performed the easier task of writing down a record of the film as shot. There are several reasons why this might be done, not least that it 'assures copyright protection of both initial subject, and final film'.

Raynauld's arguments for regarding the A versions as 'screenplays', rather than texts that 'have for too long been considered as mere advertisements[22]', are invaluable. Meanwhile, the analogies with the Library of Congress deposits suggest that the case for the B versions as 'shooting scripts' remains intriguing but not proven, and that in the present state of knowledge it is necessary to treat with caution the view that French scripts of this period displayed a surprisingly advanced recognition of the demands peculiar to the screenplay, and 'that techniques of montage, of continuity editing and of narrative inventiveness were at the forefront of the screenwriters' preoccupations, even in the early years'.[23]

Dialogue in early scenarios, 1905–12

The AM&B scenarios represent the first significant case in which scenario form can be seen to owe as much to legal matters of copyright as to the industrial demands of cinematic production. *The Serenade*, a scenario written by William Selig (whom we shall encounter again in the next chapter), and which received the Class D copyright classification on 1 May 1905, seems to have taken the opposite approach to a similar problem by imitating not the scene text but the dialogue of the stage play. Loughney argues that '[b]ecause it contains dialogue and instructions for the director and actors, it is truly a recognisable screenplay and is the earliest known document of its kind yet identified'.[24]

At first glance, this claim, like the text itself, beggars belief. Here is the beginning of Scene 1 (the illiteracy and typographical errors are in the original—the text has been tidied up in Loughney's presentation of the same material):

> SCENE:—Garden scene—with balcony projecting from upper part of house. (to left of Stage)

> Enter Freddie,Cornet under his arm stops beneath Balcony, and begins to serenade, Fannie, during the serenade,, Fannie appears on Balcony,

> FREDDIE.

> (Stops playing) Ah! My loved one,my own sweet Juliet,come fly with me,to a bower of rose's do not turn me away, but whisper that one dear short but sweet word, that means, all in life to me, say you will this very night, elope with me, and be my wife.

Fannie.

Yes I would go with you anywhere, fly with you to the end of the
Earth,were it not for my father,

OLD MAN.

(listening behind Balcony window) Ah! Ha! I see it all now, the Villain, that bargain counter three cent Dude, wants my daughter to
elope with him,Oh! the Scoundrel! the Wretch! I'll fix him.[25]

So it continues, for another eight desperate pages. If the AM&B scripts
look like stage plays but without dialogue, *The Serenade* is a sloppily presented and exceptionally badly written draft, apparently intended for
theatrical staging, dialogue-intensive and virtually unfilmable.

Suggestively, however, the title page proclaims it to be 'A Dramatic
Composition. In Four Scenes. By W. N. Selig'. This is followed by a 'caution' that 'Stage representation, Moving Pictures, etc. [are] positively
prohibited, without the written consent of the author'. As with the
AM&B scenarios, then, *The Serenade* is a multi-purpose text, but this time
the intention is still more explicit: the same text can be both used for
copyrighting purposes and considered as a scenario for either theatrical or cinematic production. Though the latter looks highly unlikely,
Loughney points to the existence of a different version (in 12 scenes)
released in September 1905,[26] and more recently has proposed, after
viewing the *The Serenade* film, that it derives from the Selig scenario. His
contention is that this and similar texts were created opportunistically
in the hope of exploiting either the theatrical or cinematic audience, or
both.[27] If so, this well illustrates the fly-by-night quality of much of the
work being produced by the early American film entrepreneurs, though
it is harder to agree that *The Serenade* is 'a recognisable screenplay',
because the textual form has not been adapted at all to the industrial
demands of cinematic production.

On the other hand, still closer than the AM&B scenarios to the theatrical play script is the much later *From the Manger to the Cross, or Jesus
of Nazareth*, a Kalem production from 1912 written by Gene Gauntier,
two troublingly different versions of which appear to have been jointly
submitted for registration as a 'dramatic composition', and copyrighted
on 2 December 1912.[28] The film itself was copyrighted on 23 October
1912, and released in January or February 1913.[29] As with the AM&B
texts, then, the registration for copyright as a dramatic composition
was made after the film had been shot, even though the production

was a lengthy one: the title page of the published text records that it took 'over three months in the photographing',[30] and some scenes (the 'Flight into Egypt' sequence) had already been shot before Jesus had even been cast.[31]

The dates and terminology carry a more general significance, since no satisfactory method for the copyright classification of films was established 'until 28 August 1912, when two separate classes (L and M) were created especially for motion pictures—Class L for fictional films (photoplays) and Class M for non-fiction and animation films'.[32] *From the Manger to the Cross* was copyrighted as LU 56, indicating that it was the 56th licence granted to a then unreleased (U) 'photoplay' (L).[33]

Loughney's account of *From the Manger to the Cross* draws on the film and on the 29-page pamphlet that Kalem chose to publish, a decision Loughney reasonably suggests may have been a promotional device,[34] though it is highly likely that it was also bound up with the developing issues in the copyrighting of films and scenarios. Loughney describes this as 'the earliest example of a fully developed modern American screenplay'.[35] The title page is followed by a three-page 'synopsis', a three-page 'light[ing] plot', and the 21-page dramatic work that comprises the bulk of the printed pamphlet and which is, roughly, 'evenly divided between dialogue and stage directions'.[36] In this sense it presents, at least to the reader familiar either with the theatrical play texts of the time or the screenplays of later periods, a more satisfying balance between scene text and dialogue than the earlier scenarios considered above.

Loughney observes that the stage directions 'are precise and indicate the directional movements of the main actors in every scene',[37] citing the beginning of the third scene as an example:

Street in Nazareth, showing doorway of Joseph's carpenter shop; women pass by, going to and from the well for water; huge jugs on their heads. Joseph discovered working. Enter Mary, right upper entrance; passes diagonally across to left first entrance, turns, smiles at Joseph, drops eyes and exits.

There is indeed a fairly close resemblance between this and the action in the corresponding scene in the film. However, as noted previously, a measure of *disagreement* between the scene text and the film tends to be more revealing, since it makes it less likely that the written text is simply a transcription. For this reason, stronger evidence for the scenario as a shooting script is that it makes no mention of the appearance, in the most readily available version of the film, of a camel that conspicuously follows Mary into the shop as she exits scene 3.[38]

More problematic is scene 5:

> SCENE V.—*Street in Bethlehem. Left center an ancient inn, street thronged with people.*
>
> (*Enter*) JOSEPH, *left upper. He is leading a donkey on which is seated* MARY. *Comes down through crowd to inn and calls.*
>
> JOSEPH
>
> Canst give us lodgings for the night, for my wife is very weary?
>
> LANDLORD
>
> What you ask is impossible. My house is filled, but in yonder street there is a stable wherein you might find shelter for the night.
>
> (*Exit* JOSEPH and MARY *left first entrance.*)

This gives a good indication of the general balance between dialogue and scene text in the scenario. In the film, however, the action above is presented in a single, continuous shot, without dialogue titles. This in itself is unremarkable: intertitles would be created in post-production, need not correspond to those in the scenario, and could be omitted or added at will. The problem is that the scene in the film is performed in pantomime: no words (in intertitle or otherwise) are exchanged, and instead the Landlord indicates with a resigned parting of the hands that he has no room available, followed with a gesture to indicate the direction in which Joseph should go to find lodgings. Consequently, neither the scene text nor the dialogue text of the scenario corresponds satisfactorily to what is seen on the screen.

Again, this discrepancy does not necessarily compromise the argument for the scenario as a shooting script. It is worth mentioning, however, that accompanying the published scenario in Kalem's copyright application was a separate, three-page, typewritten 'description of the motion picture photoplay ... to accompany application for copyright'. The wording implies that the typescript is a synopsis of the film, and if that is all it is, it is not surprising that Loughney does not mention it. However, a closer examination suggests that the typescript is a great deal more interesting, and the scenario more troublesome, than at first appears. It might reasonably be argued, for instance, that the much briefer typescript version of scene 5—simply, 'Joseph and Mary seek shelter in a stable cave in Bethlehem'—not only accords with the typescript's stated aim of *describing* the action, but also would illustrate how the pre-production 'outline' scripts that we shall consider in the next chapter functioned: by presenting a very brief *indication* of action to be improvised during the shooting.

Such discrepancies leave the question as to the precise relationship between the film and the published scenario—and, indeed, between either of them and the three-page typescript—as one of speculation. Several possibilities suggest themselves. First, some version of the scenario might well have been to hand during the filming: the director attempted to follow the action closely, the discrepancies arise from the vagaries of production and the substantial differences between Gauntier's titles and those in the film can be explained by the autonomous creation of intertitles after filming. This might appear to be supported by a note in the published text, in which Gauntier asks that 'if the drama be shown by means of motion pictures, wherever possible each scene is to be enacted in the exact location as pointed out by leading authorities'; although, since the document in which this note appears was submitted for copyright after the film had been shot, this is far from conclusive.

The second possibility is that the three-page *typescript* could have been used as an 'outline' script from which the director and actors improvised; meanwhile the 21-page pamphlet version was compiled relatively independently, possibly after shooting, with its exact formal similarity to contemporary theatrical play scripts indicating that its functions included securing copyright. (Perhaps significantly, the 'Parts' of the typescript have become the more theatrical 'Acts' in the published version.) In 1911, a scenario writer, George Rockhill Craw, had been advised by the Copyright Office to submit his work as a 'drama', leading him to assume (and to recommend to others) that dialogue should be added to scenarios for this very reason, whereas intertitles would expose the text as a work intended for film and not theatre, thereby compromising the application. During the public debate that ensued, Solberg recommended 'that the safest course is to print and publish, and then register as a book'.[39] Coincidentally or otherwise, Gauntier's script, published the following year, exactly corresponds to these recommendations.

A third possibility—that *neither* of these scripts functioned as a pretext for the film—remains, though this seems less likely, since Gauntier certainly 'conceived' the film. It is worth noting, however, that Robert Henderson-Bland, who played Jesus, makes no direct mention of a script in his book-length and (ironically) rather self-regarding recollections of the film. Only at the end does this Jesus remember where He came from, in a belated acknowledgement of Gauntier, 'who conceived the idea of making the film [...] and portrayed the Virgin Mary'.[40]

In the current imperfect state of knowledge, some conclusions can nevertheless be drawn to explain the peculiar conjunction of theatrical form and cinematic function in the texts explored in this chapter, and they all follow from AM&B's response to the initial refusal of the Copyright Office in 1904 to register the *Bulletin* copy of *The Suburbanite* on the grounds that '[t]he term "dramatic composition" as used in the copyright law has the ordinary meaning of [...] a play consisting of dialogue and action'.

AM&B seem to have responded, consciously or otherwise, on three separate but interrelated fronts. The first was conceptual: perhaps feeling unable to do anything about the absence of dialogue, they maintained that dialogue need form no part of a dramatic composition. Their success in this regard opened the door to the idea of a new kind of dramatic writing, and that idea is perhaps the seed of the form that we would today term the 'screenplay'.

The second was industrial: at some point, AM&B decided that the same text that was submitted for copyright purposes could also function as a pre-production planning document, though it is not entirely certain which of these two functions was conceived first. Moreover, if Loughney is right and the paratexts indeed fulfilled the functions of pre-production casting and set and lighting design,[41] it would suggest that, as early as 1904, AM&B was using the scenario in ways that many film historians, notably Janet Staiger, have tended to associate with a somewhat later date—around 1909—when demand for an ever-increasing supply of films led producers to begin using the script as a mechanism for organising productions more efficiently. One of these methods, as we shall see in the next chapter, included bundling the dramatic text in with a range of other materials such as a plot synopsis, location breakdown and list of the characters.[42] Certainly, these documents seem to have been a standard part of American film-making almost from the beginning of narrative cinema.

The third was formal: AM&B now created texts that resembled as closely as possible the theatrical play scripts of the time. The report-mode narrative form of *The Suburbanite*'s 'Bulletin' copy was framed with set descriptions and paratexts so that, dialogue aside, the scenarios from *The Chicken Thief* onwards could be passed off as stage plays. This had a material dimension: the script was constructed as a relatively substantial artefact. The uncinematically prolix dialogue of *The Serenade* and *From the Manger to the Cross*, scene texts that are relatively hypotactic compared to 'outline' scripts, the luxuriously wasteful presentation of the material in using entire pages merely to indicate act divisions, and the bundling of the paratextual materials with the scenario all contribute to a textual form that exceeds the requirements of the dramatic actions the scenarios depict. The result, however, is a material (and, in the case of *From the Manger to the Cross*, published) document that could pass as a relatively substantial play text instead of a brief cinematic sketch.

What the copyright submissions did *not* do, however, was create a legal category of text that was peculiar to film writing. Instead, the Copyright Office was content to pass both narrative prose (*The Suburbanite*) and documents formally resembling play scripts, with or without dialogue, as 'dramatic compositions'. To the extent that these texts were capable of performing the industrial functions we would now associate with the screenplay, and could be subsumed under the contemporary umbrella term 'scenario', a number of distinctions can become blurred. It is easy to think that the Copyright Office erred in failing to create a distinct classification for films in 1901, and that the opportunity to establish either a formal or a legal foundation for the development of film writing was missed. Nevertheless, these legal wrangles caused film producers to concentrate on two modes of writing—narrative prose and dialogue—that required only the addition of a technical vocabulary, and a conception of the shot that was more cinematic than the continuous three-dimensional stage scene, to bring such a text into being. By 1912, when *From the Manger to the Cross* was published, that had already happened.

3
Outlines and Scenarios, 1904–17

The AM&B dispute was a local reaction to a general problem of duping in early cinema. The use of catalogues was another and, as in the case of George Méliès' Star catalogues, one effect was to circulate beyond the immediate industrial confines of the production a range of textual materials that, however problematically, contribute to the origins of the screenplay. Copyright also helps to explain the textual form the AM&B scenarios took. For both AM&B and Méliès, however, the real purpose was to secure copyright on the film itself, so what we might call today 'original screenplays' were being created in the service of 'original' films.

The *Ben-Hur* case and 'scenario fever'

While the companies resorted to law to protect their own property, they displayed an altogether more cavalier attitude towards original materials generated by anybody else. The important *Ben-Hur* case of 1907 arose because the companies had not previously troubled themselves about copyright law in creating film adaptations of pre-existing literary texts. In 1907, the publishers Harper and Row initiated legal proceedings against the Kalem film company on the grounds that Kalem's 1907 film of *Ben-Hur*, for which Gene Gauntier had written the adaptation, infringed Harper's copyright in the source novel. Gauntier apparently worked on the script for just two days, and the action focused largely on the chariot race, but '[t]here was enough story left in the film for the publisher of the novel and the estate of the author to sue Kalem and win, establishing the copyright law in the area of film rights'.[1]

It would be four years before the case was finally settled, but its effects were felt much sooner, as anxieties about copyright deterred the studios from adaptation and prompted them to concentrate on 'original' stories. Lacking, at this stage, in-house story departments of sufficient depth to create enough material for the burgeoning industry, one response was to invite the public to submit potential film stories for consideration. So began the first wave of 'scenario fever'.

The Supreme Court gave the decisive ruling on *Kalem v. Harper* on 13 November 1911:

> An exhibition of a series of photographs of persons and things, arranged on film as moving picture and so depicting the principal scenes of an author's work as to tell the story, is a dramatization of such work, and the person producing the film and offering them for sale for exhibition, even if not himself exhibiting them, infringes the copyright of the author.[2]

Crucially, Kalem had created a form of written scenario by paying someone 'to read Ben Hur and to write out such a description or scenario of certain portions that it could be followed in action'.[3] With this decision, the Supreme Court arguably brought the category of the 'adapted screenplay' into being, by offering a legal clarification of the ways in which this intermediate text negotiated between the source novel and the produced film. As Torey Liepa explains,

> At issue in the *Ben-Hur* case was whether or not copyright could be extended beyond the unlicensed reproduction of words from an original text to wordless actions—in this case to silent film pantomime. Kalem argued that copyright should not extend to ideas, but only to specific, written expressions of those ideas. [...] Justice Oliver Wendell Holmes Jr. disagreed, decreeing that pantomimic actions were in fact subject to copyright, and that motion pictures constituted 'a particular, cognate, and well-known form of reproduction'[.][4]

The ruling endorsed not only the principle of the AM&B copyright claims—'that a dramatic composition does not necessarily require dialogue'[5]—but also suggested that it cut both ways, since, equally, a film without words could infringe the copyright on a written text.

The decision introduced a level of professionalisation into the area of screenwriting, since studios and adapters now had to be more scrupulous in acknowledging and paying for the use of source materials. On the other hand, it did not establish any comparable level of protection for screenwriters themselves, who were still burdened by having to produce what Liepa terms 'pre-commercial' texts. The ruling in *Kalem v. Harper* offered protection to the writer of a previously published source text; but unlike the writer of a published source novel, or the producers of a commercially screened motion picture, the screenwriter had 'published' nothing whatsoever.

These factors help to explain the entirely contradictory views advanced by film scholars as to whether 'scenario fever' was fuelled or restrained by the 1911 *Kalem v. Harper* ruling.[6] Anxieties about the costs of adapting published sources, the exponential growth in film production and the primitive status of story departments in the early 1910s all gave studios incentives to accelerate the solicitation of story ideas from the public, directly and indirectly, via advertising, advice columns in trade journals, writing schools, story competitions and so on. Yet despite the proliferating methods by which the public was induced to pass ideas to the studios, the extent to which the latter actually used them is unclear: *Kalem v. Harper* seemingly granted the public at large access to the film industry, but it also 'render[ed] their material entirely susceptible to piracy from above'.[7] Consequently, it is impossible to judge how much of it was unconsciously borrowed or secretly stolen by the companies.

Identifying the point at which the 'fever' subsided is also not straightforward. The demands of the 'continuity' script that accompanied the development of the feature film in 1913–14 (considered in the next chapter) required a fully professionalised approach to the final preparations of the written text. This provided further grist to the manual-writers' mill by suggesting that only those versed in the more esoteric arts of script writing could enter the portal, but it also suggested that the studios' recently created writing departments would function as a closed shop by professionalising the craft. It has been argued that a final outbreak of scenario fever followed the end of the First World War, but if so, a series of lawsuits containing accusations of plagiarism within material submitted by amateurs, alongside suggestions that the studios had indeed been stealing some of that material themselves, was enough to convince the industry finally to close the doors to outsiders.[8] They would not open again until some years after the next world war was over.

The 'outline' script

The period of 'scenario fever', whatever its precise boundaries, was not one in which scripts possessed any uniformity of style or presentation. Although the theatrical play script had become a model for screenwriting as early as 1904, AM&B soon abandoned the experiment of writing fully detailed scenarios for the joint purposes of production and copyright. The text that Gauntier had hurriedly prepared for *Ben-Hur* must have been something very different. In all probability, it would have looked rather like the texts presented within the Méliès catalogues: that is, in Edward Azlant's description, 'simply lists of the scenes to be shot, in the order of their eventual appearance in the edited film'.[9]

Ben-Hur, however, was made in a more industrialised environment than the 'cameraman' system in which Méliès worked. Gauntier was being employed as a professional writer to turn pre-existing material into a script for filming. Although the fatal error was to fail to ask permission for the adaptation of the source novel, in other respects the process resembles that described by Epes Winthrop Sargent, and which Staiger proposes as a model for scriptwriting in what she terms the 'director' system: 'outside writers were invited to contribute suggestions, for which they were paid from five to fifteen dollars. These mere synopses were developed in the studio into scripts, since few of the writers possessed the knowledge of picture-making requisite to enable them to develop the script.'[10]

What Staiger terms the 'outline' script arose, in her analysis, from a transformation in the mode of production around 1907 from the one-person 'cameraman' system to the 'director' system, the key difference lying in a division of responsibilities between directing, filming and writing. She associates this with the need to generate an increasing supply of stories for the burgeoning film industry: 'When the 1907–08 shift to fictional narratives occurred, film production was able to take as a model the stage director who controlled the choices of scenery, costumes, and acting, and used a script as an "outline" of the narrative.'[11]

In many respects the outline represents a step backwards from the detailed theatrical scripts prepared by AM&B, even though the form of those owes more to the demands of copyright than to the medium of film. Given the constraints on the length of films of this period, and the still small number of people who would need to consult such a document, the outline could quite literally be written on the back of an envelope. According to Gauntier herself, at the Kalem studio in the fateful year of 1907, it was common practice for writer Frank Marion to hand to director Sidney Olcott a used business envelope on the back of which, in his minute handwriting, was sketched the outline of six scenes, supposed to run one hundred and fifty feet to the scene—as much as our little camera would hold. A half dozen words described each scene; I believe to this day Mr. Marion holds the championship for the shortest working scenario.[12]

Such practices apparently continued sporadically into the early 1910s. According to Louella Parsons, who at that time worked as a story editor for Essanay before becoming the doyenne of the gossip columnists, '[m]anuscripts came in on pencil tablets, torn envelopes and even on bits of wallpaper'.[13] Given its nature, a text like this was hardly likely to survive; consequently, many of our ideas about the scripts of this time are dependent on commonsense assumptions, combined with the recollections of the film-makers themselves, caveats as to the reliability of which must always be applied. This casual approach to the scenario was far from universal, however, and would soon become obsolete. Moreover, such accounts describe scripts that are 'toward the more informal end of the continuum', and Staiger notes that more detailed forms were also in place at this stage, though the example she cites from 1909 is of a model that is less detailed than that developed at AM&B five years previously.[14]

The J. Searle Dawley scenarios, 1910–11

Staiger proposes that the next transformation, the 'director-unit' system accompanied by a 'scenario' script, was occasioned by several industrial developments. First, more complex narratives necessitated the drawing up of a scene plot that facilitated the shooting of scenes nonchronologically—although, as we have seen, a similar document was already in use at AM&B in 1904. Second, the growing sophistication of film narratives required clearer preparation at the writing stage, but this was complicated by the decision of distributors and exhibitors, around 1908, to standardise film length at 1,000 feet. 'Thus both shooting out of final continuity and the standard of clear, continuous action militated for a script written prior shooting', although this was not obligatory, with D. W. Griffith's working practices being the most conspicuous exception.[15]

Five scenarios held in the J. Searle Dawley collection at the Margaret Herrick Library (MHL) in Los Angeles illustrate one approach to script writing under the director-unit system. Dawley was originally hired by

Edwin S. Porter as a director for Edison in May 1907, moving with the company when it relocated to the Bronx later that year. An unpublished, seemingly self-authored biography dating from the 1930s claims that he directed 194 single-reel films for Edison, for 'most of which he wrote the story as well as directed'.[16] In 1946, he recalled that there were few 'picture writers' in those early days, although he singles out Bannister Marwin, who was paid $25 per story, as one of the best; and although there were almost no copyright laws, Edison paid $100 per story to respected authors like Rex Beach, Roy Norton, Richard Harding Davis, Carolyn Wells and Sir Gilbert Parker. Yet in a 1921 article, Dawley recalled:

> In those days we never worked with a script. Scenario? No such animal anywhere around. I found it difficult in the beginning to figure out 'bits of business.' There was nothing to go on really. Then again, we never 'shot' with any logic, as far as I could see. We would go out on location. Suddenly Porter would declare: 'By jove, Dawley, here's a good place to take pictures.['] And we would take pictures in that place. I wasn't used to anything like this. On the stage we had our scenery and the plot. In pictures we found our sce[ne]ry and made up our plot as we went along.

In 1946, Dawley recalls a slightly later period when,

> [i]n 1912, the Edison Co sent me with a company of players to make pictures across the continent. We started out without scripts or stories. It was my job to pick up interesting locations on the way and build stories around them. The only planned script for the entire trip was to be a picture made in Cheyenne called the 'Charge of the Light Brigade' written around Baliclava.

Dawley's recollections, like those of many early film-makers, are often contradictory, unclear and unreliable. However, the Dawley papers do show that, whether or not his earliest pictures were made without scripts, a written scenario was being used for some films, shot on location in spectacular surroundings, as early as 1910, well before the continent-wide trek he dates to 1912; perhaps they were one and the same excursion.

The location shooting is important, because it helps to explain why the scenarios appear to be both pre-production planning documents and invitations to extempore improvisation. The two earliest date from

June 1910: 'Home Making' (scenario dated 13 June 1910, film released as *An Unselfish Love* on 20 September 1910) and 'Railroad Picture' (21 June 1910, released as *The Little Station Agent* on 4 November 1910). As the Edison synopses make clear, both of these were filmed in the Canadian Rockies. The remaining three were shot in Colorado in June and July 1911: 'Earthwork Construction Story' (11 July 1911, released as *The Big Dam* on 23 September 1911), 'Pictures on the Wall' (19 July 1911, released as *The Sheriff* on 16 September 1911) and *Leaves of a Romance* (no. 703, 20 June 1911, released 7 October).

These typewritten texts appear to be multi-purpose documents: pre-production scenarios that would be on hand during the shooting and then used in post-production, with pencilled comments in the left-hand margins recording how much footage was expended in filming each scene (unless these handwritten annotations represent an estimate). In a later era, they might be described as 'shooting scripts'. The picture becomes clearer in some respects, and more complicated in others, if we use 'Earthwork Construction Story' as an example. Font and minor aspects of lineation aside, the following reproduces exactly the complete, two-page, single-spaced and apparently professionally typewritten text:

July 19th, '11

Length 1000 feet

#701

Earthwork Construction Story

Scene 1-   Parlor

Hero proposes to girl and she accepts- she shows him letter from Heavy, asking for her hand- Hero takes pen and writes across bottom "Sorry old chap but she's mine for life Ralph Sergeant" (Show hand writing this note) Puts letter in envelope and addresses same.

2-   Heavy's office

Show him drawing plans – letter received – he opens same – shows his dissatisfaction and hatred – flash letter on screen so that it may be known that it is the same letter as in scene 1.

3-   Six months later

Office connected with Hero's house. He and girl who are now married are working together upon plans of a large construction on which they expect to bid.

4-   Office of Construction Co.

Heavy waiting for reply on his bid – Hero and girl enter – business – Hero called into office (Subtitle about Hero winning contract)

5-Hero comes out of office and shows contract to wife. Heavy revengeful – president calls attention to time limit in contract – Heavy notices this point.

6-   Earthwork Construction

Heavy directing Hero in background – hits upon an idea and leaves.

7-   Home

Close view of Heavy making up as Italian laborer.

8-   Earthwork Construction

Heavy gets job from Hero who does not recognize him.

9-   Night view of Earthwork Constr.

Heavy disabling big machines.

10-   Next day

Big machines break down – delays work.

11-   Lunch hour

Heavy shows men ad – indicates that better wages will be paid – incites them to leave.

12-Paying off the men – big gang of men leave – Hero pleads with them to stay – they refuse to do so – indicates that they are going to get better jobs as shown in advertisement.

----

13   <u>Home</u>

Hero discouraged – wife tries to cheer him up –

14-   <u>Ex. Telegraph Office</u>

Heavy steals telegraph blank and takes message on same

15-   <u>Wood</u>

Heavy engages messenger to deliver telegram.

16-   Earthwork

Fake telegram given to hero – contents to state that he can get so many men if he will come at once – he reads telegram and leaves Heavy in charge.

17-   <u>Home</u>

Tells wife what he is going to do and leaves.

18-   <u>Camp – noon hour</u>

Men about to go to work – Heavy gets them interested in poker game.

19-   <u>Home</u>

Friend of hero informs wife of conditions- she puts on man's coat- takes revolver and leaves with him.

20-   <u>Camp</u>

Wife demands to know why the men are not at work – Heavy laughs at her – gets mad and reveals his identity – she pleads with men – they turn to her side – start to attack Heavy – she stays them and bids him go at the point of revolver – he leaves – men go to work

----

21-   Men working with all their might and main – girl urging them on.

22-   SUBTITLE: THE WORK IS FINISHED ON TIME

Men cheer –pick up wife on shoulders and carry her off triumphantly.

23-   Home

Hero comes on discouraged and disheartened – President arrives – indicates that he has lost – wife enters – explanation and general rejoicing.

The typescript ends with a column listing the characters: 'Hero, Hero's wife, Heavy, Wife's friend, President, Messenger Boy, Laborers.'[17]

The length of 1,000 feet does not record how much footage was actually shot, but instead indicates how long the release print will be, due to the industrial standardisation noted above. These one-reelers would play for around 15 to 18 minutes. Each project would be numbered (in this case, 701) for studio record-keeping purposes; it does not mean that 700 films had actually been made prior to this point. Like all of the Dawley scenarios, the typescript of 'Earthwork Construction Story' is attached to a backing of lightweight card, on which is typed the film title and number, and also the words 'Stage Director'. This suggests that it was in Dawley's possession during the shoot: as Tom Stempel notes, it has been folded in thirds, so as 'to fit neatly into the director's coat pocket'.[18]

Pencilled annotations in the left-hand margin document the footage shot for most (though not all) scenes, while scenes 2 and 7 have 'Monday' written next to them, this word presumably having been inserted either in anticipation of the filming or to record what was shot on each day. More detailed annotations on other Dawley scenarios give a clearer insight into how they were used during the filming. Brief, pencilled remarks on the typescript of *Leaves of a Romance* reveal Dawley noting picturesque scenes of valleys and waterfalls and suggesting places for their insertion, while on the paper backing are what Stempel suggests are additional scenes shot ('#1 Distant view of valley from Helen Hunt's grave', #2 [illegible], and '#3 Water fall at cascade').[19] The *Kinetogram* of 1 October 1911 duly notes 'the exceedingly beautiful photography and scenery throughout'.[20]

The *Kinetogram* was an Edison promotional device, 'A Semi-Monthly Bulletin of Moving Picture News', and its synopsis of 15 September 1911 reveals important differences between 'Earthwork Construction Story' and the released film. The title has been changed to *The Big Dam*, and names have been supplied for the Hero ('George D. Bedford') and Heavy ('John Dillon'). More significant are the indications that Dawley's crudely melodramatic plots were secondary to the Edison company's desire to exploit cinema's potential for spectacular scenic realism. As with each of the five Dawley films, the *Kinetogram* makes great play of the commercial appeal of the magnificent settings. This was nothing new. As early as 1902, in a 'Special Supplement of Colorado Films', a Selig catalogue was enthusing that '[t]he very name of Colorado will attract hundreds, yes, thousands and the exhibitor first on the spot will reap a golden harvest. Look over this list and read carefully the descriptions with each subject. If you don't see dollars sticking out of every one you must be blind indeed.'[21] Not surprisingly then, the *Kinetogram* synopsis of *The Big Dam* indicates Colorado as the location, and '[w]e are shown wonderfully interesting scenes of the progress of the work'.

These scenes do not, however, appear in the scenario. They would apparently have been inserted around scene 6, which is one of the scenes that have no footage recorded in Dawley's script. The same holds true for scene 21, for which the corresponding synopsis in the *Kinetogram* records that '[t]he contract is finished on time and we see the tremendous dam completed with the wagons driving away one by one'. For these scenes, the writer—presumably Dawley—has made no serious attempt to preconceive the visual effect of the film, in this case the pictorial realism that appears to be *The Big Dam*'s real *raison d'être*; instead there is, in effect, a gap in the written text that will be completed by the shooting and editing of the film.

Collectively, the scenarios suggest that Dawley's method at this time was to work out the simple plots in advance, improvise on set and then revise the film at the editing stage, fitting the story to the pictures almost as much as the other way around ('we found our sce[ne]ry and made up our plot as we went along'). With two or more films being made simultaneously, spectacular footage could be inserted into whichever film it would fit (quite literally, given the thousand-foot requirement) with the least disruption to the story. Already, then, we can see a tension between two potentially opposing conceptions of the function of a screenplay—to ensure narrative coherence, or to provide a pretext for other, essentially pictorial, spectacular or improvised potentialities within film—that in different ways have been locked in struggle ever since.

Selig studio scripts and others, 1908–13

A comparison of Dawley's scenarios for Edison to those being written contemporaneously by writers for William Selig's studio suggests little consistency in practice during these years. Selig, who founded the Selig Polyscope Company in Chicago in 1896, was sued by Edison in 1905 for patent infringement, but later joined forces with him and others to form the Motion Picture Patents Company in 1908. The following year a Selig employee, Otis Turner, described the company's working practices in ways that suggest that at this stage the director-producer was also a writer. Turner told the interviewer that 'I write all my own scenarios for the Eastern producing end [in Chicago], and Francis Boggs, an independent producer for the Selig Co., now located on the Pacific Coast for a year, writes all of his[…]we confine ourselves largely to melodramatic subjects', but also to comedies and 'fine spectacles of Western scenery'.[22]

If these subjects look indistinguishable from those being filmed during the same period by Dawley, by 1910 the Selig studios had nevertheless developed a method of scenario construction that accommodated industrial production in ways that the Dawley scripts do not. The Selig papers at the MHL contain production records for a series of short subjects produced as one- or two-reelers. Possibly the most detailed and revealing is the typewritten script for *Across the Plains* (1910), a Western adventure directed by Turner and written by Chris Lane, at this stage entitled 'The First Settlers'. Its ten pages comprise a title sheet, list of characters, a two-page breakdown of the film's 77 scenes and finally the scenario describing the action of the scenes themselves.

This set of documents represents a considerably more sophisticated approach to narrative film-making than the more happenstance methods of Dawley. There is a division of labour between director and writer, possibly contributing to the more complex narrative storytelling. *Across the Plains* divides the story into four sequences, each with its own title: scenes 1–32 comprise 'The First Settlers'; in scenes 33–49, 'The Whites Barricade Themselves Against the Indians'; in scenes 50–67, 'the following day, the Indians go on a buffalo hunt'; and finally in scenes 68–77, 'after the hunt the Indians prepare for a barbacue' (sic). Each of the 77 scenes appears directly to represent a shot (anticipating the numbered continuity of the silent Hollywood feature), whereas the Dawley scripts tend to present the story more theatrically, each number indicating a scene (anticipating the master-scene form). The use of the shot rather than the scene as the numbered unit of segmentation is seen clearly on the first page, which contains 11 shots:

"THE FIRST SETTLERS"

1. Prairie. With hills in background.

Old fashioned caravan dis, crossing the prarie (sic), the wagons contain, Men, women, and children, supposedly the first settlers. One old prarie schooner has a horse and a cow hitched together, another is drawn by a pair of mules etc. Several old time Plainsmen on horseback are riding alongside of the caravan.

2. Wagon seat. Showing interior of wagon.

Sam Martin a manly young fellow and his sweetheart Sallie Sims, dis. on wagon seat, Sam is driving, they are apparently very attached to one another. In the interior of wagon can be seen a few women, wives of the settlers, one is seated on floor of wagon, another holds a small baby in her arms.

3. Tall grass. near where the caravan is passing.

Indian dis. crawling stealthily thru the grass, trailing the caravan.

4. Top of hill. Looking down into the valley below.

An Indian dis. crouching close up to the camera and looking down into the valley below, where the caravan can be seen passing on its way.

5. Down in the valley.

Close up of the caravan, passing thru the scene.

6. Another part of valley.

The Indian of scene 2. dis. trailing the caravan.

7. A bit of prarie.

Several buffalo dis. grazing and wandering about.

8. Prarie.

Caravan dis. passing thru scene.

9. Another part of prarie.

Two Indians dis. mounted, having just ridden in, one of them
is pointing in direction of the Caravan, the other indicates that they
have been seen, both wheel their horses about and start to exit.

10. Prarie.

Caravan dis. it is coming to a halt, the plainsmen who ride
alongside, are pointing in direction where the two Indians can be
seen riding swiftly away. The Plainsmen whip up their horses and go
in pursuit of the fast riding Indians, The others are pouring out of the
wagons and excitedly watching the Indians and their pursuers.

11. A bit of prarie.

The two Indians dis. riding swiftly toward camera, pursued by
the Plainsmen, who are firing at the Indians, all exit.[23]

As with the Dawley scripts, internal evidence suggests that the scenario
represents a combination of material written in advance of filming ('Sam
Martin a manly young fellow and his sweetheart Sallie Sims') with, as
the script progresses, more makeshift scenes leaving room for improvisation. Scene 18 has a note: 'It may take a scene or two for the plainsmen
to catch up with the wounded Buffalo. If so they can be inserted here',
while another at scene 56, which shows the shooting of a buffalo,
enthuses that 'As much footage can be obtained here as desired, and
inserted here, such as the Buffalo Fight, and any other good stuff that
can be taken.' Possible places for inserting such footage are indicated
in scenes 60 and 61. Scene 15's 'Register a typical Indian village scene'
seems to use an imperative verb, while scene 26 contains the narrative comment that 'This scene is to register that they did not leave the
Buffalo on the prarie where it was killed—but carried it along as food.'
The scenarios are formally distinct from the many handwritten,
post-production records of editing in the Selig archive. The materials
pertaining to *The Argonauts* (General Film Co., 1911), initially entitled
'In the Days of '49',[24] include a handwritten, five-page, 18-scene scenario, which is not as professionally written as *Across the Plains*, in
places using a prose narrative in a series of master scenes rather than
a series of shots. There are annotations, apparently of actors and props
required, in the margin against each scene. More significant is that the
Argonauts material also includes an editing sheet, the scenes of which

exactly correspond to those in the scenario, along with two draft lists of intertitles and two images, of a clipper ship ticket and newspaper article, to be used as inserts.[25] Formally, the editing sheet is simply a staccato record of the action of each scene, unlike the relative prolixity of the scenarios. The existence of these two parallel documents pertaining to the same film strongly suggests that the scenario is pre-production and the records of editing post-production, although the tentative comments about the selection of shot material in the former may indicate that the chronological division between these stages is unstable, and that, once again, the scenario may combine a record of material already filmed with an anticipation of the action still to be shot.

Either way, the large number of editing records in the Selig archive shows that a process of industrial record-keeping for editing purposes was already firmly in place as early as 1908. Records were completed by hand on a standardised Selig Polyscope form, which in the case of *The Crooked Path* (Selig Polyscope, 1909), for example, enters the production number of the film (here, #206) and the name of the producer (Francis Boggs) at the top, followed by the title of the film; columns in the form below provide for the scene number and footage shot, room for a description of the action in the scene and any remarks. For this film, there are recommendations for tinting ('blue tone', 'amber', etc.). A list of (inter)titles, again handwritten, is supplied on a separate sheet.[26]

Another form completed by Boggs, for *The Cowboy's Baby* (Selig Polyscope Co., 1908), shows how the narrative construction of a film of this time would often only reach its definitive form in post-production. It ends with a note to 'Tom': 'This picture runs 1045 feet, including announcements and letters. I think this will trim close to 1000 feet. Should it become necessary to cut out a scene to bring it down—take out scene no. 18—(It is 50 ft.).'[27] Similarly, *The Engineer's Daughter* (1909) includes another 'note': 'This picture was made over entirely [with exception of some scenes] [...] as the thread over the story has been changed somewhat, all of original picture except above scenes will have to be thrown out.'[28]

Even more revealing of the role of the scenario in production is the appearance of an 'assembly', indicating the editorial arrangement in narrative sequence of the scenes and titles, among the script materials for several Edison one-reelers in the early teens. Of particular interest here is *Aunt Elsa's Visit*, the scenario of which, dated 10 January 1913, takes a form quite similar to that of Dawley's *Earthwork Construction Story*, but also incorporates titles:

Scene 1-   Dining room- well-to-do
            <u>SUBTITLE: NO COOK AND AUNTY EXPECTED!</u>
            All seated at breakfast table, father, mother, young
            lady twins and small boy brother – confusion at meal –
            shows they have no cook – one of the young ladies
            exits to answer bell – returns with mail – gives father
            letter – reads – ["]Dear Will: – Expect me on the third
            to pay you that long promised visit – we haven't seen
            each other since I was eight years old, then you were
            five. Your old maid, sister, Elsa. San Mateo, Cal." All
            more upset than ever.

Scene 2   <u>Same</u>
            <u>SUBTITLE: MORNING OF THE THIRD. NO COOK YET</u>
            The boy just finishing breakfast – starts to go – he
            is called back – it is put up to the others to meet
            aunty at the station – the girls refuse on account of
            engagements – boy puts up awful kick but they give
            him money and he consents to go.

The synopsis, which appears to have been drawn up for publicity
purposes ('To see the film with its refreshing comedy is a delight'),
is dated three weeks later, 31 January. A list of titles on 10 February
gives the length in feet that each title would require, and the content of the titles (which, as is common at this time, give the names
of the characters and actors on first appearance) is inserted verbatim within the scene breakdown specified in the assembly of
17 February, as here:

SCENE 3-   INTERIOR—-DINING   ROOM—-FATHER   KISSES
            FAMILY—-
SUBTITLE:- The day that Aunty is to arrive.
SCENE 4:-   INTERIOR—-DINING   ROOM—-FAMILY   SEATED
            AROUND TABLE—-
SUBTITLE:- "The girls are going to have a party. Take this money
            and keep your aunt out all day."

Not surprisingly, both the titles and the scenes of the assembly accord
more closely with the film than does the scenario of five weeks earlier.[29]
    The texts examined in this section show that from 1908 onwards the
scenario was routinely being bundled with other documents relating
to pre-production, such as location plots and scene breakdowns, along

with post-production records of footage shot and expenditures incurred. Collectively, these reveal much about the transformation of the story idea from the scenario to the release print of the film. The documentation accompanying the scenario had acquired a certain level of consistency in appearance and function prior to the industry's embrace of the multi-reel 'feature' film in 1913–14. As we shall see in the next chapter, however, it was only with this later development that the presentation of the dramatic material itself became more or less regularised with the introduction of the 'continuity' script.

Moreover, it is important to note that the short story and scenario forms persisted until much later in the decade for short films, especially when those films were made by relatively autonomous directors or companies. An important case is that of Anita Loos, one of whose early scripts, for *The New York Hat* (directed by D. W. Griffith in 1912), has achieved some prominence, partly because the surviving film illustrates well some of the narrative conventions in American film of this period. The only surviving contemporary textual record, however, is a post-production synopsis. The form in which Loos is likely to have written *The New York Hat* can be gauged from the slightly later texts reproduced by her biographer, Cari Beauchamp, who records that '[m]ost of Anita's scenarios were three to five typed pages told as stories. That was perfect for a director like Griffith, who rarely used scripts'.[30]

Beauchamp's book reproduces six such present-tense stories written between 1912 and 1915, intended for one- or two-reel pictures, and a single example of the more obviously cinematic scenario: *A Ride with Billy*, which begins with a one-paragraph synopsis followed by the cast of characters and then the 25-scene description of the action, told in the now familiar form in which the progression of actions within a scene is broken down by use of the dash:

> 1. O'Neils' kitchen—Amy is wrapping up lunch at table—Marie stands at mirror admiring herself—enter Mrs. O'Neil—Amy grabs hat from table and pouts it carelessly on her head—picks up lunch—kisses mother goodbye—waits for Marie who is still primping in front of glass—Marie, without kissing her mother, slowly joins Amy and they leave.[31]

In the short film, then, it was still possible for a director to work from a scenario in the form of narrative prose, though as *A Ride with Billy* suggests, for all but the simplest films (or the most idiosyncratic directors), a more common procedure was to recast the story into scenes, with the dashes indicating both the progression of the action and (possibly) opportunities for further subdivision into shots.

The Mack Sennett scenarios, 1916–17

What none of the materials considered so far reveals is the spoken dimension to much storytelling for film. This does emerge clearly, however, in the surviving materials for films made by Mack Sennett, especially those compiled at the Triangle studio from the years 1916 and 1917. The Sennett materials show that in a relatively autonomous company, especially those making shorter films, scripts could take any form that best suited the needs of the unit. In this case, the written texts are essentially a pause or intervention in a process of storytelling that is as much oral and improvisatory as written and textual.

Despite the meticulous archiving of the Sennett collection at the MHL, there is an element of chaos to these materials. It is the norm for the main title to change multiple times, beginning with a dummy title for the initial story synopsis ('Haunted House Story', for example, became *Done in Oil* [1916]), and the stories themselves were in a state of flux, often changing almost beyond recognition in the progress from conception through to post-production. The file for *Her Nature Dance* (Triangle, 1917) appears to contain materials for two or three different story ideas, connected only by motif or title; the story outline 'The Nature Dancers' of 13 October 1916, for example, otherwise bears no resemblance to the scenario for 'Saved by the City Dump (Nature Dance)' of 9 November.[32] This suggests that, not surprisingly, previously discarded ideas were picked up and recycled for later use, in a further complication of the assumption that individual productions were discrete, integrated and developed in a linear fashion.

The perfect Sennett file for present purposes would contain a complete run of the most important documents: dated examples of all of the three key pre-production stages (the story synopsis or outline, the scenario and the 'rehearsal continuity'), together with a record in the (post-)production report of the dates of production, thereby confirming which written materials were created prior to filming. In the event, none of the files is ideal, though several pertaining to the later films, such as *A Maiden's Trust* (1916) and *A Clever Dummy* (1917), do contain the bulk of these documents. Looking at several files together it is possible to compile a quite accurate composite picture of how the written texts worked in the process of film production.

The pre-production writing process would generally pass through three more or less clearly defined stages. First came a story synopsis or outline, of differing degrees of detail, length and complexity. Next, the story would be reworked as a 'scenario', which usually rendered the story idea into recognisably cinematic form, with the inclusion of 'cuts' from shot to shot. Both the synopsis and the scenario could, and frequently did, exist in several, usually chronologically consecutive, versions. By contrast, the final preparatory phase usually exists only in a single iteration, as the 'rehearsal continuity', a term often typed on the scripts themselves. It shows the effects of the extensive period spent on rehearsals, which often exceeded that expended on developing the story in the first place; the production report for *His Busted Trust* (Triangle, 1916), for example, records that four days were spent on the story and five on rehearsals. Even in the rehearsal continuities, however, there are frequent indications of room for improvisation. After shooting, the problematically termed 'continuities' (cutting sheets) often show multiple attempts to edit the material in different ways, while the often barely literate 'final synopsis' is a record of the film as shot, including intertitles, and again tends to reveal substantial differences from the story as it stood even at the rehearsal continuity stage.

Some examples will show how the process worked in practice. The documents in the folder for *Done in Oil* (Triangle, 1917) are in many cases undated, and there is no production report.[33] Nevertheless, the internal evidence, supported by knowledge of the process from other Sennett files, suggests that the sequencing of items in this folder is accurate. Following these items in order shows how the project developed from a rough idea delivered orally to the film as shot.

The sequence begins with a five-page story outline ('Haunted House Story') which, very revealingly, is actually a transcript of a piece of oral storytelling 'as related by Mr. [Clarence] Badger':

> To begin with we have this haunted house; establish that it is haunted; we don't establish it on the opening of the story; we show Swickard as a sort of a crafty character type, the owner of this house; He owns this haunted house – it has the reputation of being haunted, and it is a bug bear on his hands, and it is impossible for him to rent it and it is impossible for him to sell it.

Badger goes back on himself to clarify, alter or add to events, even remarking of one idea that it 'might be stretching it a little bit too far'.

The second item is a transcript of a story conference between Badger, John Grey and Hampton Del Ruth, with the latter in effect tutoring Badger in how to improve the story. Next, a three-page 'scenario' shows the effect of the story conference: the seller is now a real estate agent who has to sell low because of the house's reputation, but after finally selling it, is swindled into buying it back at a greatly inflated price after being conned into thinking there is oil underneath. Beyond this, however, the ideas rather run out, and the scenario ends lamely 'Ad lib.' Item 4 is a five-page, undated 'rough rehearsal' (identified as such on the typescript) which clearly records the story at a provisional, pre-shooting stage ('Rodney enters—might run across bonfire—or something—finds a piece of charcoal and writes on inside drum something [in] regard to money being hidden in the basement or whatever we decide on'). Despite the improvisatory quality, however, this has much of the detail in shots and transitions associated with the more rigorously prepared continuities considered in the next chapter:

FRONT OF HAUNTED HOUSE

Open up with Swickard chaing (sic) signs

REAL ESTATE OFFICE

Rodney reading letter that Mace and girl will arrive at a certain time

FRONT OF HAUNTED HOUSE

Swickard has sign up and leaving

INTERIOR TRAIN

Mace, Fuller and Luther on –

REAL ESTATE OFFICE

Take Rodney away

STATION

Train arrives – Mace, girl and governess get off the train – Rodney enters and greets them – all exit

PARK NEAR STATION

All enter – Mace leaves them on bench – tells governess to keep eye on them – get some biz in park with governess – Mace exits

The first dated texts in the folder (items 6 and 7) are from 13 November 1916 and are designated 'scenarios' by the MHL archivists, as is the undated fifth item. It is impossible to be certain that these post-date the 'rough rehearsal', but certainly item 6 suggests an advance in detailed conception. It is a peculiar amalgam of the two characteristic Sennett forms of the short story and the paratactic inventory of actions, rendered more unusual still by very specific suggestions for expository intertitles to preface individual scenes (which are unnumbered), such as the first: 'Under title "Real Estate Agent Unable To Sell Haunted House" we see real estate agent on exterior of a rather nice bungalow changing sign which reads "For Sale Completely Furnished $5000" for a sign which reads "For Sale completely Furnished $500".' By the fifth scene, however, the familiar style is back: 'Int House: Father, daughter and agent on: Father and daughter delighted—they start to make deal—sweetheart looks in window at them', and so on. The numerous indications of interior, exterior, type of shot and so forth make this much more cinematic than item 7, a present-tense prose story from the same day.

The absence from the *Done in Oil* folder of a production report or a precise means of dating the remainder of the synopses and 'continuities' (a term that usually, and in most cases clearly, designates a post-filming cutting sheet in the Sennett files) makes it harder to track the story through to production and post-production than is the case with some of the other films. The main interest of *Done in Oil* lies in its demonstration that story conferences, rather than the revision of textual iterations, were the predominant means of story development, and that many of the written 'scenarios' represent a temporary halt to development for purposes of taking stock, as it were; in no sense can they be regarded as a 'blueprint' for production.

A second example, from the following year, gives a stronger indication of the sheer instability of the Sennett stories during the creative process. *A Clever Dummy* (Triangle, 1917)[34] began life as 'Automat Story', a two-page, nine-paragraph, present-tense story outline, which was committed to paper on 8 September 1916. In this version, a penniless inventor is in debt to a lawyer who has invested in the inventor's new creation—an automaton servant girl. The inventor writes to an aunt, asking for money to patent the invention. Her condition is that he must never marry without her approval, and as she has never met him, she solicits a reference. Sennett's films inhabit their own closed universe: so the inventor has of course already been married in secret, the referee is the lawyer, and the automaton has been unfortunately destroyed. 'This places the young man in the position where he has no invention to show his aunt and no money to make a new invention; neither does he care to put his wife out of the house, nor does he know any way to hide his wife from the aunt.' So his wife will impersonate the automaton. The lawyer intends that his own daughter marry the inventor, so that he can gain access to the aunt's fortune; to this end he installs himself at the inventor's house along with his daughter, who becomes the victim of the wife/automaton's jealousy. The daughter, however, has a lover, who has 'learned by some means' about the aunt's forthcoming visit and tries to thwart any potential liaison by arriving at the house disguised as the aunt. The inventor 'overhears him plotting', and when the real aunt arrives the inventor mistakes their identities, ejecting the real aunt and treating the fake one royally.

> Many complications arise; the young inventor's wife does some favor for the old maid aunt who has returned to assert herself, thus getting in her good graces; the scheming lawyer is found out and punished, as is the sweetheart of the girl in his impersonation. The old maid aunt approves of the young inventor's marriage and turns over the money to him.

The story is grammatically well presented, unlike some of the others, while the plotting is tight in some areas, provisional in others. An undated handwritten note indicates that the embryonic tale could be a potential vehicle for the company's juvenile lead (playing the inventor), if the central conceit can be made sufficiently credible (!). Some eight months lapsed, however, before the company set to work on it again in earnest, generating two 'scenarios', each of three pages (together with a further copy of each, with handwritten alterations), both dated 17 May 1917. Attached stenographic notes suggest that, again, these scenarios are the record of a story conference, which helps to account for the staccato, unparagraphed succession of incidents: 'Open story up on garbage can at back of house—pair of shoes along side of it—Ragpicker comes along—picks up shoes', and so on. There are very frequent indications of cuts from shot to shot, anticipating the editing stage.

Aside from the idea of the automatic figure, however, the story has been transformed beyond recognition. There are now four characters: an inventor, his daughter, the inventor's assistant ('Juvenile') and 'Janitor', to be played by Sennett star Ben Turpin. The inventor is an older man; the automaton, to the extent that these things can be sexed, is male. The assistant is part-creator of it, and is in love with the daughter, as is the Janitor. The father disapproves of both, however, so each takes revenge: the assistant hides the automaton, while the Janitor substitutes himself for it. The father unwittingly presents Turpin as the automaton at a demonstration for proposed investors, who, in testing the invention to near-destruction, are actually torturing the Janitor. The assistant and the daughter then successfully exhibit the real automaton, saving the father from disgrace; accordingly, he blesses their union and throws the Janitor out of a window. Much of the second scenario, completed on the same day, retains the material verbatim, but there is some tightening up of the motivation: the father's disapproval of the assistant is occasioned by a quarrel, and the Janitor substitutes himself for the automaton in order to be near the girl.

The 'rehearsal continuity' of the following day (the term is typewritten at the beginning of the script) is again largely similar, but with a radical alteration to the ending: the Janitor/automaton is successfully sold to the investors, who cart him off in a box in a truck, occasioning a chase scene as the inventor, assistant and girl pursue them, accompanied by the real dummy. The 43 'subtitles' (intertitles) in a separate, and presumably later, document further clarify the motivation and deepen the ironic parallels, as with title 3: 'The daughter favored her father's partner who had modeled the dummy after a lovesick janitor.' The final, post-production, four-page and substantially illiterate 'final synopsis' shows that further significant changes were made at the shooting and/or editing stages: in a risqué twist the girl changes clothes in front of the dummy, while the ending has been altered once again, as the Janitor/dummy exploits the opportunity provided by the demonstration to steal money from the prospective buyers and runs away with the cash, successfully pursued by the 'Manager and the whole gang'.

To the extent that distinct and regularised formats can be identified in American film writing prior to the emergence of the feature film in 1913–14, it seems sensible to propose that there were not two kinds of script in use during this period, but three: the theatrical play script, the outline script and the scenario. The word that appears most commonly in contemporary discourses to designate a document used in the preparation of the dramatic action is 'scenario', but what emerges is not so much a generic distinction as a continuum, with the 'outline' at the minimalist end of the spectrum and the 'scenario' at the more detailed.

The form of scripts was not consistent between studios and film units, which had their own ways of working; instead, different prototypical approaches to the two most common methods of segmenting a narrative—via the scene or via the shot—were being explored. Writers were constructing documents appropriate to the particular tasks at hand: prompts to a director during a semi-improvised shoot, preparing a production relatively fully in advance, attempting to negotiate the minefield of copyright or creating a text that might serve more than one purpose in more than one medium.

From 1908 onwards, the scenario was routinely being bundled with other documents relating to pre-production, such as cast lists, location plots and scene breakdowns, along with post-production records of footage shot and expenditures incurred, for legal, commercial and industrial purposes. Collectively, these documents reveal much about the transformation of the story idea from the scenario to the release print of the film. The pre-production scenario was used for story conferencing and rehearsal purposes, but it was not slavishly adhered to: the material would change both in performance and in the process of editing. Each of these production documents had acquired a certain level of consistency, in function if not in appearance, prior to the industry's embrace of the multi-reel 'feature' film in 1913–14. Hollywood now adapted to this new development by installing a more centralised, producer-driven mode of production, with a standardised form of script at its heart: the 'continuity'.

4
The Continuity Script, 1912–29

Prior to 1913, a script could exist in any form comprehensible to the relatively small number of people directly involved in making the film. Around 1913–14, however, a set of developments within American film production meant that the studios began to take a different approach to the texts written in preparation for filming. In Staiger's analysis, the 'director-unit' system was by 1914 in the process of being replaced by the 'central producer' system, a more centralised mode of production whereby the studio maintained quality and economic control over the multi-reel 'features' that had now become the norm for narrative film-making. The script form that emerged has been most widely dubbed the 'continuity'.

The continuity had a dual function. First, it represented a more specific visualisation of the action as it would appear on the screen, precisely anticipating the number and type of shot and the anticipated footage, for example, so that all of those working on the film would understand exactly what was required during production. Second, it assisted powerful studio managers in overseeing and anticipating the budgets of large numbers of longer, more complex feature films.[1] These functions inevitably led to the metaphor that has become ubiquitous: the continuity is a 'blueprint' for the film.

Its utility was enhanced by the range of textual documents with which the script was customarily packaged or archived, and which became fairly standardised for Hollywood feature films around 1914. These documents themselves, however, did not greatly differ from similar materials that had been used at some American studios in the pre-feature era. Although the process varied from film to film, they would now include some or all of the following: (i) relatively infrequently, a copy of the source text, which could be either a property bought by the studio or a story developed in-house; (ii) a synopsis of the story, usually no more than a single paragraph or a page in length; (iii) a list of the characters, perhaps accompanied by indications of costume; (iv) a 'scene plot' or list of locations, recording which scenes (identified by number) were to be shot in which location; (v) the 'plot of action' or 'continuity script' itself, presenting the action usually in terms of a series of specified shots, which we shall discuss in detail below; (vi) a 'title sheet' detailing the dialogue and narrative intertitles, which will sometimes appear in more than one iteration: a provisional list, drawn up before filming, to assist in the understanding of narrative continuity, and a later version, completed after the filming but prior to the final editing of the film; and (vii) a set of post-production documents detailing the footage shot and the costs of production.

Both the terminology and the selection of the documents risks obscuring some important aspects of creative labour. The continuity script itself represents the final stage of pre-production work on the story, and shares with the accompanying documents the industrial functions of planning, budgeting and preparation for filming. Before the creation of the continuity script, however, there must often have been some form of 'scenario' that developed the story or adapted it into a series of scenes and that became redundant for production purposes after the continuity script had been completed. This meant that the writer of the story and the compiler of the continuity were likely to be different people: beginning around 1913, 'a separate set of technical experts began rewriting all the stories. Although the companies might hire famous writers to compose original screenplays, their material was then turned over to these technicians who put it into continuity format.'[2] The continuity, then, was in many respects similar to what we would now term the shooting script, with two important differences: it was prepared not by the author or director, but by a specialist team of continuity writers; and its functions went beyond a breakdown of scenes into shots, to include budgeting and instructions for other workers on the film, including actors.

A second reason why the 'scenario' stage can disappear from view results from the problems surrounding the term 'synopsis'. In their book *How to Write Photoplays* (1920), John Emerson and Anita Loos advise novices that:

The first step in preparing a photoplay is to put it into plain English, telling the entire plot in from 500 to 1,500 words. This is called a synopsis. Unless you are experienced in scenario and continuity work, just tell your plot. The editor will do the rest. [...] If your story is accepted, the editor will have it written into continuity form by a staff man. Learn continuity, but don't attempt to sell stories in that form until you have thoroughly mastered it. Tell your story in the synopsis just as you would want it written as a short story.[3]

As mentioned in the introduction, this shows that the term 'synopsis' can refer not only to the capsule account of the story but also to the story itself, which is superseded by the continuity script in studio records. A similar point may be made regarding the somewhat later 'treatment', which became a standard stage in the process in the 1920s and remains highly prominent today.[4] This translated the source material into a much longer prose form than that of the synopsis; it was often augmented by sample dialogue, usually taking on the appearance of the fairly lengthy short story told in the present tense. Again, the treatment is of interest to historians of particular film projects, but is not primarily a *production* document.

French visitors to Hollywood during the late 1910s were impressed by the efficient division of labour and began reporting both the American introduction of the continuity stage in pre-production and the terminology. In 1923, the director Louis Delluc commented on 'the importance, in America or Germany, of the "continuity writer" [phrase in English]. It is time to realize that an idea for a scenario, however good it is, is not a scenario',[5] while in 1925, the critic Juan Arroy was less impressed that in Hollywood

> the production is divided up in this way: the rights to some literary work are purchased, it is assigned to be adapted by an experienced scenarist, and then the d[é]coupage is assigned to a specialist 'continuity writer' [in English], then it is given to a director to be shot, and finally the film passes into the hands of the *monteuse*. All these functions are absolutely separate, and there is no point of contact among them which would permit each of these artisans to review the work of his predecessors, to apply his critical sense, and to correct their faults.[6]

('Découpage' refers roughly to the division of scenes into shots; the 'monteuse' was an editorial assistant to the director in France.[7])

It should be stressed that this kind of analysis, which suggests that writing proceeded through a relatively efficient series of discrete stages, can be contested. Patrick McGilligan, for example, remarks exasperatedly that:

Before 1926, at least to judge by the official credits, there were no screenwriters. The expression per se barely existed. The profession was fragmented into specialties. [...] There were subspecies of gag-writers, continuity writers, treatment writers, scenarists, adaptors, titlists, what-have-you. [...] If one believes the myths, there were no scripts, just disconnected bits and pieces of paper with enormous gaps allowing presumed geniuses such as DeMille, Von Stroheim, and D. W. Griffith to extemporize as they roared along.[8]

While the 'myth' is largely contradicted by the documentary record, it is not quite so outlandish as McGilligan suggests. The continuity script is at once a narrative form (and one bound up with a complementary narrative of linear film production—the production 'line'), and an arrangement of many different kinds of material, any part of which—the scene text, the formatting and especially the titles—could be re-worked by one or more writers relatively independently of the remainder of the text. Each of the two dominant readings of Hollywood film—as a narrative medium or as a cinema of multiple attractions—is dependent to a considerable extent on which of these perspectives receives the greater emphasis.

The script becomes a co-product of a team of specialists, including, but not necessarily confined to, the story writer, the adapter, the continuity writer and the intertitle writer. Of course, it was possible for a single person to encompass more than one, and possibly even all, of these functions, and possible for more than one of them to be performed in the same iteration. As an effect of this process, the continuity script, especially with the addition of titles, becomes a palimpsest: a scenario has the continuity writer's technical directions laid upon it, followed by the dialogue, intertitles and handwritten production annotations. In such cases it is not so much that the scenarist's work is re-written as that it is preserved but augmented. Staiger's comment on the general relation between scenarios and continuities serves well for both the microcosm of the iterations of an individual script and for the macrocosm of historical change between eras: 'The framework for the continuity script already existed in the scenarios of the period.'[9]

Before considering the continuity script in detail, it is worth introducing two caveats about the apparently obvious connection between script form and industrial function in the screenwriting of this period. If we are interested in a piece of dramatic writing for film as a purely industrial document, we need to focus on the continuity. Subsequent critical debates about the 'blueprint' metaphor have therefore tended to revolve around its division of conception from execution: for example, around whether or not the film really is little more than a straightforward realisation of material that has been planned in its entirety on paper in advance. Such studies have therefore tended to focus on the relationship between the continuity and what came *after* it. These emphases, however, tend to marginalise what we might term the more 'authorial' status of the 'scenario' text; but if we are interested in the 'creative' screenwriter—in what scenarists such as Marion Fairfax or Frances Marion, for example, were actually writing—then we may wish to consider the textual forms that came *before* the continuity and that have been partially obscured by its technical construction. For such purposes, the figure of the palimpsest is more appropriate than that of the blueprint.

A second caveat concerning the industrial model returns once again to the thorny question of the relation between copyright and textual form. In August 1912, two separate legal developments combined in ways which, in Torey Liepa's analysis, helped to bring the Hollywood studio system into being and restructured film writing so that it became part of in-house production. On 16 August, the Sherman Antitrust Act began proceedings against the Motion Picture Patents Company (MPPC), which until that point had largely controlled east coast film production, leading ultimately to the rise of independent producers who would soon begin to move the centre of American film production to the west. Eight days later, President Taft signed the 'Townsend Agreement' into law, bringing into being the copyright classification of films (as mentioned in the discussion of *From the Manger to the Cross* in Chapter 2). Liepa suggests that the passing of copyright laws protecting the business interests of newly powerful studios against freelance film writers instigated, among other things, the development of the 'continuity' script, which then formed a template for film writing for the remainder of the silent age, since 'the written codification of editing patterns, as well as the inclusion of greater descriptive detail and dialogue [...] were believed to bring unpublished screenwriting closer to copyright'.[10] In the event, however, attempts to secure copyright on unpublished scripts proved fruitless until as late as 1978.

Thomas Ince and C. Gardner Sullivan

One of the figures most closely associated with the introduction of the central producer system, and by extension with the development of the continuity script, is Thomas H. Ince, who worked at the New York Motion Picture Company before forming Triangle in 1915 with D. W. Griffith and Mack Sennett. Ince, who created 'Inceville', the prototypical Hollywood studio, in 1912, occupies a significant position in histories of American film writing. He has been credited with 'pioneer[ing] the adoption of both scriptwriting and character dialogue in the silent cinema, and in so doing creat[ing] a space in silent films for the audible dialogue that would emerge by the end of the 1920s'.[11] Staiger, and more recently Liepa, see these developments in the 1910s as being shaped by the shift from the 'scenario' to the 'continuity' script, which itself was in the service of the transformation of American film-making along quasi-Fordist lines that emphasised efficiency and the rationalisation of the workforce. Finally, Staiger uses Ince to advance what is perhaps the most crucial (and contested) claim in her presentation of Hollywood as an industry: 'Ince's use of the continuity script resulted in a two-stage labor process—the work's preparation on paper by management followed by its execution by the workers.'[12]

Ince's reputation as an industrial innovator can be exaggerated. As Edward Azlant observes, although Ince can be credited with taking 'to highly sophisticated levels' the twin functions of the continuity script (' "planning and construction," one procedural or organizational, the other qualitative or aesthetic'), nevertheless he 'certainly did not invent or institute the organizational use of the screenplay'. Scenario departments had existed beforehand, while, as we have seen, the use of accompanying documents pertaining to other aspects of production predated Ince by several years; indeed, they were established some time before their description by the prototypical screenwriting guru Epes Winthrop Sargent in the 1911 article that Azlant cites. More problematically, Azlant is inclined to credit Méliès and Porter (problematically, as noted in Chapter 1) with developing rudimentary forms of continuity, a form that was 'reportedly used at Biograph by 1908, and was clearly indicated by a sample format reproduced by Sargent in his July 29, 1911, article on screenwriting in *Moving Picture World*'.[13]

Although these qualifications are significant, nonetheless the sample pages Staiger reproduces of a crucially early example of an Ince script—*The Raiders*, directed by Jan Hunt in December 1913—do tend to bear out her arguments for the significant advance in industrial organisation represented within the script. Following the paratextual title sheet containing the cast of characters and the shooting dates, and the scene plot breaking down the scene locations, what Staiger describes as the 'continuity script' itself commences as follows:

SCENE 1   INTERIOR EVANS CABIN

TITLE: IN THE MOUNTAINS OF KENTUCKY, BILL EVANS, THE MOONSHINER, AND HIS WIFE AND DAUGHTER.

Bill Evans, tall gaunt mountaineer moonshiner seated at breakfast table with wife and daughter—checked table cloth—homely furniture and props—close of breakfast—demijohn of moonshine on table—Evans pours out a drink in a tin cup—wife tall angular Kentucky type—wearing wrapper—Mary, the daughter, young and pretty—hair in braids—Mary puts on sunbonnet and slips silently unnoticed from cabin—Evans drinks his moonshine and talks with his wife—rifle leaning against the table at his elbow—another rifle over fire-place background—

SCENE 2   PRETTY SET OVERLOOKING WOODED ROCKY MOUNTAIN TRAIL BELOW

TITLE: JACK KEANE, MARY EVANS' SWEETHEART

Close up Keane, handsome young moonshiner—blue jeans—hickory shirt, etc—watching trail below with rifle across his knees—flash—

SCENE 3   EXTERIOR OF CAVE.

Bill Gale (heavy) a big raw-boned moonshiner on guard at cave entrance with rifle slung across his knees, seated by the entrance [...]

Clearly, this represents a much more fully visualised pre-text for a film than any of the scenarios considered in earlier chapters. There is some specification of shot type and a measure of detail in the presentation of mise-en-scène. The second function of the script, to aid the efficient production of the film, is implicit in this degree of detail, and explicit in the accompanying paratexts that organise the shooting of the scenes out of narrative sequence, while handwritten annotations on the scenario itself show the scenes being crossed off as they are filmed. In this way the scenario functions, alongside the other documents in the continuity, as both a pre-production planning document and a post-production record of the filming.

The year after *The Raiders* was filmed, the company was joined by the most widely noted of Ince's writers, C. Gardner Sullivan, who had been writing scenarios since 1912. Sullivan has been described as 'the most important screenwriter of silent films',[14] although it is clear from a comparison of his scenario for *Satan McAllister's Heir*, shot almost exactly a year after *The Raiders* at the end of 1914, to the earlier script that he was working within already established conventions. In what the title page describes as the 'scenario', what mainly distinguishes *Satan McAllister's Heir* from *The Raiders* is the amount of prescriptive detail concerning how the action should be shot and performed:

SCENE 1. CLOSE UP ON BAR IN WESTERN SALOON

A group of good Western types of the early period are drinking at the bar and talking idly—much good fellowship prevails and every man feels at ease with his neighbor—one of them glances off the picture and the smile fades from his face to be replaced by a strained look of worry—the others notice the change and follow his gaze—their faces reflect his own emotions—be sure to get over a sharp contrast between the easy good nature that had prevailed and the unnatural, strained silence that follows—as they look, cut—

SCENE 2. CLOSE UP ON SATAN AT HITCHING RAIL BEFORE WESTERN SALOON

TITLE: "SATAN" McALLISTER, THE RICHEST, MEANEST AND MOST HATED RANCHER IN THE WYOMING VALLEY

Satan is tieing his horse to the rail—he finishes and looks brazenly about him—Satan is all that his name implies—he is a sinister gunfighter, a man-killer and despite the fact that he is without fear, a bully of the worst type—he delights in hurting and abusing people and dogs, and the more forlorn appearing they are the greater his delight in tormenting them—everybody is afraid of him and hates him—he knows this and revels in it—he exits, looking for trouble at every step—

SCENE 3. CLOSE UP ON BAR: SAME AS 1.

Flash back to the men at the bar—they show Satan is coming and wait uneasily, none of them knowing but that he will be singled out for Satan's abuse—[15]

The clear directions for shooting and editing are complemented by the detailed but only obliquely physical description of the villain in scene 2, which amounts to a general recommendation about how the role is to be performed. As Stempel remarks, '[t]he Ince scripts are, in effect, letters to the production team, including but not limited to the director'.[16]

Nevertheless, the nature and significance of the Sullivan scenarios in relation to the production process can be overstated. Although he remarked in 1916 that '[a]ll of the business, no matter how unimportant, is... written into the scene', so that '[e]ach scene in our continuity is practically a short story in itself they are so fully described',[17] this is clearly an exaggeration. While the 'business' is indeed carefully described, and there is more comment in matters of interpretation of character and indications as to how characters are to be played than is the case in most screenwriting either earlier or later, there is relatively little use of description. Unlike the mode of realism in prose fiction, *Satan McAllister's Heir* (more so, indeed, than *The Raiders*) is almost devoid of redundant physical detail: the characters in the saloon are 'good Western types', while Satan 'is all that his name implies'—but the reader will have to supply that from his or her imagination. This may be because 'Inceville' was so densely populated with contracted actors and contained enough established sets that there was no need for the writers to be specific as to visual appearance: the characters and locations were already to hand.

Neither Staiger nor Stempel has found any evidence to support what appears to be the myth that Ince scripts were stamped 'shoot as written', although the occasional typed instruction to that effect has surfaced.[18] Stempel concludes that '[t]here is... more than enough evidence to conclude that Ince did not consider the completed screenplay the end result, but merely the first step in the process of making a film. It was not necessary to follow the script exactly, as historians have assumed Ince's directors did.'[19]

Moreover, while there is a great deal more shot specification than will be found in the later master-scene screenplay, an element of confusion is introduced because, in the technical vocabulary of the time, no distinction was ordinarily made between a scene and a shot: a scene *is* a shot. In this way the scenario or continuity form can be distinguished from the later 'master-scene' screenplay. This problem appears to have exercised Ince who, as Azlant shows, would frequently alter the scenarios for this very reason:

the bulk of Ince's notations involve aesthetic matters, such as further segmentation, condensation, or omission of actions, changes in plot development through cut-backs, changes in the language of leaders, and even some blocking of camera and subject positions within scenes.

Above all, it is the segmentation of actions to construct a film plot that clearly was Ince's primary, and eventually his almost exclusive, concern. If much of screenwriting resides in the design of film narrative through segmentation and arrangement of actions, then Ince's notations actually represent a final rewrite of the screenplay more than any incursion into the visual domain of the director.[20]

Azlant's description of Sullivan's later *Selfish Yates* (1917) holds good for these texts generally: 'The script obviously lies somewhere between a master-scene script, segmented only by scenes, and a densely detailed shooting script or continuity, prescribing so many shots as to constitute an exhaustive segmentation or blocking of the activity, thereby becoming a definitive version of the ensuing film.'[21] As we shall see, other companies of the time were most certainly producing scripts that were more precisely detailed, in this respect at least, than Ince's.

Perhaps as significant as any innovations or improvements Ince may have brought to the scene text is his increasing concentration on speech. Liepa credits the Ince–Sullivan partnership, particularly in the Westerns written for William S. Hart, with developing a vernacular style of dialogue that typified the studio's commitment to realistic detail and anticipated trends in the American cinema of the 1920s, 'featuring more and more speech in its films and increasingly placing the demands of genre and spectacle above those of narrative—until the desire to speak burst off of the celluloid in audible form at the end of the decade'.[22] By 1915, dialogue was accounting for more than half the intertitles in Ince's films, and Liepa describes two of his 1916 features as 'almost full-fledged "talkies"'.[23]

The Immigrant (Paramount, 1915)

Before exploring the Ince scenarios in a little more detail, it is worth noting that the screenwriting work at his studio was at least matched by that at some others. A good example is *The Immigrant*, a typical example of the then-dominant genre of romantic melodrama, written for Paramount by Marion Fairfax in 1915. The 38-page scenario begins with Masha, the titular heroine, being saved by the gallant Harding from unwanted advances aboard a ship bringing her to America. Also on board is the villain, a successful engineer named Walton, who by underhand means employs Masha at his New York engineering company, where Harding (in an example of the crude coincidence typical of melodramas of this period) is just beginning his own career. Walton (implicitly) rapes her, then offers to marry her—for which she has 'a certain thankfulness'. Three years later, Walton is still keeping Masha as his mistress but not as his wife (which she resents), and experiencing Harding's honesty and professional success as a threat. Much of the remainder of the plot hinges on Walton's decision to sabotage a huge dam Harding is building out west: Walton destroys the dam but is killed as a result, the heroic Harding is injured rescuing a child but is saved by Masha and the romantic couple can finally be united.

In general, the film bears out the critical commonplace (D. W. Griffith being an unavoidable example) that the technical advances in American cinema of this period co-exist with a residual addiction to the simpler forms of Victorian melodrama, arguably as a result of the commercial, mass-market ambitions of Hollywood in general. This does not mean that the storytelling itself has not advanced: the greater length of film stories after 1914 demanded more from their writers than the mere repetition of existing formulae, and although the story of *The Immigrant* is crude in various ways, it is much more carefully constructed than any of those considered in the previous chapter. The dam plot is remarkably similar to that of Dawley's *Earthwork Construction Story*, for example, but Fairfax brings in a number of effective dramatic ironies resulting from Harding's ignorance of Masha's true marital situation.

The careful structuring of the plot is matched by a highly sophisticated formal presentation of the script, described on the cover sheet as 'An original by Marion Fairfax'. The following extract comprises the first and the beginning of the second page of the copy in Fairfax's own papers:[24]

1. Main title: "THE IMMIGRANT"
2. Producer's Title:
3. Subtitle: A THOUSAND SOULS – A THOUSAND DESTINIES.

Scene 1.

Long shot of Transatlantic liner, at night. Lighted. (Moonlight)

Ship under full headway.

4-5.   Subtitle: FIRST CABIN

J. J. WALTON - THEODORE ROBERTS.

Scene 2.

Smoking room. (Lighted)

Walton, playing cards, – keen sensual determined face. At a glance a man of wealth and standing – Walton a big bug.

6-7.   Subtitle: SECOND CABIN.

DAVID HARDING - THOMAS MEIGHAN.

Scene 3.

Second deck. (Moonlight)

Harding, looking at the moon, bored—lonely.

8-9.   Subtitle: STEERAGE

VALESKA SURATT

as

MASHA, THE IMMIGRANT.

Scene 4.

Steerage deck. (Full shot) (Moonlight)

Immigrants lying about—crowded, hot. Russians and Slavs. Masha frees herself from group, rising, stretching impatiently as if rebelling against the confinement between decks. She forces her way to the rail and stands looking out over the water, her face full of passionate longing.

Scene 5.

CLOSE UP of Masha as above.

Scene 6.

Steerage deck. (A little longer shot)

Below-decks officer, passing, sees Masha – is strongly attracted to her and very curious. He touches her arm. She turns, draws back, flashes a frank smile and waits. He says to her, "Do you by any chance speak English?" She laughs in a spontaneous way – a frank pleasant laugh – and replies:

10. Spoken title: "YES – I SPIK ENGLISH. I HAVE BEEN TO AMERICA BEFORE – I HAVE GO TO SCHOOL."

Officer comments upon this with exaggerated interest, delighting Masha. He then asks her what she was thinking of when she was looking out over the water so earnestly, – and watches her face grow tender as she replies:

11. Spoken title: "MY SISTER – MY MOTHER – I GO TO THEM."

She starts to tell him about her people in America.

The script is typewritten on dedicated stationery, the numbers pertaining to titles (numbers 1 to 11 in the extract) being separated from the remainder of the text by a vertical red line. Also appearing in red type are all of the 'titles': main title, producer's title, 'subtitles' (narrative and descriptive intertitles) and spoken titles. The use of red type ordinarily indicated that the titles were provisional and could be replaced during the editing. Fairfax's text is certainly a pre-production script: at scene 20 'Harding makes arrangements with steward and pays the difference in the fare. (Show that he hasn't much money)', while scene 133 calls for a hacienda, 'None of it too civilized looking, if possible to get.' Yet it is also presumably a revision, with fractional numbers having been inserted for new scenes to maintain the previous version's scene numbering, while in other places a series of scenes in a previous iteration has been conflated to create one new scene.

That the producer's title has yet to be supplied is a further sign of the text's provisionality within its production context. Such internal evidence alone suggests that while Fairfax may have composed the story, the scene text and even, perhaps, all of the titles, the script has been prepared by studio specialists trained in how to format the scenario—although it is not inconceivable that Fairfax could have done this herself. While titles could be and generally were written by specialists, this was not invariably the case. Sullivan claimed in 1916 that at Inceville all of the writers created their own intertitles: 'I feel that the subtitles must come from the author at the time he is writing the play, for no outsider could be so thoroughly filled with the story and imbued with the atmosphere while simply watching the finished production.'[25]

The scenario reflects technical advances in editing and composition in the cinema of this period, with none of the theatrical awkwardness of entrances, exits and other transitions in the Dawley and Selig scripts. By contrast with the later scenarios we shall consider in this chapter, Fairfax's prose is remarkably lean and cinematic, with the description and report modes being prominent in the scene text, and little sign of authorial narration or comment. Type of shot is frequently though not invariably specified. Perhaps most striking of all, however, are several different modes of rendering speech, all of which are visible in the above passage, and in more condensed form in scene 138:

> Living room. (Hacienda)
>
> Walton walking up and down, waiting – evidently on a tension. Japanese servant announces Mr. Munsing. (Harding's secretary) Walton says impatiently to bring him in – Munsing enters. Walton greets him, says, "WELL, you're here at last are you?" Secretary protests that he came the minute he could. Walton says, "What word have you?" Munsing replies:
>
> 70   Spoken Title: "THE DAM IS ALMOST COMPLETED – WE'RE READY FOR YOU."
>
> Walton says, "Very well, Now, Munsing, your work is all cut out for you – are you going to be able to put it through?" Munsing says, "Yes, – I've got everything ready." Walton says, "Have you got men that you know you can trust?" Munsing says, "Yes," Walton looks at him – then says grimly:
>
> 71   Spoken Title: "BLOW IT OUT TONIGHT."
>
> Munsing says, "All right." Walton starts to carefully outline plan – Munsing listening very earnestly.

The dialogue is presented throughout in three different ways, the first being the dialogue intertitles. The formal separation of the spoken and subtitles from the other elements of the scene text—the two distinct numbering sequences for the scenes and the titles are especially notable—is an indicator of their autonomous position in the production context, since the physical title cards themselves would of course have to be prepared and filmed independently of the dramatic action. A second kind of speech is that reported directly within the scene text ('WELL, you're here at last are you?'). Noting a similar phenomenon of a 'large amount of incidental dialogue, never to appear in the leaders, which Sullivan supplies the various characters' in *Selfish Yates*, Azlant proposes that the purpose is to indicate character motivation and physical expressibility. This 'coexpressibility' of verbal and physical action occurring simultaneously functions differently to the cognitive material of the 'leaders' (a contemporary term for titles), which explicitly directs the spectator to a particular understanding of the action.[26] It is also likely that by this date spectators and actors were sufficiently well versed in lip reading 'silent' movies that a certain amount of dialogue could be reliably delivered in this fashion, obviating the need for interrupting the dramatic action with titles. This may also account for the third kind of dialogue, that where only the gist of the conversation needs to be supplied ('Walton says impatiently to bring him in', 'Secretary protests that he came the minute he could', 'Walton starts to carefully outline plan'). Here the 'coexpressibility' is so easily readable that the spectator need register only the import of the physical gesture of which the speech forms a part.

A second version of *The Immigrant*, also at the MHL but this time in the Paramount files, allows us to place the script in its industrial context.[27] This explicitly divides the script into five 'parts', in place of the 'subtitles' (intertitles) indicating passage of time and mood in Fairfax's script. The main story difference is a radically condensed coda, which cuts out Masha's explanation to Harding that she was never married to Walton. The Paramount papers contain a note crediting Fairfax with both the 'original story' and the 'scenario', a copy of which appears within the compilation of papers that comprise the full continuity. This begins with seven pages of typewritten paratextual materials that preface the scenario itself. The first of these is a cover sheet stamped 'master file', which gives the name of the 'photoplay', indicates that it is an original, identifies Marion Fairfax as both 'author' and 'author of scenario', indicates that the negative was finished on 16 November 1915 and gives the names of the director, assistant director and photographer. Finally, it records the length of each of the five 'parts', coming to a total of 4,614 feet. The next two pages give instructions for the colouring of scenes, titles and inserts; finally, there are four sheets of titles, these comprising both 'sub' (inter) titles and spoken titles.

The copy of the scenario that follows does not directly incorporate these titles but instead tells the editor where each title is to be inserted. The Paramount Files version, then, represents a disaggregation of the script into its component parts, what we might think of as the scene text (the Fairfax 'scenario') and the dialogue text (the title sheets). Clearly this text, or rather collection of texts, has therefore been compiled for the use of different specialists: the director and camera crew shooting the visuals, the writers and makers of the titles, and the editor who will combine them.

There are many indications that the Paramount version is almost certainly the later of the two, not least that the red typescript for intertitles in the version in Fairfax's own files would conventionally indicate that they are temporary, whereas the version in the Paramount files serves the function of post-production record-keeping. The typing differs, and while the material is often identical, there are innumerable minor changes of wording. The Paramount version records the footage required for each intertitle, and where these have been altered it appears to have been mainly in the interests of clarifying the action. For example, spoken title 26 in the Fairfax version ('IT'S UNDERSTOOD YOU POLITICIANS ARE TO HAND US THE BIG STUFF. THERE'S A NEW CHAP ACROSS THE HALL WHO'LL GRAB THIS'), becomes in Paramount spoken title 27: 'IT'S UNDERSTOOD YOU POLITICIANS ARE TO HAND US THE BIG STUFF. THERE'S A YOUNG ENGINEER BY THE NAME OF HARDING ACROSS THE HALL WHO'LL GRAB THIS.' An even clearer example is an insert of a telegram, which in Fairfax insert 65 is 'ORACLE, ARIZONA. J. J. WALTON, FLAT-IRON BLDG. NEW YORK. DAM NEARS COMPLETION. MUNSING.' Here the narrative point could be missed, but not in Paramount's version (insert 69): 'DAM COMPLETED IN TWO WEEKS. COME AT ONCE. MUNSING.' Moreover, Fairfax's clearly pre-production description of a Hacienda at scene 133 ('Quaint terrace—rough pergola to one side—rustic table under old tree. None of it too civilized looking, if possible to get') has been entirely omitted from the Paramount version.

The comparison suggests that the Paramount text represents a later iteration than that held in the Fairfax collection, and that at least some of the changes—the presentation of the intertitles separately from the scenario, for example—would have been carried out by studio staff rather than by Fairfax herself. In this sense it can reasonably be claimed that the version held among the writer's own papers is closer to her own intentions, and that a comparison of the two texts gives some insight into the ways that a 'creative' author's work would be restructured by studio specialists. Meanwhile, in the absence of further documentation it is hard to know exactly how much of the version preserved in the author's own collection is her unaided work; at the least, it is highly unlikely that Fairfax is personally responsible for the highly polished and professional-looking typing and formatting of that earlier text either.

The Scarlet Letter (MGM, 1926)

We can be confident that the better-known Frances Marion was not responsible for the material form of her scenarios, since in the words of Cari Beauchamp, her distinguished biographer,

> Frances preferred dictating, in part because the secretary was an audience whose reaction she could gauge, but most often she and Anita [Loos] wrote by hand on long yellow pads. Both also claimed never to learn to type, as if the skill would make their careers and success appear premeditated, but in reality they were seen using typewriters on occasion.[28]

The generic appearance of continuities at this time suggests that they were invariably subject to final polishing by studio staff.

What this leaves uncertain—from the continuities deposited as part of the studio records, at any rate—is the extent to which 'creative' writers might incorporate within their scenarios anticipations of the shooting and editing, a function that in most readings of the system has been ascribed to specialists. The question arises in the case of a script such as that for *The Scarlet Letter*, because by 1925 Marion was among the most eminent and experienced of writers and would certainly have been familiar with the conventions of the continuity (in later years she was to claim that she, Anita Loos and Bess Meredyth 'were asked our advice on virtually every script MGM produced during the thirties').[29] *The Scarlet Letter* was a particularly difficult adaptation because it 'was on the Hays office "blacklist" of books that could not be filmed', and the project could only begin to proceed once Lillian Gish, who was to play Hester Prynne, assured Hays that she would be 'personally responsible' for the film.[30] Marion herself was brought in after several other unsatisfactory versions had been attempted.

As an indication of the liberties Hollywood felt able (or obliged) to take with major literary works, the eight-page treatment by Wyndham Gittens, dated 1 July 1925, is beyond parody. Gittens recommends 'the simple device of making the principals boy-and-girl lovers', proposes that 'there need be no hint of "sin" other than the reaction of the minister', suggests making the scarlet letter represent 'some term of reproach less shocking than "adulteress"—or, failing a suitable word, by changing the symbol to another letter which will permit of this evasion', and believes 'a "happy ending" should be given to the story'.[31] There goes American Literature.

Marion's own 113-page script bears a cover and title page, dated 30 December 1925, which describes it as a 'scenario'. There is also a studio slip stating this is a 'complete OKAY script from F. Marion'. The scenario contains 372 'scenes', the term being used indiscriminately for scenes and shots.[32] Scene 30, for example, shows Hester in the countryside, and although the following six 'scenes' take place in the same location, in each case it is the indication of a different shot ('CLOSE SHOT OF HESTER; LONG SHOT; SEMI CLOSEUP GROUP OF PURITANS; SEMI LONG SHOT OF HESTER; SEMI CLOSEUP GROUP OF PURITANS') that generates a new scene/shot number.

Beauchamp implies that this text in its entirety is the work of Marion alone: 'Frances's solution was to open *The Scarlet Letter* with scenes and camera directions to establish sympathy for the conflicts Hester faces.'[33] It is difficult to prove the point about these directions from internal evidence alone, but the script gives a very clear sense of Marion's own distinctive authorial style. Marsha McCreadie cites scene 10 as demonstrating 'that she understands film very well in its use of an image for a visual equivalent for emotion':[34]

SCENE 10   SEMI CLOSE-UP AT WINDOW

> Close to the window is a rustic cage with a bird in it. But a black shawl has been thrown over the cage; for the bird's song is forbidden to mount on the Sabbath. A shaft of sunlight has fallen upon the cage. Hester's face, as she gazes at the cage, becomes wistfully sad. Why should she hide its song, Hester asks herself in this moment of faint rebellion. She draws the black shawl away.

Certainly, the script contains remarkably few dialogue titles for a continuity of this period, other than in certain dramatic scenes, especially those between Hester and Dimmesdale. Moreover, as in the combination of reported speech within the scene text and parenthetical narratorial commentary in scene 29, it often preserves a clear sense of authorial commentary while minimising the intrusion of purely technical direction:

SCENE 29   SEMI CLOSEUP REVEREND DIMMESDALE AND MISTRESS HIBBINS

> Reverend Dimmesdale listens to Mistress Hibbins. "We were passing Mistress Prynne's house – she stood

by the window – she uncovered the bird – the bird sang – and then if she didn't deliberately go running out after the bird! And if that wasn't enough, Reverend Dimmesdale, we heard her whistle!" The old lady purses up her lips and whistles – then gives an imitation of Hester calling, "Come birdie, birdie!" beckoning to the bird.

Into Reverend Dimmesdale's eyes comes a look of stern condemnation. (He has known a rigorous school of religious train-ing, and it has made him stern and severe toward the transgressor. He has no pity for the frailty of human nature, and is relentless when he sits in judgment on his parishioners who have sinned. The story of Arthur Dimmesdale is of a man who becomes guilty of the very sin he damns in others, and his spiritual growth through sorrow and repentance.)

"It is wicked of Hester Prynne to do this – and on the Sabbath," Mistress Hibbins is pleased to hear him say.

The ways in which the material text conforms to convention indicate that studio specialists would have prepared and typed the physical doc-ument itself. Conversely, there is nothing within the writing, including the technical elements of titling, camera direction and shot selection, that an experienced writer like Marion would have been unable to provide unaided. That she and Gish were, in effect, given the author-ity to bring a problematic adaptation to a successful conclusion also invites consideration of authorial status in determining the degree of input each might have had in deciding how the film would finally be made. In any event, both *The Immigrant* and *The Scarlet Letter* shed helpful light on the relationships between the authorial scenario and the studio continuity, while giving some indication of the stability of the form across different studios and throughout the period from the beginnings of the Hollywood studio system to the end of the silent era.

Love or Justice (1917)

In light of the preceding sections, it is worth returning finally to Thomas Ince, in order to examine the interaction of authorial style, continuity form and production in the studio that has been the most influential in discussions of the position of the script within silent-era Hollywood film-making. The Wisconsin Center for Film and Television Research has recently placed online a set of documents relating to Ince's 1917 production *Love or Justice*. This is doubly significant: it makes available to scholars and the public an important set of primary materials relating to an aspect of Hollywood film-making that is otherwise impossible to research remotely, and it samples a collection that is central to Staiger's work on the relation of the screenplay to the formation of the classical Hollywood cinema.

Collectively, the *Love or Justice* documents represent a sample of the full run of documents that collectively comprises the 'continuity'.[35] Leaving aside a 1924 transfer of copyright letter (which is not relevant to the production) and what the website confusingly describes as a 'detailed scenario' (which is in fact a printed pamphlet containing the source story, 'The Woman of It', by Lambert Hillyer), the collection comprises six documents directly pertaining to the production:

- A single typewritten sheet, the lower half of which contains a three-paragraph synopsis of the story (again, a romantic melodrama). Above this are the story number (no. 522), and credits for the company, cast, writer, director and 'supervisor' (Ince).
- A two-page document giving the numbers of the scenes to be filmed at each location, first the exteriors and then the interiors. The pencilled deletion of these numbers on the typescript presumably records that the scene number in question has been shot or edited.
- An eight-page 'title sheet' that combines dialogue and narrative titles in a consecutive, unnumbered sequence; aside from inverted commas for dialogue, no attempt has been made to differentiate between these different title forms. The context for these titles is provided by the next document:
- A 14-page sample of the 'continuity script' itself. The title at this stage is still *The Woman of It*, and the title page tells us it is 'by Lambert Hillyer'. The dialogue and narrative intertitles recorded on the title sheet have been inserted within the scenario, and appear in an identical sequence in both documents.
- A post-production 'complete picture report', which is a standard, one-page printed form that has been completed with details of dates of production and the footage shot. Some additional, related detail is provided on two further typewritten pages, one of which refers to Hillyer as author of the 'scenario'.
- A second post-production document, in this case a one-page budget report that breaks down the actual expenditure for labour, materials and so on.

As we have seen, a similar set of documents exists for films made by most Hollywood studios during this period, revealing their industrial functions, their standardisation in Hollywood in this period and their development from a similar, somewhat less detailed set of documents compiled to accompany scenarios from a slightly earlier period. That same context accounts for the annotations to the scenario. Over each scene a large handwritten 'OK' covers the text, presumably to show that the scene has been shot.[36] Indications of additional shots have also been inserted: '3A—close up table' between scenes 3 and 4, for example, while between scenes 6 and 7 a handwritten dialogue title has been added. The continuity, then, is not entirely shot as written, and generates three further iterations after composition: first during the filming, with the addition of handwritten annotations; a second, either before, during or after filming, with the inclusion of the (mostly typewritten) titles (assuming that the author of the scenario and the author of the titles are not one and the same person); and a third—although the scenario text itself may not change at this point—by becoming a part of the composite series of texts that comprise the continuity.

However, what might be termed a purely industrial reading does not wholly account for the nature of the scenario. Below the title and author name on the first page is a preface, which performs a very different function to that of a synopsis:

> This is a story of the underworld; the underworld of a great city, presumably New York, although the exact whereabouts will not be definitely registered in the story. I do not wish to confuse underworld with slums, for although they are often found together, they are not inseparable. The crook of today is seldom a 'tough' and almost never a tramp. Most of them have ingenuity enough to dress in a manner which does not attract attention in any surroundings. If then from time to time the Director finds statements which seem obvious and superfluous, I hope that he will attribute them to an author's desire to picture the real New York underworld as it exists today, and not as it has been so often picturized erroneously.

The whole paragraph at once separates the writer from the production process (in using first-person narration and differentiating the writer's role from that of the director) while inscribing the text within that process by implicitly making a recommendation about the overall desired effect of realism. This duality—a text that is at once personal and industrial, literary and cinematic—persists throughout.

The industrial role is evident in the specification of shot type, as at the beginning of scene 2—after which, however, the mode immediately changes:

SCENE 2.   CLOSE SHOT ON NAN AT TABLE.

> TITLE: NAN.
>   A woman of the underworld, lonely
>   despite the homage of her kind.

> IRIS IN, to get Nan's face. Hold this iris and then come in full and get her sitting at table. Nan is a woman who has lived her life in the underworld; a woman of the type which seems capable of but one real affection, and that a great and overpowering one. Love with a woman of her sort is not a pretty thing, but a savage, vicious passion that is rather hard to quell. Her attire would probably be a suit, not cut by a custom tailor, but at least thoroughly modern and up to date in style. At present she is watching the life around her in the cafe with a sort of amused smile, for despite the fact that she reigns as a sort of uncrowned queen in her surroundings, she is generally bored and many times lonely. After a survey of the room, Nan's eyes swing to the left and she sits listening, presumably to someone who is sitting there.

The paragraph contains some description and report essential to the visualisation of the scene, and even a suggestion for costume design, but overall the dominant mode is of narratorial comment. A sentence like 'Love with a woman of her sort is not a pretty thing, but a savage, vicious passion that is rather hard to quell' cannot be reconciled with a purely industrial function: it does not even possess a particular use for the actor who is to play the character. In such ways, the scenario represents a conflation of the technical and literary modes that exceeds the purely industrial connotations of the blueprint. A reading that concentrates on industrial function would emphasise material that has been adapted by the continuity writer(s) for production; but from a different perspective, what is more interesting is the material that has *not* been so adapted. In such ways the authorial voice peeps through the layers of industrial structuring.

A similar argument could be made about the titles. Liepa observes that 'Ince's writers placed particular emphasis on dialogue writing, allowing character utterances to stand alone within his films as distinct, detailed and reified elements of the mise-en-scène'.[37] Whether or not this emphasis was peculiar to Ince, title writing becomes a distinct part of film-making in this period, and one that can 'stand alone' in ways that cannot always be reconciled with an exclusive interest in narrative structure.

The continuity is an industrial version of screenwriting. Stressing the continuity as the final stage in a writing process (and this can be questioned, in light of the frequent rewriting of both scene sequencing and intertitles) obscures other forms of storytelling in the period: oral communication in script conferences, for example, or the creative work of the writer in producing the scenario. Nevertheless, as a textual form it possesses a degree of stability across both the industrial and the public understanding of screenwriting that would never be achieved again. The introduction of sound would momentarily throw screenwriting into a state of confusion, and no comparably universal set of principles would emerge in place of the continuity. Before examining these later developments, however, we shall see that the continuity's reach extended beyond the United States, to countries that were simultaneously developing alternate forms of screenwriting.

5

The Silent Film Script in Europe

Any attempt to generalise about 'national' screenwriting practices in a particular country during the silent era is dependent on a combination of several factors: a substantial textual record, an advanced industrial model that allows for the analysis of both scenarios and cinematic style within a wider economic and technological framework and a tradition of scholarship with the means to disseminate its results. Given the very low priority that has been given to screenwriting research until recently, the latter is liable to be a hurdle too far even if the other conditions have been met.

In Great Britain, for example, a written 'scenario' of sorts seems to have been in use at Cecil Hepworth's company in 1904.[1] As late as 1919, however, the director Maurice Elvey was complaining that '[t]he number of people in London who can be trusted to turn out a scenario on which a [director] can really get to work without fear of being stopped by some technical error can be numbered on one's fingers', and in 1921 his fellow director (and screenwriter) Adrian Brunel claimed that '[t]wo or three [British screenwriters] are over-worked and are over-producing—while the others chase about for commissions'.[2] Moreover, the UK has never implemented any systematic approach to the archiving of screenplays.[3] Consequently, the surviving relevant materials that have been unearthed to date are skimpy and patchy, with Eliot Stannard, screenwriter on seven of Hitchcock's first nine British pictures, by far the most strongly represented in the research of Ian Macdonald, whose ongoing studies in this field are the most likely source of future discoveries.

The most important of these to date, for present purposes, are two different versions of Stannard's 1921 adaptation of parts of Israel Zangwill's 1891 collection of stories, *The Bachelors' Club*. What appears to be the later of the two resembles the Hollywood continuity script in most respects, with a numbered shot breakdown and a paratactic prose form in the scene text, as in scene 215: 'She looks at him—suddenly perplexed—he gazes down at her—makes a half movement—then stops, thinking—'.[4] This style recalls kinds of scenario that appear to have survived into the earlier Ince continuities, such as *The Raiders* and *Satan McAllister's Heir* from 1913 to 1915, which were considered in the previous chapter. Interestingly, a 'note' in this version ('This in view of Mr. Zangwill's note to hold the affair in suspense, and not play it too strong, which I think very good indeed') appears to show Stannard as the author of the continuity and attempting to influence the direction, in contrast to the divisions of labour seen in the Hollywood studios by this time.

More significant, in the context of attempts to define distinctive or studio-specific forms of scenario construction, is the earlier version, Stannard's 'Scenario Adaptation' of Zangwill's stories.[5] Macdonald sees this as illustrating 'the English style' of scenario writing that had become standard by the late 1910s. The first scene of this text is 'Ep[isode] 1. Sc[ene] 1', the 'episodes' forming a larger unit of segmentation (which perhaps owes more to the source stories than to conventional screenwriting practice), and the 'scenes' being in a numbered sequence. This is followed by an expository 'SUB[TITLE]', a scene heading in lower-case ('Exterior picturesque and fashionable Country Town Pub. Evening'), and a lengthy paragraph of scene text. After nine sentences the paragraph is interrupted in what is (to those familiar with Hollywood conventions) a most unusual way:

> [...] Peter Parker hangs back shaking his head. The two bachelors step into the entrance of the saloon bar, still urging him to accompany them.
>
> SUB: But Peter Parker, in a fit of temporary insanity, has taken unto himself a wife, whose sole recommendation was her Bank Balance.
>
> Peter Parker, played by ...
>
> SHOT A.
>
> Close up Peter Parker from his friends' eye line. He shakes his head dolefully, hesitates, takes out his watch, looks at it, shakes his head again and is about to turn miserably away when one of his friends entering past camera, steps up to

him and taking him by arm, expostulates. Parker, planting thirst, begins to give way and then with great self discipline and determination holds out one finger and says,

SUB: "Righto, but only one."

The passage is fascinating in a number of ways. Macdonald has noted the recurrence of the 'plant' direction in a number of British scripts of this period (here, 'planting thirst'), which seems to be a direction to the actor and/or director to ensure that the required emotion is signified to the spectator.[6] The distinction in prose style between the hypotactic 'writer's version' and the paratactic 'continuity' version, adapted for shooting, is also notable. Most important for present purposes, however, is the direction 'SHOT A'. This makes the scenario a combination of numbered master scenes (each scene being indicated by a scene heading) and a separately numbered (or alphabetised) sequence of specified shots. As noted, the distinction between scenes and shots is confusingly absent in the silent Hollywood continuity—which did, however, generally accord the *intertitles* their own separate number—and the 'English style' in this respect represents something of an advance on contemporary American practice.

Meanwhile, although France was arguably the world leader in filmmaking prior to the First World War, it pursued a very different approach to industrialisation during the time at which American companies were beginning to develop the prototypical Hollywood studio system. The emphasis in France was in quite the opposite direction, towards decentralisation and a 'cottage industry' approach that has persisted ever since.[7] While Hollywood was establishing the continuity script within the central producer system, France remained wedded to a director-unit model, with a number of powerful writer-directors at its core. Combined with the effects of war, this left France in a vulnerable position and confronted with American domination of the industry after the war. As early as 1917, Charles Pathé was identifying a 'scenario crisis' and arguing for something akin to the American continuity script as one way out of it.

In retrospect, his 'estimate that the amount of work for developing a scenario for a four or five reel film would [be] a book of 200 to 250 pages'[8] is remarkably prescient, given that this is the way that the French *découpage* would indeed develop during the sound period in the 1930s. That form of script, however, would continue to be in most cases the responsibility of the director, and French cinema never did develop the Hollywood-style centralisation of production and the division of labour that Pathé and others were calling for in the late 1910s and early 1920s. There is general agreement among those working in French cinema during the silent era that there was very little in the way of formal scriptwriting, other than the often minimal work of a director in preparing the adaptation of a literary source.[9]

Nevertheless, something resembling the continuity was coming into being in the hands of writer-directors like Marcel L'Herbier, in whose work, according to a 1927 account by Jack Conrad, '[t]he montage seems to be minutely foreseen, *a priori*, in the writing of the scenario. [...] L'Herbier specifies in his decoupages the length of each shot, and this must theoretically be scrupulously respected during the shooting'. However, in a remark that looks devastatingly laconic in light both of the preceding chapter's account of the Hollywood continuity and of contemporaneous attempts in Russia to impose an 'iron scenario' on its directors, Conrad concludes that '[i]n actuality this does not happen, because it is impossible practically'.[10]

Parallel screenplay forms in Europe and the United States to 1929

The textual records of British and French screenwriting in the silent period are too fragmentary to admit of much further generalisation in the current state of knowledge. Nor is there a distinctly British style of film-making in this period that would enable worthwhile speculation on the nature of other written texts involved in their pre-production. In France, Russia and Germany, however, the combination of what might be termed a national style—forged by theoretical debate as well as an aesthetics of film—and substantial surviving scenario texts in the latter two countries has enabled Kristin Thompson to propose strong relationships between screenwriting practices, the industrial mode of production and a dominant film style during the silent period in each of these countries. In all three cases, however, by the 1920s the film industries were looking to Hollywood for a model of greater efficiency, and each identified the script as a key factor.

Even before then, however, writing for film was developing in ways that strongly resembled what we have already seen in the United States. In his study of German and Russian screenwriting for silent film, Alexander Schwarz proposes a periodisation that is broadly similar to that we have seen in the United States. After the embryonic early years, recognisable prototypical forms came into being in the pre-feature film phase between 1907 and 1913. Schwarz reproduces parts of several German texts written around 1912 that take a range of different forms: Hugo von Hofmannsthal's *Das Fremde Mädchen* (1910–13) is written in narrative prose; the more complex *Schatten des Lebens* (1912) is divided into many scenes ('Bild'), each with detailed scene text, though as it derives from a contemporary manual it should be treated with caution; the excerpt from Hermann Lemke's *Siegfrieds Traum: Ein Kino-Dramatisches Mysterium* (1912) contains two paragraphs of scene text followed by a lengthy intertitle spoken by Siegfried; and Luise del Zopp's *Maskierte Liebe* (1911) includes handwritten annotations and corrections, and a separate sheet of intertitles. Very similar kinds of text were being produced contemporaneously in Russia between 1907 and 1913: Schwarz's abridgment of what he identifies as 'the first Russian screenplay', Visilij Goncarov's *Sten'ka Razin (Ponizovaja Vol'nica* (1908), contains six scenes, intertitles and an insert of a letter; a scenario for Alexander Voznesenskij, *Jabloko Tellja (Slezy)* (1912), reads as continuous narrative prose.[11]

All of the texts from this period that Schwarz discusses have more or less precise analogues in the kinds of film-related materials being produced at around the same time in the United States. This suggests that while local demands of censorship or copyright undoubtedly played a role in the development of film writing, the formal approaches to the scenario that developed in different countries were prompted for the most part by common-sense adaptations of similar, familiar genres: the short story, the theatrical play script or the rudimentary outline form of scene summary.

As in the United States and elsewhere, the period around 1913–14 was crucial in forcing screenwriting practices to adapt to the demands of the feature-length narrative film. Significantly, however, whereas the continuity script appears to have functioned more or less consistently in Hollywood from around 1913 to the end of the silent era, Schwarz proposes a significant break in Germany and Russia around 1923–24. The later 1920s saw a movement towards greater industrial stabilisation, associated with both post-war reconstruction and envious glances towards the industrial efficiency of Hollywood. This represented a challenge to the autonomy of directors, particularly in Russia, and in this sense the more striking textual forms that we shall examine later in this chapter represent something of an assertion of directorial independence in the face of industrial or political orthodoxy.

Again, however, the similarities between these European industries and that of Hollywood are as remarkable as the differences. Schwarz finds in the development of a given screenplay in France, Germany or Russia a sequence of phases that are more or less analogous to those we have seen in the development of the Hollywood continuity.[12] Here we shall use the German model, but indicate the French and Russian analogues:

1. The 'exposé', or synopsis (the Russian term was 'tema' or theme).
2. The 'treatment', a roughly 20- to 30-page prose version that gave an indication of how the action could be structured into scenes or sequences, with rudimentary indications of possibilities for dialogue, camera directions and titles. The French equivalent was the 'scenario', and a Russian approximation the 'libretto' or (confusingly for those versed in Russian formalist criticism) the 'sjuzet'. Viktor Shklovsky described this as consisting 'of plot and dénouement, furnish[ing] the actor with an opportunity to act and provid[ing] interesting material to film'.[13] This appears to be the same kind of document as the treatment in use in Hollywood at the same time.
3. The 'Rohdrehbuch' ('rough' or 'raw' screenplay), a more specific and detailed version of the treatment, which breaks scenes down into filmable (though not numbered) shots, with intertitles, but lacks the precise specifications of camera and dialogue that would be supplied in the final iteration. In Russia this stage would occasion one of either a technical or literary scenario. This resembles certain forms of scenario and screenplay that use the master scene as the basic unit of action.
4. The final iteration, the 'Drehbuch' itself, much like the English 'screenplay' or continuity, the French term being 'découpage'. As we shall see, in Russia, too, the 'iron scenario' was posited as an antidote to the economic inefficiency that some critics attributed to the irresponsible editing practices of some directors, in the work of whom is often encountered a fifth stage: the preparation of the 'montage list', which can mean variously (and problematically) a shot list, a production record of the shooting, or a document to be submitted for the approval of the censor.

Clearly, all of these countries were developing similar screenplay forms, as well as analogous written stages in the development of a given film project. Nevertheless, as Thompson notes, visitors to Hollywood from France and Germany in the later 1910s and early 1920s pointed to differences from their own systems, with greater or lesser degrees of admiration. Moreover, in each of these countries, as well as in Russia, a distinctive style of film-making had arisen—French impressionism, German expressionism, Soviet montage—that can be associated in part with a mode of production that involves significant variation in writing practices. Finally, it is notable that the structural organisation of the models outlined above is at odds with what appears to have been happening on the ground. In all of these countries, the voices of contemporary commentators and industry insiders were repeatedly raised in opposition to the prevailing 'script crises', directorial whim, cinematic illiteracy and the general *dis*organisation of the film industries themselves, while many leading directors were attempting to resist the imposition of efficiency measures, in particular the enforced separation of writing from directing. Unlike in the relatively well structured and harmonious environment of Hollywood, textual form was a site of contention, and while this produced a degree of chaos, it also enabled major writers and directors to create some of the most enticing written texts in film history.

Carl Mayer and the expressionist screenplay

Between 1913 and 1924 the credits of a number of German films would grant the screenwriter the 'film by' credit, such as Carl Mayer and Hans Janowitz for *The Cabinet of Dr. Caligari* (1920) and Mayer for *Genuine* (1920), both of which were directed by Robert Wiene.[14] Mayer stands at the forefront of—indeed, is exceptional within—attempts to present 'Weimar auteur cinema' as an art form rather than merely popular entertainment, legitimated partly by the perception of the writer as a 'film poet'.[15] Siegfried Kracauer calls Mayer's work 'screen poems' or 'instinct films',[16] and the poetic form is evident both in the manner in which Mayer presents the scenario text and in his application of a new principle to the relationship between the written text and the film experience. Mayer places comparatively little emphasis either on what is imagined to be seen on the screen (unlike most forms of screenwriting) or on the requirements of the technical crew (unlike the silent Hollywood continuity or the various kinds of 'shooting script'). Instead, he anticipates the emotional response of the spectator; and 'anticipates' is the right word, since his writing is an attempt to capture the nervous excitement of the viewer, with all his or her doubts and speculations about the events unfolding on the screen.

In most respects his first script, *The Cabinet of Dr. Caligari*, written with Hans Janowitz in the winter of 1918–19, is atypical. Until quite recently, the understanding of the *Drehbuch* for this film was largely derived from Kracauer's influential *From Caligari to Hitler: A Psychological History of the German Film* (1947), which was itself indebted to Janowitz' own account. It was only in 1995, with the German publication of a copy previously in the possession of Werner Krauss,[17] the actor who played Caligari himself, and which David Robinson has convincingly argued to be 'the first, the last, and the only version of the *Caligari* script',[18] that historians began significantly to revise the received view of the nature of *Caligari*'s written text.

The *Caligari* script is formally divided into six 'Acts'—perhaps a legacy of the move to multi-reel production rather than, necessarily, of theatre (similarly, *Grausige Nächte*, directed by Lupu Pick in 1921, was billed as 'A Film in Five Acts by Carl Mayer').[19] Unlike Mayer's later work, *Caligari* contains lengthy titles for both dialogue and exposition:

ACT 1
1. Scene: Large, elegant terrace of a country house

(viewed from the Park)

> Evening atmosphere. Francis with a lady on his arm, Jane with a Gentleman, followed by two Gentlemen and three Ladies, step in cheerful mood onto the terrace, where a table with a steaming bowl is prepared. They sit on the wicker chairs placed there, and chat animatedly.

2. Scene: The Terrace.
(closer view, from the house)

> View over the fine, ancient park lying in the evening atmosphere. The landscape slopes away. Cheerful atmosphere. Suddenly Francis casts a look at the road outside, where two gypsy wagons with people trotting beside them slowly pass by. Francis puts down the glass he has raised in a toast and stares reflectively into the distance, while his wife quietly and meaningfully goes to him and lovingly strokes his hair. Surprised and disquieted, the guests question the couple.

TITLE: Yes, my friends, you do not know that dreadful tale of Holstenwall, which the sight of these gypsies passing by brings back as melancholy thoughts to Jane and me.[20]

Characteristic of the German *Drehbuch* is the justification of the text for titles at the left of the page, with scene text towards the right. More peculiar to Mayer's later method, in Robinson's view, are some of the detailed descriptions of character and action, such as on Caligari's first appearance:

> A spectral-looking old man, in a dark, flying cloak and high cylinder hat, trots along the street, following the procession. His hands, clasped behind his back, hold a walking stick. His head recalls that of Schopenhauer. He stands still for a moment, and before going on, solemnly leafs through the pages of a large book which he takes out of his coat pocket. Then he appears satisfied and goes on his way.[21]

This meticulous depiction of the scene, while certainly amenable to recasting as a series of shots, does much to suggest that the writers are prioritising mise-en-scène over montage in a way that is characteristic of the German cinema of this time.

Given Mayer's later innovations in writing the scene text, it is remarkable that the titles in the Janowitz-Mayer script for *Caligari* have a 'conventional narrative style', whereas in German (though not English-language) prints the titles are 'staccato', a result of 'the film production team's attempt to integrate the titles into the overall expressionist design in literary style as well as in their shape'.[22] Mayer would dispense with titles altogether for *Der Letzte Mann* (1924) and use them only sparingly in *Sunrise* (1927), while Hermann Kappelhoff states that in *Sylvester* (1923), '[n]ot only had the inserts disappeared almost entirely, they were replaced by visual motifs with no relation to the plot: the surging sea, a churchyard, a forest'.[23]

Still more important to the reassessment of *Caligari* is that the 1995 publication refutes Janowitz' contention—promoted by Kracauer—that Wiene's frame story, which reveals the events to be a story told by a madman, reintegrates an essentially radical critique of authority into a conservative frame. What this overlooks is that the original scenario also had a frame story, and one that is altogether *more* conservative: as the extract above shows, in the original Janowitz-Mayer version the story is related retrospectively from the security of an exemplary bourgeois country house, suggesting that any potential threat has been successfully contained.

Mayer's post-*Caligari* texts aspire to the condition of poetry, presenting a method and form of writing markedly at odds with contemporary American practice. A transitional phase can perhaps be seen in his scenario for the lost film *Der grüne Kuss* (aka *Der Bucklige und die*

Tänzerin, directed by F. W. Murnau in 1920), in which, according to Jürgen Kasten,

> the grammatical transpositions and abbreviations, the use of single words as independent sentences, emphasis by means of unusual punctuation and the elaboration of processes stretching over a number of scenes were not used throughout. *Der grüne Kuss* is one of Mayer's earliest screenplays. But his technique, which he later perfected, condensation of language and abbreviation for the purpose of designating the specific visual form were already employed here.[24]

The Mayer script for another Murnau-directed film of this period, *Der Gang in die Nacht* (1920–21), again appears transitional. To judge by the facsimile of a page of the *Drehbuch* reproduced in Patrick Vonderau's analysis, Mayer was still presenting the scene text in continuous paragraphs, rather than as short lines suggesting a sequence of shots.[25] Yet the syntax now has the characteristic brief, emotional punches of his better-known works: 'He fights for breath. But she just looks at him. Hot! Burning! Possessive! Pugnatious! Sparkling! Closer: But he gasps. Faster and faster! Struggling more and more. Then: a cry! You!' Vonderau suggests that this methods represents 'a stylistically heterogeneous mixture of melodrama's "canonized emotional poses" on the one hand and on the other hand an attempt to translate emotional states into intensified physical expression'.[26]

The recasting of such prose into a series of short lines in Mayer's subsequent work, beginning with *Sylvester*[27] and the better-known *Der Letzte Mann*,[28] also suggests a concern for the language as text, as poetry. Indeed, *Sylvester* contains all of those characteristics of the 1927 *Sunrise* scenario that are likely to seem peculiar to the reader familiar only with American scripts: the lineation, the liberal use of exclamation and question marks in the scene text to indicate emotional mood and, in place of the more usual film-specific transitions ('cut', 'iris', etc.), conjunctions or adverbs of time, often accompanied by an exclamation point ('Und!', 'Jetzt:', 'Und da!', 'Doch!', 'Denn:') that suggests a peculiarly child-like wonder at the scene and an insistence that the reader follow, like a child dragging an adult through the attractions of a funfair.

This is precisely the effect of *Sunrise*—arguably Mayer's (and Murnau's) greatest achievement—especially in the sequences in which the young married couple rekindle their love and start to see the world through new eyes, as in scene 72:[29]

Ansass and Indre walking along in an embrace.

And now: as though visualizing their thoughts, everything is fading away before extreme happiness.

The houses grow indistinct.

Slowly sinking into the ground?

And also all the carriages and rolling traffic?

While we see just the two strolling along.

Through fantastic spheres.

The title page of the published facsimile of the German-language typescript, with Murnau's handwritten annotations, identifies *Lied von Zwei Menschen* (*'Sonnenaufgang'* has been handwritten above) as a 'Film von Carl Mayer'. The title page of the English translation held at the American Film Institute identifies *Sunrise: A Song of Two Humans* as a 'Photo-play by Carl Mayer, Adapted from a Theme of Herman Sudermann's "A Trip to Tilsit".' That description (a translation of Mayer's 'Unter Verwendung eines Motivs aus Hermann Sudermanns: "Reise nach Tilset"') helps to explain Mayer's work as a kind of musical variation on a 'theme'.

For *Sunrise*, as was Mayer's custom (but very much against usual Hollywood practice), the writer worked in independence from the studio: Murnau had accepted an invitation by William Fox to make a film in Hollywood, leaving Mayer behind to write the *Drehbuch*.[30] Fox had brought Murnau to the United States in an attempt to marry Hollywood's commercial reach and technological innovation with the cachet of European art cinema. Yet the timing was not propitious: although the film is now widely regarded 'as a sort of fortuitous historical accident by which the resources of Hollywood were put, for once, at the service of a great film artist', it was already the beginning of the end of the silent cinema, and 'prints of the film were prepared with a synchronous music and effects track, making the film a curious technological hybrid: not silent, but not quite "sound"', contributing to its financial failure.[31] Moreover, a populist backlash had begun against German art cinema, and the film suffered as a consequence of its rumoured aesthetic radicalism and the director's secretiveness during production, so that 'this "otherness" was spoken of as difference and strangeness rather than progress and innovation'.[32]

Arguably a stronger argument in favour of the film's strangeness is found in the form Mayer used to write the script, which reveals no deference to Hollywood convention whatsoever. The page, again, is divided into two columns, with scene-text description on the right, and technical material—scene heading, camera and editing directions, and titles—on the left. Scene numbers are absent; Murnau has inserted them by hand on his copy, and they are present in the English-language typescript. Mayer de-particularises the story world, which is a Lithuanian fishing village in the source, but unidentified in the retelling. Characters' names are also absent from the German text, but supplied in the English (although mistranscribed from Sudermann: 'Ansas' and 'Indra' have become 'Ansass' and 'Indre'), and there are fewer than 20 titles. Combined with the characteristically poetic lineation, this refusal to conform to some of the most basic requirements of the conventional film scenario helps to place the reader in the dream-like state the film itself evokes.

Debates about the film often engage the question of the extent to which Fox attempted to 'Americanize' it by bringing it closer to Hollywood conventions, an argument that depends to a large extent on changes to the source story. Although in certain respects Mayer follows Sudermann's source text quite closely, there are radical changes. The short story begins with the homewrecker Buzse as a servant in the house of the young married couple, the fisherman Ansas and his wife Indra. Her father decides to throw Buzse out, resulting in her taking lodgings in a nearby house. The 'photo-play' omits this altogether, instead moving us straight to the heart of the love triangle, with Buzse a vampish outsider and the motivation left comparatively obscure. In Sudermann's tale, Indra knows full well that her husband plans to drown her, and her willingness to go with him onto the lake becomes a suicidal act of self-sacrifice. In Mayer's version, the wife does not initially realise that her husband may be planning to kill her; instead, her first intimation that something is wrong comes as the couple begin their boat trip, when the dog causes a commotion and the husband has to take it back to shore. Moreover, the tragic twist to the ending of the story—the husband drowns while the wife is saved—is eliminated, the vamp is driven out of the town and the happy family is reunited.

Although *Sunrise* can reasonably be held to be Murnau's crowning masterpiece, and perhaps the best illustration of the fertile relationships between European and American film-makers in the silent Hollywood era, the 'photoplay' credits—especially in the light of the aforementioned German conventions regarding the attribution of film authorship—allow us to place German writers generally, Mayer individually and the *Sunrise* script specifically at the centre of film production. This was in contrast to the prevailing model in Hollywood, in which with the exception of some directors of auteur status (who were often of European extraction, such as Erich von Stroheim), the producer tended to be the dominant figure. Instead, throughout his career Mayer 'was "writing films" rather than writing for film', and so 'is not adequately described as a "scriptwriter"'.[33] In the same year as he made *Sunrise*, Murnau said that 'we have a generation born and grown to manhood since the motion pictures were invented, and yet so far, no great Poet of the new art has arisen'. The remark is chosen by Lucy Fischer to preface her discussion of poetry and narrative in the film,[34] yet neither she nor the director defers to the 'film poet' who was arguably the first writer to transform screenwriting from the preparation of industrial pretexts into a medium of literary expression.

Soviet Russia: Montage and the 'iron scenario'

Anxieties surrounding the relationship between writing and film production had surfaced in Russia before the 1917 Revolution: as early as 1913 there were 'too many film-makers chasing too few ideas',[35] and the problem of under-supply became acute thereafter. In 1923, prior to the greatest advances in montage editing, concerns were being expressed over a perceived 'scenario crisis',[36] partly because the war and the Revolution had eliminated many experienced writers, but also because methods of production were perceived as wasteful. In 1924, 90 per cent of scripts were being rejected, leading not only to suggestions for higher pay for script writers but to concerted arguments for a more centralised organisation of writing in relation to film production.[37] By 1926, Soviet cinema journals were launching a 'regime of economy' campaign, with Sergei Eisenstein's cavalier approach to the shooting script of *The Battleship Potemkin* (1925) being singled out for criticism. In 1927, Viktor Pertsov, characterising the screenplay generically as a 'half-finished literary work', was still complaining of a 'screenplay famine', and therefore a 'plot famine', in the industry.[38] In December 1928, the Sovkino Workers' Conference held that '[t]he script crisis has not yet been overcome', and argued that screenwriting should be subject to centralised control within the studios, with 'specialist scriptwriters... prepar[ing] scripts for particular directors'.[39]

The familiar debates between Eisenstein and Vsevolod Pudovkin, among others, about montage editing and the role of the script need to be seen in the contexts of these endemic 'scenario crises' and the moves towards economic and political control of the film-making process. The 1920s was a period when Hollywood scripting practices and their position in the industrial process were arguably the most stable that they would ever be; unsurprisingly, there were those in Soviet Russia who looked to their ideological alter ego as providing a centralised model that could solve their chronic problem of industrial inefficiency, with the continuity script at its core. The most celebrated achievements of Soviet montage editing, then, took place against an ideological backdrop in which the wholly contrary concept of the 'iron scenario' loomed large.

It was a method propounded by Pudovkin in his 1926 pamphlet 'The Film Script':

> There is a belief that the scriptwriter should provide just the bare bones of the action, leaving it to the director to flesh it out 'cinematically'. Nothing could be further from the truth. [...] All the individual camera positions—long shots, close-ups, aerial shots, etc., all the technical devices—such as 'fades', 'masking', 'panning'—that help to link the sequence to the ones that precede and follow it, all that constitutes and enhances the inner content of the scene must be precisely calculated. Otherwise irreparable mistakes may occur in the shooting of a scene plucked at random from the middle of the script. So, the working or shooting form of the script provides a detailed rendering of every part, however small, indicating all the technical methods needed to shoot it. Of course, asking scriptwriters to write in this way is the same as asking them to become directors. Nevertheless, the work of the scriptwriter must move in this direction. Even if he fails to deliver a 'steel' script ready for filming, he must try to furnish material that approaches the ideal form.[40]

There are evident connections between this view of the script, Pudovkin's 'constructional' theory of montage in which shots are linked in sequences, and perhaps his best-known film, *Mother* (1926), the narrative structure of which is not radically dissimilar to that of contemporary Hollywood cinema in detailing the adventures of the protagonist as a causal sequence of ultimately heroic deeds in overcoming a powerful adversary.

In that same crucial year, screenwriter and critic Viktor Shklovsky used the familiar metaphor—'[t]he script should become the blueprint of the picture'[41]—while the critic Ippolit Sokolov was enthusing that in the

' "iron scenario" [...] nothing is left to chance. The picture ought to be literally preliminarily edited before the filming begins. One should not film a single frame until the entire picture is mentally edited.' Finally, '[t]he scenes and shots ought to have numbers'.[42] However, it is worth noting Thompson's observation that 'in practice [the "iron scenario"] approach to scripting seems to have remained largely an ideal goal rather than a practical method until well into the 1930s'.[43] The current researches of Maria Belodubrovskaya suggest that even this is an overstatement, and that throughout the 1930s, in the absence of a professionalised approach to screenwriting, the Soviet industry relied on directors still wedded to the montage tradition to prepare scripts, which consequently rejected the blueprint model.[44] As we have seen with both the Hollywood continuity and the French *decoupage*, in practice the 'ideal goal' of a rigid separation of written conception and filmic execution is likely always to be compromised by the exigencies of production, for innumerable different reasons.

It was in Russia, however, that the politics of the debate were most acute. Noting a distinction in terminology, Richard Taylor points out that '[a]n "iron script" [...] was a full script delivered to a director ready for filming. A "steel script" [...] was one that could not be altered. By 1926 there was, of course, also an association with Stalin, "man of steel".'[45] By the end of the decade the dearth of suitable screenplays could be traced as much to the political problems of censorship, and the ideological question of what might constitute permissible and appropriate themes, as to the industrial mode of production, for which something akin to the Hollywood continuity script could have been adapted. Cinema lay at the intersection of industry and ideology, and writers were legitimately anxious that in a new production economy that put the script and not the director at its centre, they would be uncomfortably exposed.[46]

In light of these developments, Eisenstein's theoretical pronouncements, as well as his work on *October* (1928), appear remarkably courageous. In a short essay in 1929 he gives a general, theoretical justification for taking a position that is directly opposed to the blueprint model of the iron scenario. Eisenstein proposes a radical separation between the written text and the director's cinematic interpretation, describing them as two different 'languages'.[47] He gives the example of a survivor of the *Potemkin* mutiny, who had stated that 'A deathly silence hung in the air.' Eisenstein remarks that a writer might choose to place these words in the script, because it sets out the emotional requirements. [...] And the scriptwriter is right to present it in his own language. [...] Let the scriptwriter and the director expound this in their different languages. The scriptwriter puts: 'deathly silence'. The director uses: still close-ups; the dark and silent pitching of the battleship's bows; the unfurling of the St. Andrew's ensign; perhaps a dolphin's leap; and the low flight of seagulls.

The prose libretto, then, could function as a scenario precisely because it *didn't* need to anticipate the film in anything more than approximate narrative or emotional terms. By contrast, for Eisenstein (repeating a phrase he had first uttered in 1928), '[a] "numbered" script will bring as much animation to cinema as the numbers on the heels of the corpses in the morgue'. Consequently, he stated openly that 'we are opposed to the usual form of numbered detailed script (*Drehbuch*) and [...] in favour of the film novella [libretto] form'.

However, between the polarised concepts of the 'iron scenario' as a production blueprint, on the one hand, and of the writer and director working with fundamentally different 'languages' demanding only the freest translation between them, on the other, lies a range of textual possibilities. Nor were positions necessarily as entrenched as it at first appears. By 1928, Pudovkin had changed his mind and, with Osip Brik, was creating another kind of pre-production document that allows for a directorial latitude akin to Eisenstein's approach to the libretto. Brik's 'treatment' for *Potomok Cingiz-Chana/Storm over Asia* (1928) comprised a typewritten list (with handwritten annotations) of scenes, shots or actions, each no longer than a few words or a short sentence: the first three, for example, are 'steppe', 'snowy steppe', 'Mongolian steppe'. Pudovkin translated this into an equally elliptical form of numbered shooting script ('Landscape. Barren mountains', 'Mountains, mountains', 'a wild animal' and so on), with approximations of shot length.[48]

Brik himself had in 1926 advanced perhaps the most radical conception of the screenplay we have so far seen when he proposed that '[t]he screenplay should be written, not before shooting, but afterwards. The screenplay is not an order to shoot, but a method of organising what has already been shot. And we should therefore ask, not how a screenplay should be, but what should be photographed.' As Richard Taylor remarks, however, 'this extreme attitude contributed to the chronic shortage of screenplays that affected the Soviet cinema in the later twenties'.[49]

Soviet cinema of the 1920s therefore provides two completely opposite directions for screenwriting. The first shadows Hollywood, moving from the initial 'tema' or idea through the prose libretto to the 'iron scenario' that in theory (if not in practice) could be filmed as written. The second is an almost precise inversion of this: a conceptual hostility to the idea of rigid pre-production causes the director to use the libretto as the first stage in a deconstruction of the narrative, proceeding through a series of sequence outlines for filming and ending with, in Brik's words, '[t]he re-working of material in the screenplay [which] is the last stage of the work'.[50]

Some examples from the work of Eisenstein, the most excitingly unsystematic of the Soviet film-makers—and therefore a stimulating contrast to the idea of Hollywood as a factory of serial production—show the range of textual materials that could result, including drawings, diagrams, storyboards and voluminous annotations.[51] The written scenarios themselves were prepared with different collaborators, and they were rarely more than provisional. The major unit of segmentation is the act or sequence—*The Battleship Potemkin*'s script is formally divided into four acts, *October*'s into five—but in contrast to Hollywood practice, Eisenstein at this time had no use for the division into scenes.

Eisenstein's drastic irreverence towards the 'shooting script' is well indicated by his approach to *Potemkin*. Alexander Lyovshin, his assistant, recorded that after each day's shooting in Odessa, rehearsals for the following day involved crew members who 'walked or ran through the rehearsed *mise-en-scène* while Eisenstein made corrections in the shooting script. Although 75 percent of the shooting script was ready in advance, most of the remainder was determined in these rehearsals.'[52] The quality of improvisation extended to most of the film, which was expanded from a 46-shot sequence initially planned for a much larger project, *The Year 1905*, after Eisenstein arrived in Odessa: as the director recorded, '[n]o scene of shooting on the Odessa Steps appeared in any of the preliminary versions or in any of the montage lists that were prepared'.[53]

Jay Leyda reproduces what he describes as 'the director's shooting script', though the document is undated, and Leyda is careful to note that '[i]t represents a particular stage in Eisenstein's work on the film', after some footage had already been shot, and with—not surprisingly—only a rough approximation of the intertitles.[54] This version preserves Eisenstein's insertion of certain shot breakdowns, which are (presumably) illustrations of the rewriting that Lyovshin observed, and which reveal some of the director's process of translating what is in many ways a quite straightforward narrative in the scenario into more vividly realised shot series. Most notable in this respect is a radical rewrite of the Odessa Steps sequence, with Eisenstein's handwritten insertion of all of the shots of the child's pram as well as notes for the use of sculptures at the Opera House, including one of stone panthers. Even so, in this version of the scenario almost every shot is from within the diegesis, and contributes to narrative progression, as does the overt division of the scenario into four sequences (not the five acts of the film as released), with somewhere between 100 and 140 shots in each.

By contrast, the script for *October* (1928), written in collaboration with Grigori Alexandrov, represents a quite remarkable kind of narrative deconstruction, although this is partly because, again, the scenario was provisional, and 'a full version of the shooting script never in fact existed—scenes were constantly re-worked during shooting'.[55] As Schwarz's chronology shows,[56] there were no distinct stages between synopses, screenplays, shooting scripts and production: all were subject to continual revision, largely in reflection of the political compromises that were forced upon the project. Eisenstein had been urged to produce another work of populist propaganda, along the lines of *Potemkin*; instead, the script shows that the intellectual 'formalism' that caused *October* to run afoul of the authorities was prefigured in the early written, planning stages, and was not simply an effect of editing and the pressures of production.

Where the text of *The Battleship Potemkin* is purely functional, an indication of the content of each shot, from the beginning the scenario for *October* has literary qualities in excess of the requirements of any blueprint:

1   Gold,

2   precious stones,

3   shimmering lights covered the tsarist crown, the imperial sceptre and the autocratic orb.

4   The gold glittered,

5   the lights shone,

6   the gems sparkled,

7   until ... until women's bony fists rose out of the queues of the hungry,

8   until calloused workers' hand brought machines to a standstill,

9   until angry leaflets lifted into the air,

10   until the hungry trenches ceased firing,

11   until the people rose up and brandished their fists.

12   But see, they have risen.

13   and they have brandished their fists.

14   And with that the crown began to grow tarnished and dull,

15   with that, the blinding radiance faded,

16   with that, the oppressive, crushing idol became visible...

17   The idol of autocracy, standing

18   on a massive, polished stone, against a sky darkened by ominous clouds.

This is something other than a simple shot list. An almost universally observed rule of screenwriting is that because the viewer experiences the film as a series of actions unfolding in the here and now, the script must report events in the present tense. The use of the past tense in *October* (at least in this translation), by contrast, introduces the idea of literary narration. This quality is accentuated by repeated recourse to the rhetorical device of anaphora: successive shots begin with the same word or phrase ('until' in shots 7–11, 'with that' in 14–16), until they come to resemble lines of poetry, again suggesting the stylistic and rhetorical organisation of the literary rather than the screen text.

Nonetheless, this sequence functions well enough in indicating the content of each shot—more so, indeed, than most Hollywood continuities. Soon, however, this literary style introduces complications, as in the use of similes:

45   The orators of the petty-bourgeois party poured forth like balalaikas.

46   The telegraph machines tapped away like trilling nightingales.

     TO ALL... TO ALL... TO ALL...

47   But, like ammonia hitting the nostrils, a question sprang to the eyes:

     T-O A-L-L?

Each simile, by definition, introduces a comparison between two terms, which cinematically suggests either a juxtaposition two shots (a cut from the orators of shot 45 to be followed by a shot of balalaikas in a succeeding shot 46) or the use of superimposition, a method Eisenstein used extensively in the film. The scenario proposes no solution, however, and the problem starts to become insuperable at shot 47, the simile of which introduces images that would produce a distractingly comic effect if visualised. This use of analogy is surprisingly prominent: shot 114, for example, notes that 'As the drowning man clutches at a straw, so the failing government reaches for the machine gun'. At times the numbering seems to be used to provide a narrative rather than visual breakdown of the action, as at 188: 'The Bolshevik Party programme was transformed into a weapon against infantry, cavalry and artillery', or, more extensively, at 206–10:

206 The Smolny prepared for a Congress of Soviets.

207 Its preparations were as intensive as for a major campaign.

208 The outcome of the insurrection more or less depended on the armed soldiers.

209 In short, the outcome was in the hands of the Petrograd Garrison.

210 And this is where the Smolny directed most of its preparatory work.

These could be rendered as titles, but again, the scenario does not give any indication of this, or of how the narration might otherwise be incorporated within the montage.

Clearly, this is an incomplete scenario, but in any case it would not be adequate to the demands of a system such as Hollywood's, which utilised a rather impersonal division of labour. In its very form, then, it reveals something of the nature of the relationship between Eisenstein and Alexandrov, his co-writer and co-director; the cinematographer Eduard Tisse formed the third member of what could be considered Eisenstein's principal production team. As in the later case of *Citizen Kane* (Orson Welles, 1941), and indeed the screenplays of Ingmar Bergman, to both of which we shall return, such a literary form of scenario is a statement of a kind of artistic authority over the whole production, and is therefore associated with ideas of the cinematic *auteur*.

It is not surprising either that Eisenstein proved incompatible with the American studios with which he attempted to work in the 1930s, or that *October* should have alerted the Soviet authorities to a potentially troublesome 'formalism' in a director who had failed to produce the straightforwardly effective propaganda they thought they had commissioned. It was to be his last major silent film. *The General Line*, which Eisenstein had placed to one side to undertake the *October* assignment, was never satisfactorily completed. In the summer of 1929, Eisenstein made ultimately abortive plans to add sound to *The General Line*, now retitled *Old and New*, and compiled detailed notes for the music, to be composed by Edmund Meisel.[57] Although these annotations were compiled separately from the film's scenario, which the director was also preparing to publish in Germany, this attempt to reconfigure for sound a film that had already, partially or wholly, been shot according to the practices of the silent cinema was one symptom of cinema's remarkably rapid transition to sound. In this brief transitional period, from around 1927 to 1931, screenwriting itself had to be radically transformed to accommodate the new technology.

6
The Coming of Sound

By 1927, the continuity script had, for around 13 years, provided Hollywood with a clearly structured and relatively efficient means of structuring a story idea within the context of film production. The appearance in that year of *The Jazz Singer* represented little less than a heart attack, its effects immediately visible as the studios struggled to find ways of adapting their writing practices to cope with the shock. In time, the screenplay would be overhauled, with a measure of consistency re-emerging once the transition to sound had been completed, although an inter-studio consensus comparable to that surrounding the continuity would never fully return.

In the interim, sound presented screenwriters with two overlapping sets of questions. The first was, essentially, simply one of formatting: How should dialogue be incorporated within the script? The second engaged the studios' short-term need to salvage what it could from projects that had been undertaken with silent cinema in mind, but that now needed to be reconfigured for audiences that were unwilling to turn back the clock. Several solutions were attempted: the accidental inclusion of dialogue within *The Jazz Singer* suggested that audiences might temporarily accept the 'part-talkie', films that had originally been shot silently could be reconfigured for sound, or the studio could simultaneously produce silent and sound versions of the same film. All of these methods produced different headaches for the writer.

The beginnings of the sound film: *The Jazz Singer* (1927)

The Jazz Singer tells the story of Jakie Rabinowitz, the son of a Cantor who despairs of his son's desire to pursue a career on the stage. After running away from home to follow his dream, Jakie, under the name Jack Robin, finds himself forced to choose between standing in for his dying father to recite the 'Kol Nidre' for Yom Kippur in synagogue or performing at the opening night of the Broadway show that would make him a star. He effects a reconciliation by choosing the former, although in a dramatically weak conclusion the show is merely cancelled until the following night, when Jakie's performance of 'My Mammy' (in blackface) in front of his mother brings the film to an appropriately melodramatic conclusion.

It was not the first film to feature sound, Warner Brothers themselves having already released *Don Juan* (1926); nor was it an all-talkie, the first example of which was *Lights of New York* (Warners, 1928). It was not even planned as a 'talkie' at all, and the 'Adaptation and Continuity by Alfred A. Cohn, from the Stage Play by Samson Raphaelson' is, for the most part, a typical example of a silent continuity, with 401 numbered scenes (shots) and a separately numbered sequence of 162 titles.[1] As initially conceived, its technological advance was supposed to lie in its application of the Vitaphone sound-on-disc apparatus, which was more fully integrated into the dramatic action than had been the case with *Don Juan*. The continuity includes parenthetical indications for the use of the sound recordings, and suggests some apprehension about what may be achievable. In scene 43, as the young Jakie prepares to sing at Muller's Café, 'The player plays the introduction to "Mighty Lak a Rose" and the boy starts to sing. (The various shots for this will have to be in accordance with Vitaphone technique and its necessities.) Vitaphone singing stops, when cut is made.'

However, the film does, famously, contain two moments of spoken dialogue: briefly, when the adult Jack Robin at Coffee Dan's excitedly exclaims 'Wait a minute! Wait a minute! You ain't heard nothin' yet', and a later and more extended section when he speaks to his mother, for whom he is playing the piano, before he is stopped by his irate father. These words were unscripted, and no suggestion that dialogue is to be heard is present in the continuity, which instead contains examples of the three ways of representing talk that had been in place since the 1910s (as seen in the 1915 continuity for *The Immigrant* in Chapter 4): written intertitles, spoken words that are to be filmed in such a way that makes it possible to for the spectator to lip-read, and words of which it is necessary for the spectator merely to get the gist. All three can be seen in the following short passage:

218.   CLOSE-UP MOTHER

> Her lips form the word "diamonds" in a startled manner as her eyes reflect the glitter of the jewel. She looks up at Jack and says:

TITLE 73:   "Are you sure it's for me, Jakie?"

219.   MED SHOT BOTH

> Jack laughs as he says of course it's for her. She shakes her head at this unheard of extravagance. She tells him he shouldn't have spent so much money for her. Jack laughs heartily.

220.   CLOSE UP JACK

> He tells her that it's nothing at all, adding:

TITLE 74:   "I got so much money, Mama, Rockefeller is jealous of me—and Henry Ford is always trying to borrow from me."

The Jazz Singer's script falls some way short of being an accurate 'blueprint' for the film. For example, scene 311, which does not appear in the film, is merely a sketch, with no attempt at this stage to indicate how the apparently dialogue-intensive scene is to be created:

> Sara tells Yudelson that she is going to get Jakie [in hopes of persuading him to sing in his father's place at Yom Kippur]. The latter tells her it's no use, but she is insistent, and he agrees to go along. Sara tells Mrs. Rubin to remain there until they return.

Other directions are hesitant: in scene 2, 'A shot may be made from an auto or truck down the street showing the teeming life of the ghetto'; scene 6 is a long shot of tenements, 'Looking upward from the street piano. This may be a very effective shot.' And ironically, of course, the continuity contains no reference to what would immediately become the film's main claim to fame. Even when it became known that speech would be heard, the full significance of the innovation was not immediately apparent: an article in *Motion Picture News* of 8 July 1927 correctly predicted that 'what dialogue there is in *The Jazz Singer* will probably be purely incidental'.[2] Nevertheless, Warners rapidly put together a publicity campaign that incorporated references to the innovation of audible speech, as well as to the Vitaphone technology more generally. The revolution had begun.

The 'part-talkie': *The Shopworn Angel* (1928)

As with *The Jazz Singer*, *The Shopworn Angel*, released by Paramount on 29 December 1928, made much of its incorporation of sound. Unlike that for the earlier film, however, the 'Final Continuity' by Howard

Estabrook, dated 6 September 1928 but with extensive revisions from the 7 and 8 September, at this date bearing the marginally different title *The Shop Worn Angel*,[3] was compiled in preparation for the production of a 'part-talkie', with indications of sound effects throughout and audible dialogue entering in the final sequence.

The continuity is prefaced by two single-spaced pages of additional material incorporating short notes on 'theme' (the basic plot idea), a longer 'digest' (summary), which occupies most of the first page, and a page of 'character notes' on the participants in the film's love triangle: the title character Daisy, her sugar daddy Bailey, and the young officer William, with whom she falls in love. The story and characters combine the familiar melodramatic tropes of the sympathetic good-time girl, the 'woman with a past' that catches up with her, and the fashionable Great War setting seen also in *Wings* (1927), *Hell's Angels* (1928), which we shall consider below, and the more realistic *All Quiet on the Western Front* (1930).

The continuity itself is divided into nine 'sequences', lettered A to I, and is the first script we have so far examined to utilise this larger unit of segmentation—though it will not be the last. Pencilled annotations in a copy of the 6 September script held in the Paramount files renumber the film as a continuous series of 342 shots.[4] In most respects, sequences A to H follow the familiar conventions of the silent continuity. Each is prefaced by a short synopsis of the sequence and a tally of its scenes and titles, with sequence A, for instance, having 39 scenes and a total of 12 intertitles and dialogue titles. Each 'scene' is in fact a shot, numbered consecutively within each sequence (so sequence B commences with scene 'B-1'), and the script is often very specific as to the type of shot and editing required: E-8 ('CLOSE UP OF DAISY—across Bailey's shoulder'), for example, is followed by the reverse shot E-9 ('CLOSE UP OF BAILEY—across Daisy's shoulder'). It also looks backward to an earlier version of the continuity, indicating where scenes have been eliminated (e.g. 'B-17—OUT'), and retains the standard silent practice of distinguishing between pantomime and titles, as in a passage from scene A-20, in which the heroine has failed once again to attend a rehearsal. The stage manager first 'speaks emphatically into the phone, registering—"Well, she can't get away with that stuff! I've stood all I'm going to!"'; the crucial plot point, however, is presented in a title: 'the next time she misses a rehearsal or show ... she's fired!'

Where sequences A to H diverge from the conventions of the silent continuity is in the creation of separate columns: a little over four inches for the 'ACTION', and then a further inch and a half for 'SOUND

EFFECTS', with these headings provided at the top of each page, in order to synchronise the matching of each to the other:

ACTION:	SOUND EFFECTS:
FADE IN – A-1 Impressive view of Congress, with President Wilson delivering his memorable address of April 2, 1917.	Very subdued, far away effect of military band playing: "Star Spangled Banner". (NOTE: This must be very soft and in no sense an invitation to make audience stand up. It is merely atmospheric music, to create high mood.)
LAP DISSOLVE INTO:	
A-2 CLOSER VIEW – of the President, speaking the historical words:	
TITLE 1. "Many months of fiery trial and sacrifice are ahead of us. It is a fearful thing to lead this great, peaceful people into war …"	
The President continues his impressive address.	

A striking illustration is provided by scene A-25, in which Daisy takes a shower. The sound effects column having suggested 'In Old New York' for incidental music, the continuity advises shooting the scene in two different ways to avoid censorship problems in certain American states, while also specifying that the two versions should be of equal duration in order to maintain sound synchronisation. In addition to anxieties about the possible effects of censorship, the continuity is often tentative or suggestive in other respects. For instance, there is advice on how scene A-5 might be photographed, but there is also an indication that it might not appear at all, while two alternate approaches to the filming of scene A-7 are outlined. After scene B-13 the continuity indicates the potential for cuts if the film is perceived to be too long, while sequences B and C both offer alternate endings.

Historically, the most significant element of the script is the concluding sequence 'I', dated 7 September 1928. This is prefaced with a note that dialogue as well as sound effects will now be present until the end of the film, and a revealingly oxymoronic reference to 'sound titles'—that is, audible speech—in the enumeration of the sequence elements: 'Scenes: 19. Titles: None. Sound titles: 27'. The dialogue is spoken in two specific scenes of this sequence: the wedding, which begins the sequence, and Daisy's broken-hearted return to the stage, which ends the film. The scenes sandwiched between these two, in which the broken-hearted Daisy wanders in New York, contain no actual dialogue.

Throughout sequence 'I' there is no columnar separation of action and sound effects. Instead, spoken dialogue is centred, rendered in upper-case and in inverted commas. This represents a variation on the presentation of dialogue in theatrical stage plays, although two kinds of tautology suggest a measure of improvision in finding a solution to the rendering of speech: it is both 'SOUND' and 'DIALOGUE', and the scene text frequently feels the need to indicate that the character whose speech is presented is actually talking. Both kinds of redundancy are seen in this extract from the wedding scene:

- SOUND -

THE DRONING VOICE OF THE CHAPLAIN INTONING THE WORDS OF THE MARRIAGE CEREMONY. [...]

- DIALOGUE -

The Chaplain says:

"INTO THIS HOLY ESTATE THESE TWO PERSONS PRESENT COME NOW TO BE JOINED. [...]"

While this mode of presentation substitutes for the parallel columns for action and sound effects earlier in the continuity, a quite different use of columns is introduced at one point in sequence 'I's wedding scene, to indicate double exposures:

DOUBLE EXPOSE ABOVE
DAISY'S HEAD – BLENDING
MULTIPLE LAP DISSOLVES OF –

Daisy's thoughts –

(a)   Daisy at wild, drunken
party. A revel in striking
contrast.

(b)   Daisy being kissed by
unidentified men.

(c)   CLOSEUP – of Daisy's arm,
with bracelets. A cigarette in
her hand.

(d)   Daisy's luxurious bed,
disordered, disarranged, and
empty. Roses on the floor.
Rose petals sprinkled over
the sheets.

(e)   A street – pedestrians. Daisy
comes furtively along,
registers seeing someone,
hides in doorway, as
William, in civilian clothes,
passes through, apparently
looking for her, registering
that he has seen her and
that she has disappeared.
He exits, still searching.

DOUBLE EXPOSE ABOVE
WILLIAM'S HEAD –
BLENDING MULTIPLE LAP
DISSOLVES OF –

William's thoughts –

(a)   Vivid, flashing scene on
battlefield in France.
William advancing
bravely in close
foreground.

(b)   CLOSEUP – of
Distinguished Service
Medal.

(c)   A home-coming
transport ship, moving
to pier, loaded with
hundreds of soldiers,
frantically greeted by
great crowds.

(d)   CLOSE VIEW – William –
(in uniform) meeting
daisy in ecstatic
happiness, crushing her
into his arms.

(e)   A beautiful scene before
a little vine-clad cottage,
bordered with roses.
William and Daisy in
foreground, ideally
happy, playing with a
little baby.

While the technical questions posed by this particular series of shots are unconnected to the problem of sound, a measure of the difficulties they caused is that the scene was reworked in a separate document of 10 October.[5]

The slightly haphazard construction of the continuity is a consequence of the awkwardness and transitional nature of the 'part-talkie' itself. Reviews of *The Shopworn Angel* remarked on the ungainly effect, the *New York Times* regretting that 'producers have seen fit to tag on to the end a talking chapter, which, while it does not actually hurt the picture, at least unlocks the tongues of people who have been silent for most of the time',[6] while the *Los Angeles Times* considered that the

> [f]inal scenes with the spoken word, after the bulk of the picture has been shown silent, burst upon one's ears with the sudden and disturbing effect of a calliope. The dialogue is intelligent enough in *The Shopworn Angel*, what there is of it, but somehow it seems rather unnecessarily dragged into an otherwise enticing vista.[7]

Silent and sound versions: *The Last of Mrs. Cheyney* (1929)

The coming of sound brought with it an end to the trans-national advantages of the silent movie and the creation, for a short period, of simultaneously shot versions of the same film in different languages, such as *The Blue Angel* (in German and English, 1930) and *The Threepenny Opera* (in German and French, 1931). In an indication of the chaos threatening the film industry, a *Los Angeles Times* article published in the wake of *The Shopworn Angel* recorded the statement of its director, Richard Wallace, that his next film, *Innocents of Paris*, was due to be made in four versions: two different silent edits for the American and European markets, and two talkies, with different songs in the French and English versions.[8]

Relatively straightforward was *The Last of Mrs. Cheyney*, an adaptation of a comic stage play by Frederick Lonsdale, which was initially slated for release in both silent and sound versions, although in the event only the latter was released. Nevertheless, it had a complex history as a silent continuity that went through many iterations before being reworked for sound. The two scenarios completed by Hans Kraly are perhaps most instructive in offering directly comparable silent and sound versions of the same material, the silent scenario, dated 20 February 1929, being 'okayed' by Irving Thalberg on 22 March,[9] and the sound version being similarly 'okayed' on 2 March.[10] The primary story difference between the two is that the silent version begins with a 22-scene sequence in which Mrs. Webley is robbed in the street outside the house of Mrs. Cheyney, who invites her indoors while Mrs. Cheyney's butler Charles succeeds in recovering the stolen items. This is omitted in the sound version and replaced by exposition, during a telephone conversation, that offers a different explanation of how the women first met. Otherwise the versions are remarkably similar in terms of story and scene structure, which allows for a clear understanding of how analogous material is presented, especially regarding dialogue.

In many scenes there is no difficulty at all. For example, the sound version repeats a 26-shot sequence set in a florist's shop almost verbatim from the silent version (sound scenes 11–36, silent scenes 33–59), with the exception of some minor changes in wording and an abbreviated version of one speech. It is possible to do this because, as we saw before, continuities routinely include within the scene text relatively insignificant dialogue that is to be understood via pantomime or lip-reading ('The saleswoman greets her with a smiling: "Good morning, madam!" '), reserving intertitles for particularly significant or representative speeches (as when the saleswoman asks, 'Your favourite Madonnas?'). All of this material from scene 35 of the silent continuity can be presented in the sound version (scene 12) simply by removing the distinction between titles and other dialogue.

Other scenes show the relative strengths and weaknesses of the two formats. Mrs. Webley is a chatterbox, and both scripts indicate that '[t]he torrent of words flows on' (silent scene 23, sound scene 7), but in the silent version this is followed by a title of just 15 words, whereas the analogous speeches in the sound version are inevitably more prolix and occupy about a page, running into the age-old problem of how to write the dialogue of a bore. Elsewhere, however, the sound version benefits from the opportunities for rapid duologues. For example, silent version scenes 122–25 present the following exchange:

INT. STUDY – CLOSEUP DILLING AND MRS. CHEYNEY

Dilling once more bends toward her and says:

TITLE: "I phoned you five times yesterday. Each time I was told you were out. Were you?"

She shakes her head. Dilling nods with a smile. "Ah, I thought as much!" Mrs. Cheyney tells him:

TITLE: "Twice I answered you myself and told you I was out."

In the sound version, the parallel episode occurs in the middle of a lengthy conversation in scene 61. As one might expect, the dialogue in the silent version is more condensed, and therefore arguably crisper, but the sound version is more nuanced:

> He moves toward her and the conversation continues in low tones. Meanwhile, Dilling takes a step nearer to Mrs. Cheyney and says:
>
> > "Since noon yesterday, I've called you up five times. Each time I was told you were out."
>
> She says, with mock gravity:
>
> > "What a shame!"
>
> He asks:
>
> > "Were you out?"
>
> She shakes her head:
>
> > "No. Each time I was in."
>
> He nods:
>
> > "I thought so."
>
> Mrs Cheyney tells him:
>
> > "Twice I answered it myself and told you I was out."

Perhaps the most curious aspect of the sound version occurs in the final scene (332), which begins with the same redundant method of rendering dialogue as we have seen above and in *The Shopworn Angel*, whereby the scene text informs us that a character is speaking. Suddenly, after about half a page, something resembling modern practice intrudes, continuing through to the end of the scene (and the script) some four pages later:

> He takes a step toward her, asks:
>
> > "You liked him?"
>
> Mrs. Cheyney answers:
>
> > "I adored him."

Dilling moves a little closer. In the dialogue that follows he works his way gradually down the table toward her, the CAMERA FOLLOWING him. He speaks without looking at her, drawing patterns on the table with his forefinger. But he comes ever nearer. He says:

"How much is that?"

MRS. CHEYNEY

As much as a woman can ever like a man she is not in love with.

ARTHUR

Like to go with him?

MRS. CHEYNEY

I'd hate it. [...]

Within the same scene the formatting has changed: no longer is the dialogue presented in treatment form, framed by narration and inverted commas; instead, for these last few pages of this adaptation of a theatrical play, *The Last of Mrs. Cheyney* has hit upon the stage play format itself as being an appropriate means of presenting dialogue within the continuity. It would become the default method as Hollywood fully embraced the sound era.

Remaking a silent film for sound: *Hell's Angels* (1930)

Hell's Angels is an oddity in many ways, not least because among other things the dramatic action is largely a frame story for the spectacular flying sequences that became an obsession with Howard Hughes, who eventually took charge of the filming himself after falling out with a series of directors.[11] Shooting had begun on a silent version in October 1927, but the film would not be finally exhibited until May 1930. The lengthy period of production is explained partly by Hughes' perfectionism regarding the scenes of aerial combat, but of wider significance was the coming of sound. With this in mind, late in the day (around May 1929) Hughes decided to reshoot the dramatic sequences, occasioning major recasting and the recruitment of Joseph Moncure March. The poet and writer, newly arrived in Hollywood, wrote a more or less completely new script that was dialogue-intensive and with scenes which, with some significant exceptions and aside from a few camera directions, were in stage-play form. The two friends in the silent version, Seaton and Cowan, have become brothers (the demure Roy and the womanising Monte) in March's, and the rewrite takes pains to dramatise their relationship as well as those between each of them and Helen, the third major character. March's script is divided into two 'Parts', which are subdivided into 'sequences' and further subdivided into 'scenes': for example, Part One has three sequences, the first of which has four scenes.[12]

The sequence-and-scene structure proved beneficial when Howard Estabrook was brought in to overhaul the writing once again for a sound version, dated 27 September 1929.[13] A cutting continuity of a silent version was compiled as late as 26 August 1929,[14] probably specifically to assist Estabrook, since the silent version had already been abandoned and a copy of the cutting continuity appears in his personal files. He had to work to incorporate the silent material (referred to in his continuity as 'S[ilent] V[ersion]') alongside much of March's dialogue: in effect, he was attempting to reconfigure both a silent movie and a text that substantially resembled a stage play as a workable script for a sound film. In the following account of Estabrook's script, 'S.V.' refers to the silent cutting continuity, 'March' to the Joseph Moncure March script that Estabrook inherited and 'Estabrook' to the 27 September sound continuity that incorporates much of the material from each of the other versions.

Estabrook's nine sequences (A–I) shadow those in March. The first four scenes of sequence A, which begin to map out the dramatic relationships between the film's three principal characters, are structurally similar in all versions, and at several points Estabrook specifies where footage from S.V. is to be retained. The two scenes that close this sequence in S.V. are jettisoned. Conversely, sequences B (detailing the brothers' adventures in Oxford) and C (the declaration of war), some scenes of which Estabrook incorporates almost verbatim from March, do not appear in S.V. at all. Sequence D, which famously incorporates a Technicolor ballroom sequence, is radically different in S.V. On screen, sequence E is substantially given over to the stunning Zeppelin footage that had already been filmed, using some dubbing and title cards, devices which are less distracting than might otherwise have been the case because the airmen are speaking German (today one might use subtitles). S.V. shows that the Zeppelin sequence originally contained 332 shots and 26 titles, but Estabrook simply records that 1,409 feet of material from S.V. is to be inserted at scene E-5. Aside from this, the dramatic storyline in the rest of this sequence and the beginning of the next differs significantly between S.V. and the sound versions, much of the S.V. material being jettisoned. The transition between Parts One and Two in March is marked as an 'intermission' in Estabrook.

Sequence F shows both March and Estabrook rather self-consciously incorporating references to the potential of sound, especially in scene 3 (which has no direct equivalent in S.V.), in which the sound of a Victrola running down dramatically shadows the sense of doom engulfing the airmen in the mess hall:

VICTROLA: Smile!

> Smile . . . .
>
> S –
>
> mi –
>
> le –

Sequence G, which dramatises Helen's betrayal of Roy in France, is not present in S.V. Conversely, Estabrook's sequence H (like March's) consists in its entirety of the words 'Bombing sequence', 'The Battle in the Clouds', and 'MONTE and ROY are captured on enemy ground', referring to material previously filmed for S.V., like the Zeppelin episode in sequence E. The concluding sequence I, in which Roy shoots the cowardly Monte to prevent him betraying the British to the Germans and is then executed himself, is broadly similar in all versions, although March presents it in two alternate forms.

Although *Hell's Angels* is a spectacular oddity, and the history of its writing is very much bound up with both the personal concerns of its maker as well as its creation at a critical juncture in the development of film technology, it is nonetheless representative of those approaches to Hollywood film-making that are less concerned with linear storytelling as the dominant mode. In some narrative genres, the story is essentially a connecting tissue holding together a varied set of attractions, and the most obvious example is the musical.

The emergence of the musical

Entire genres are unthinkable without sound: the screwball comedy, for example, is dependent on rapid-fire, wisecracking speech, and the prominence of this new element of dialogue is inextricable from the development of the master-scene script, as we shall see in the next chapter. Perhaps the most important new film genre ushered in by sound, however, is the musical. With *Don Juan*, the attraction of the technology had lain in the possibilities of eliminating the cost of live musical accompaniment, rather than in furthering cinematic realism via the reproduction of the human voice. Later, the 'integrated musical', in which the songs contribute to the development of the storyline, would become one of the genres that most significantly helped to define classical Hollywood style. In the interim, however, at the beginning of the talkies, came what might be termed by contrast the 'unintegrated', backstage musical: dramas set in Broadway theatres in which the primary function of the songs is less to advance the narrative than to display the potential of the fledgling sound technology.

Several continuities for films such as these evolved from projects initially conceived with silent cinema in mind. For example, the continuity by Sarah Y. Mason, dated 11 September 1928, for *Broadway Melody*[15] is mostly silent, but by the time the film was released in 1929, James Gleason and Norman Houston would be co-credited as writers along with Mason, and *Broadway Melody* would become not only a talkie but the first musical to win an Academy Award for Best Picture. Like many silent scripts, *Broadway Melody* lays considerable emphasis on means of indicating sound visually. In scene 3, a series of close-ups and dissolves— a policeman blowing a whistle, a fiddler, a ticket tout calling out and so on—is designed to give an impression of a multitude of sounds occurring simultaneously.

As with some of the other scripts we have seen during this transitional period, such as *The Last of Mrs. Cheyney*, the rendering of dialogue is formally inconsistent. Most scenes have titles for dialogue. However, in a sequence in the theatre dressing room (scenes 48–56), dialogue is indicated differently, beginning as follows:

TOP OF STAIRS – SHOT TOWARD DOOR GIRL'S DRESSING ROOM

A fat wardrobe mistress standing inside the door is bawling out the effeminate dress designer, as the file of girls with elaborate headdresses attempts to enter the dressing room, but the headgear will not go through. She indicates violently to him "There you are!" He says cuttingly, like an old gossip:

"I designed the headdresses not the building."

Shrugging off the blame. The wardrobe mistress gives him a cutting thrust "I know that, or it'd have been done in lavendar (sic)," as she starts to engineer the girls in, making them leave the headdresses outside.

Script pages 29–33, from scenes 48–56, continue in this vein, although at one point in scene 52 a dialogue title is indicated, for no obvious reason. Had Mason been following the conventions previously detailed in connection with *The Jazz Singer*, one would have expected to find both titles and indications for speech used regularly throughout the continuity. The anomaly of scenes 48–56 raises the possibility that Mason was establishing the basis for a talkie, but was uncertain of her ground and had not yet distinguished between audible and unheard dialogue.

For Universal's 1929 adaptation of Philip Dunning and George Abbott's play *Broadway*, Edward T. Lowe, Jr., initially compiled a silent, 898-shot continuity. A synopsis by Lowe, dated 2 February 1929, then divides the material 'in scene groups, with notes regarding the revue numbers, off-scene music, and dance selections', an arrangement that informs Lowe's 'sound script', which tracks the silent version shot by shot. Instead of reproducing the often very substantial scene text of the earlier version, however, the 'sound script' is a more technical document. It borrows the shot numbers and headings from the previous iteration, but otherwise confines itself to dialogue and brief indications of sound (street noises, indistinct voices, orchestral music and so on). The document can only be fully understood when read in conjunction with the silent continuity; in this sense, it resembles, in function at least, the list of titles compiled separately from the scenario of a silent film.

The grouping of the scenes in the synopsis, and the arrangement of the sound script, also indicates some of the ways in which sound effects, dialogue and song were being incorporated within a system that is otherwise still heavily indebted to the conventions of the continuity. An 'S' designates scenes that will be shot silently but then synchronised for the sound track in post-production. In places, a series of discrete scenes in the silent version is replaced in the sound script by a single, continuous stretch of dialogue, which consequently appears as one scene. Here we can see the beginnings of the transition to master scenes that is a corollary of the introduction of dialogue in Hollywood cinema. This change is particularly noticeable in *Broadway*'s sound script because, in common with many of the other texts seen in this chapter, dialogue is being reserved for particular scenes or sequences rather than being integrated continuously within the narrative. Similarly, the script indicates the presence or insertion of dances and songs, but not the words of the musical numbers.

A text that better integrates dialogue and songs within the musical continuity—or, perhaps, simply represents a later stage in the production process—is the otherwise undated 1929 script for *Gold Diggers of Broadway* (Warner Bros., 1929), marked as 'final' and with a note that the dialogue is not to be altered in production. The title page casts an interesting light on the conventional understanding of a 'backstage musical', because it describes the text as the 'CONTINUITY of Front Stage and Back Stage Story of "THE GOLD DIGGERS" (of Broadway) by Avery Hopwood'.[16]

The distinction between front-stage and back-stage stories is significant. The back-stage story is rendered in scenes that closely resemble the master-scene format of later years. For example, scene 11, in which the chorus girls change out of their costumes, continues for three pages largely comprising dialogue, with speakers' names and dialogue indented (although the dialogue continues to the right margin, as was generally the case at this time). The scene text, which totals less than one-fifth of the lines in the scene, specifies that a moving shot is to pass along the length of a dressing table before pausing on a small cluster of characters. Shot specification of this kind occurs frequently, but less so than might be expected of a silent continuity, partly because the interest in such scenes is deflected away from telling the story in shots and towards telling it in dialogue, and partly because, in consequence, there is no attempt to use shot type as a method of subdivision.

The back-stage scenes are written with a level of detail that resembles both the silent continuity and the dialogue-intensive master scenes of the sound era, but the handling of the front-stage scenes is markedly different. Within the film, this material is substantially the work of contributors other than the writers—composers of music and lyrics, choreographers and designers—and the continuity defers to these collaborators. Prefacing the dramatic script is the list of characters (of which only Ann Collins, played by Ann Pennington, as has been cast at this point), following which is a list of the songs, indicating which character sings the song and the location of the scene in which it is performed. Within the continuity itself, scene headings for the front-stage scenes merely indicate 'theatre' or 'stage', without elaboration, and with minimal description of the content of the scene. For example, scene 2 notes simply that Ann is leading the chorus in their performance of 'Song of the Gold Diggers'. In the next scene the words of the song are printed out in full beneath its title ('Dig, Little Diggers, Dig') and credits (words by Al Dubin, music by Joe Burke).

If song lyrics enter screenwriting as a relatively autonomous element within the musical continuity, choreography presents a different set of problems. The text of the continuity for the 'Song of the Gold Diggers' scene records that 'This is number where chorus are dressed as forty-niners and dig the audience for gold'. The wording suggests that the design and choreography, as well as words and music, have already been established, or are at least being planned by others. The main choreographer of the front-stage numbers of *Gold Diggers of Broadway* was Larry Ceballos, but it was with the giddy surrealism of Busby Berkeley that choreography entered film in ways that, as far as screenplays are concerned, became literally unrepresentable in words. While the dramatic narrative of the Warner Brothers musicals on which Berkeley worked after 1932 would be directed by others—Lloyd Bacon on *42nd Street* (1933), for example—Berkeley's celebrated designs operate in an autonomous fantasy realm that belongs to neither the front nor the back stage story, and requires no substantial input from writers.

42nd Street passed through a series of textual versions, culminating in a 'final—master' of the 22nd.[17] This is a typical 'final' script of the period in that it represents a hybrid of the earlier numbered continuity and the evolving master-scene script. As in the continuity, scene (or more accurately, shot) headings routinely indicate what kind of shot (full, medium, close and so on) is to be used. This becomes potentially illogical during lengthy, dialogue-intensive scenes, as here:

136. INT. MED. SHOT CORNER OF "YE EAT SHOPPE" RESTAURANT (FORTY-SECOND STREET AND EIGHTH AVENUE)
Peggy and Terry occupy a table in one corner. At a table, by himself, opposite, sits Billy, interestedly reading a copy of *Variety*. At a table directly in front of Terry and Peggy sit Ann and Lorraine.

The discussion between these characters, and a waitress who enters at the end of the scene, continues for 13 speeches, several of which are prefaced by possible indications of eyeline matches, as when Peggy 'suddenly notic[es] Billy, who is eyeing the scene disapprovingly[.] [Peggy] smiles, and turns to Terry'. However, no further shot segmentation is specified, even though the likelihood is that the scene will be edited as a series of shots, rather than presented as the single medium shot specified in the header. Here we can see that the conventions of shot specification in the continuity are coming into conflict with the demands of the dialogue-intensive scene, for which the master scene script, without subdivision into shots (which can be determined later), appears more appropriate.

Equally important is that *42nd Street* resembles *Gold Diggers of Broadway* in the contrast between the detailed exposition of the dramatic narrative on the one hand, and on the other the vagueness or silence concerning the non-narrative elements: the songs and Berkeley's dance/design routines. Some striking examples occur when the two elements come together towards the climax, as the performers deliver a series of songs. The script has no trouble in presenting this as a series of shots, because the location is clear: Billy and the girls are on the stage, and although little attempt is made to specify the visual appearance and spatial organisation of the scene, the action has been accommodated readily enough within the conventions of the continuity script. The songs themselves (by Al Dubin and Harry Warren), however, are unidentified, their presence merely cued:

333. FLASH   MED. SHOT   ORCHESTRA LEADER
and nearest musicians, all in immaculately full dress. Leader taps baton on music stand and orchestra starts introduction.

334. CLOSE SHOT   PEGGY AND LEADING MAN
She gives him tremulous look; he gives her an encouraging firm handclasp and approving nod of head. Music goes into verse. Peggy and leading man go into their duet.

335. FLASH.   MED. SHOT. BACKSTAGE RIGHT
Andy, very excited, lining up chorus girls for their entrance. Duet heard off.

The song that was used here was 'Shuffle off to Buffalo'. Similarly, soon afterwards Billy sings:

343. FLASH FULL SHOT ORCHESTRA   SIDE ANGLE
as orchestra leader starts Billy's number.

344. CLOSE SHOT   BILLY
singing number.

Again, no details of the number (which was 'Young and Healthy') are given. The only song mentioned by name in the script is '*42nd Street*' itself:[18] at shot 362 'Peggy finishes tap, lights flood up, disclosing whole company behind her on stage, joining her in final tap, in the "*42nd Street*" number!'.

The songs, then, operate relatively autonomously of the dramatic material. Berkeley's work, meanwhile, is barely anticipated at all. 355–61 are 'ALLOWED FOR TRICK SHOTS after production number is set', but to all intents and purposes the responsibility is passed to Berkeley, creating a lacuna in the script. What is most significant is that the lacuna survives right through to the cutter's copy of the final script, where the cognate shots form part of a sequence boxed in blue ink and marked 'Berkeley' in the margin. The cutter was using a copy of the same script as was used for the 'final—master' (dated 22 September 1932), in which the sequence is instead marked in pink as 'Buzz'.[19]

Berkeley's material is largely intractable to verbal representation, which may explain its absence. A second explanation is that Berkeley musicals were in effect a special case of the unit system of production, with the choreographer working semi-independently of the director and writers of the dramatic material. Moreover, Berkeley's work erased the temporal and spatial organisation of classical Hollywood editing. The continuity script was designed partly to complement Hollywood's visual style: the laborious if logical use of scene headings and divisions facilitated the segmentation of time and space into sequential narratives, while the editing positioned the spectator securely in relation to the shot and the story world. Famously, this is what Berkeley's routines avoid, by escaping the diegetically motivated action: having begun on the stage set established by the narrative, he would routinely dissolve the realistic frame and take the spectator on a surrealistic fantasy unrelated to the constraints of theatrical time and space.

Unlike the essentially conservative ideology of the classical Hollywood style, which situates the spectator within a narrative and a field of vision that imposes boundaries to the possibilities for transgression, it speaks volumes that a textual form designed to meet those needs barely attempted to accommodate the erotic release supplied by Berkeley. No written text could possibly do justice to such mind-boggling sequences as the 'We're in the Money' number from *Gold Diggers of 1933*, for example, in which a troupe of chorines, naked save for the pair of gigantic gold coins with which each dancer gamely struggles to protect what remains of her modesty, is examined from any angle that Berkeley could possibly get past the censor.

Berkeley is an exceptional figure in many ways, but the impossibility of accommodating his work within the narrative continuity form typifies the nature of screenplays written for musicals. Moreover, the development of this genre also reveals much about screenwriting of the period more generally. All of the written texts considered in this section are hybrid forms: the 'sound script' for *Broadway* is not so much a later iteration of the silent version as an accompaniment to it; *Gold Diggers of Broadway* comprises two formally distinct modes in representing the back-stage and front-stage action; *42nd Street* is a kind of incomplete text, a dramatic narrative dependent on supplementation by the Berkeley material it cannot accommodate. In consequence, several textual elements familiar from the silent continuity fall by the way-side: without supplementation, the script becomes relatively useless for the purposes of estimating timings or budget, and many scenes are not effectively visualised within the written text. The genre can appear anomalous in these ways when considered alongside the integrated narratives of contemporary Hollywood genres such as the gangster film or the historical costume drama. As the following chapter will suggest, however, the composite nature of the musical screenplay, which draws together dialogue, scene text, song lyrics and separately-choreographed dance sequences, is in many ways representative of classical Hollywood screenplays in general.

7
The Hollywood Sound Screenplay to 1948

If the numbered continuity had become standardised within the Hollywood of the 1920s, the hasty conversion to sound had resulted in an ad hoc approach to resolving the technical questions confronting the script at a time of rapid industrial change. There is little consistency, at this transitional time, between scripts or often within the same script, regarding such matters as how to present dialogue, where to position the speakers' names and how, in particular, to overcome the problem that, with intertitles having become obsolete, precisely rendered speech and action now occurred simultaneously. As Staiger remarks, '[e]ach studio adapted the old script format differently'.[1] This prompted suggestions that the Hollywood studios should collectively introduce an agreed, standard format for the presentation of scripts.

They certainly considered such a move. The first item in the 'Proceedings of the Research Council, Quarterly Meeting, December 15, 1932'—published in summary form in the Academy of Motion Picture Arts & Sciences' *Technical Bulletin*, supplement 19, December 23, 1932—concerns the 'standardization of format of scripts'.

> **Problem:** Since the introduction of sound, there has been no generally recognized format of scripts. As a result the placement, order, numbering and display of the various parts—dialogue, action, set descriptions, camera instructions, etc. vary widely among the studios and are constantly subject to change. This unnecessarily complicates the work of those who handle the scripts during production. [...]

> **Proposed:** To conduct such surveys as may be necessary to establish the basis for the various present practices. To correlate this information and secure general agreement on a recommended form of script

that will be most legible, graphic, and convenient in practical use by actors, directors, writers, executives and the various production departments.[2]

That Darryl Zanuck chaired the meeting, and Irving Thalberg was an ex-officio member of the Council, demonstrates the importance attached to this initiative. Staiger argues that '[t]he form that eventually became standard (the master-scene) was a combination of theatrical and pre-sound film scripts, a variant of the continuity synopsis used in the 1920s'.[3] The evidence she presents is a facsimile reproduction of two pages from a 1938 script for the Warner Brothers film *Juárez* (1939); with this, Staiger concludes her history of screenwriting practices in *The Classical Hollywood Cinema*.

Clearly the analysis is not intended to be exhaustive, but the implications are significant: that the Research Council's proposal resulted in a standardised form of screenplay that was adopted collectively by the studios; that the agreed form was the master-scene script; and that this was adopted relatively quickly, by the end of the 1930s, with *Juarez* functioning as a representative illustration of these developments. Such conclusions would tend to support the thrust of the argument in *The Classical Hollywood Cinema*, namely that the studios introduced standardised methods of production in the interests of economic efficiency.

The problem is that neither *Juárez* individually nor surveys of the Hollywood sound screenplay generally support any of these conclusions. Nor, indeed, does a second analysis by Staiger, published in the same year as *The Classical Hollywood Cinema*, which proposes that the sound film screenplay of the classical era represented a modification of the continuity.[4] Rather than effecting a step-change from the numbered continuity to the master-scene screenplay in the 1930s, the introduction of sound resulted in a hybrid form in which the conception of a scene, as a unit of temporal continuity and spatial integrity, is compromised by the need to draw attention to specific elements within the scene. This leads to an element of confusion, because the word 'scene' tended to refer both to master scenes and shots, with a new shot and a new scene each introducing a new 'scene' number.

This confusion persisted at least into the 1950s, and is clearly illustrated by a two-page document in the files of the screenwriter James Seymour, headed 'SHOOTING SCRIPT FORMAT' and dated 26 March 1944.[5] Seymour had been one of the writers on several of the Warner Brothers musicals discussed in Chapter 5, including *42nd Street*, *Golddiggers of 1933* and *Footlight Parade*. By 1943, however, he was working on a series of British films, and it is likely that this document represents the distilled advice of a seasoned Hollywood veteran to his new British colleagues. It is worth quoting in full:

> From a technical picture-making point of view, a Shooting Script has two primary purposes:
>
> 1)   To give the Production Department a clear idea of epoch, sets, characters and times of day and thus simplify 'breaking down' the script for shooting schedules, costume plots, etc., and to allow an approximate estimate of actual minutes of shooting and screening time.
> 2)   To give Producer and Director a clear idea of what the writer considers the emphases and climaxes, by cinematically underlining the writer's intentions.

This should in no sense hinder the Director's creative camera-work or restrict his complete freedom of decision or action. The writer's suggestions of shots should act merely as springboards which may assist and stimulate the Director's inspiration. This corresponds, in music, to a composer's orchestration of his symphony to supply guide-posts for his Toscannini (sic).

The purpose of a Shooting Script is definitely NOT to make entertaining READING at the expense of concise clarity. All the entertainment value in it should be translatable to and capable of expression on the screen. It is not intended to gloss over with clever writing or hide behind words story or character weaknesses or inconsistencies, which inevitably become bald and magnified in screening.

For the convenience of all concerned, it would be wise—and a simple matter—to adopt a single tech[n]ical procedure in the writing of Shooting Scripts. There are two common errors: either to break the script up into too many scenes or not to break it up into enough. The following might be suggested as a practical and simple technique:

> 1.   Number all scenes and indicate 'Inserts' [here 'without number' has been scored through and replaced with the words 'as such'].
> 2.   If it is not a direct cut from one scene to the next specify the desired transition, as 'Fade Out' and 'Fade In', 'Dissolve To,' etc.
> 3.   New scenes and scene numbers should show a change of set (ie. Master Scenes)[,] that is—'Exterior' or 'Interior' and various

portions of a large set as 'a corner', 'an alcove', 'by the fire-place', etc.

4. A new scene and scene number should be used for a new 'set-up' only to achieve a definite desired dramatic effect, such as a 'Close-Up' for an individual's important reaction or dramatically important piece of business to which the audience's attention is to be drawn. This, in effect, underlines with the CAMERA things to be 'punched over' for story values.

5. New scenes and scene numbers should NOT be used merely for a change of CAMERA ANGLE within a master scene for no other reason than to break up what seems to the writer a too-long dialogue scene. Thus a dualogue (sic) would not be broken up into alternating close-ups of the speakers—except as specified in Paragraph 4 above.

6. In general, then, nothing should be included in the Shooting Script which has not a definite reason for being there. The aim should be—as far as the technical format is concerned—to make perfectly clear to Producer, Director and Production Department the author's intentions without any vagueness. It is then the Director's task to effect those intentions by his skill and artistry without his having to cudgel his wits to find out what the author is driving at.

While point 3 demonstrates the concept of the 'master scene', point 4 shows how it is 'broken up' by indications of a new camera 'set-up', either for a specified shot (such as the close-up) or for what the writer considers a 'dramatically important piece of business'. Mean-while, point 5 stresses that particular kinds of master scene, notably dialogue-intensive scenes, may continue for considerable length with-out additional segmentation by the writer.

It is possible, though unlikely, that Seymour is here offering advice on the transformation of an earlier iteration—a master-scene screenplay—into the next stage, a shooting script. If so, however, the same writers would generally work on each iteration, including the 'final' iteration being a shooting script that could then be subject to further modifica-tion by the director. Moreover, as we shall see, the various drafts through which a text would proceed in the classical era generally show writ-ers bearing shot segmentation in mind once work on the screenplay, as opposed to the synopsis or treatment, was underway. This leads to an additional source of confusion: just as 'shot' and 'scene' can be synonyms, so 'screenplay' and 'shooting script' can both refer to the final iteration prior to shooting.

The screenplays of this period were hybrids, and inconsistent hybrids at that. Moreover, there is a gradual but perceptible evolutionary change, through to the end of the classical studio era around 1960, whereby shot segmentation, camera angles and parenthetical speech direction became progressively less common, thereby bringing the shooting script into closer alignment with the master-scene screenplay. The research for the present study broadly confirms two of Claudia Sternberg's conclusions, drawn from her sample of 43 screenplays from the beginnings of the sound era to 1969: first, that during the classical sound era scripts 'occupy a middle position' between the master scene script, in which 'only changes of time and location directly designate cuts', and the numbered script in which 'each cut is predefined';[6] and, second, that 'screenplays up to the 1950s tended to contain more detailed camera and shot instructions. Since then the *master scene* script format, which only registers changes of place and time, has become the standard form'.[7]

It seems best to consider the continuity and the master-scene screenplay in their pure forms as two ends of a continuum, the former segmented by shot and the latter by scenes, with most scripts in practice falling somewhere within the spectrum. Nevertheless, the coming of sound did have the effect of introducing into screenwriting the dialogue-intensive scene, a development which occasioned the recruitment of experts such as playwrights from the East Coast.[8] If the title-writers of the silent era had become redundant, the specialist dialogue writers had entered to take their place.

Just as the dialogue-intensive scene in film can appear cinematically uninteresting—Hitchcock's 'pictures of people talking'—so such scenes in screenplays often take on the appearance of the stage play, with a general absence of camera directions or even much in the way of scene text. Since the default mode of filming and editing such scenes quickly became the establishing shot followed by a succession of over-the-shoulder shots/reverse shots, there was often no need for further indications of shot type even when, as in the classical Hollywood system, screenplays would generally include such directions elsewhere. In short, the introduction of dialogue had the effect of creating a more hybrid kind of screenplay, with dialogue-intensive scenes often rendered in what now appears master-scene form, and other scenes not.

Meanwhile, analysis of a range of screenplays from different studios suggests that, while the intentions of the Research Council are clear enough, no inter-studio agreement on screenplay format seems to have been implemented. Instead, the picture is a great deal more complicated, and messier, with considerable evidence that there was a greater or lesser degree of standardisation *within* studios, but little *between* them. Even within a studio widespread variation can occur, largely as a result of differing modes of production: writer-director teams such as Billy Wilder and Charles Brackett at Paramount might have their own methods of working, while a powerful producer such as David O. Selznick at MGM would bring different specialist contributors to a project at various stages of script development, resulting in a still more hybrid kind of text. Moreover, screenplays themselves were (and are) inherently unstable. During the course of a given production a range of script documents would be generated, while even a 'final' draft was unlikely to represent a 'blueprint', the release print of the film differing substantially as a rule from any given iteration of the screenplay.

Juárez (1939)

Juárez is not a master-scene script, though this is not apparent from the two script pages reproduced in *The Classical Hollywood Cinema*. One of these shows the transition between scenes 41 to 42, which indeed is occasioned by a change of scene ('DISSOLVE TO: 42. AN ASSEMBLY OF PEONS AND POORER-CLASS TOWNSFOLK'). The other (excerpted from scene 32) contains no numbered transitions at all. This does capture something of the flavour of the screenplay, many scenes of which are indeed lengthy, dialogue-intensive and uninterrupted by numbered shots. In many other scenes, however, this is not the case. Immediately following the DISSOLVE at the end of scene 42, scene 43 is:

CONTINUATION OF SCENE 42

This scene has already been shot. The speaker has said that he will not sign the plebiscite; he has run out of the shot and up the stairway; he has yelled, "Viva Juárez—Viva la República!"! The French soldier has lifted his revolver, and the peon, mortally wounded, has fallen over the railing of the balcony.[9]

By contrast, a note at the beginning of the screenplay indicates only a rough approximation of a prologue that, in the event, did not appear in the film:

NOTE: The following "Napoleon scene" will be preceded by a prologue establishing and showing in several alternating "tableaux" the contrasting careers of Juárez and Maximilian from their birth to manhood.

There will be no dialogue spoken by the characters shown in these "silent" scenes, but a narrator's voice will explain them.

The Napoleon scene is, therefore, the first scene of the picture in which the actors actually talk, and consequently through its development our main protagonists are brought into story contact.

This shows that, in contrast to a silent continuity script which, in theory, posits a clear distinction between a completed stage of conception (writing) and an anticipated stage of execution (filming), the *Juárez* screenplay is a transitional or living document, an intervention in a process that has already begun and has many difficulties still to overcome.

This provisional status perhaps accounts for an uncertainty that is apparent in most screenplays of this period, and is well illustrated here. While, as noted, there are many scenes that continue for several pages of (mostly) dialogue, without occasioning any change in the numbering, in others the screenplay is explicit in its shot specification, and in such cases it is the indication of shot that generates a change in the number, as here:

263.   EXT. COURTYARD CONVENT OF LA CRUZ   NIGHT

shooting over a large circle of *Juarista* infantry, on the doorway. The Imperialists emerge to find themselves hopelessly trapped.

CUT TO:

264.   REVERSE ANGLE

shooting from the doorway over the Imperialists, to show them hemmed in by the circle of rifles. They look around them in bewilderment. Mejía raises a pistol to fire, but Maximilian takes him by the wrist and draws down his arm.

MAXIMILIAN:
It is useless, Tomás.

CUT TO:

265.   MED. SHOT ESCOBEDO

> emerging from the *Juarista* ranks. Pan with him toward the
> group. [...]

The screenplay specifies those shot selections that seem essential to a
visualisation of the scene, and each such specification would generate a
new shot number in the screenplay. Conversely, in a dialogue-intensive
scene, which may read analogously to the dialogue of a stage play, no
such directions need intrude.

Presentation of the text elements

The specific terms of the Research Council's initiative seem modest
enough: 'a recommended form of script that will be most legible,
graphic, and convenient in practical use'. This is a simple matter of
formatting, as opposed to (for example) prescriptions concerning the
degree of permissible narratorial commentary in the scene text. Formatting might involve nothing more complicated than the capitalisation,
margins and indent settings of different elements—'the placement,
order, numbering and display of the various parts'—so that scripts generated at different studios would have a similar appearance and therefore
be straightforwardly 'legible' in this literal sense. The extreme standardisation of the master-scene script in some of today's screenwriting
discourses (see Chapter 10) suggests that it would have been perfectly
possible for the relatively centralised, oligarchical studio system of the
classical era to have agreed upon a standard screenplay format shortly
after the introduction of sound.

   The objective was also achievable because, even if 'the closer we
look at Hollywood's relations of power and hierarchy of authority [...]
the less sense it makes to assess filmmaking or film style in terms of
the individual director—or *any* individual, for that matter',[10] Zanuck
and Thalberg were members of the Research Council, and among the
elite:

> studio production executives like Louis B. Mayer and Irving Thalberg
> at MGM, Jack Warner and Hal Wallis at Warner Bros., Darryl Zanuck
> at 20th Century Fox, Harry Cohn at Columbia, and major indepen-
> dent producers like David Selznick and Sam Goldwyn [...] were the
> men Frank Capra railed against in an open letter to *The New York
> Times* in April 1939, complaining that 'about six producers today
> pass on about 90 percent of the scripts and edit 90 percent of the
> pictures.' And these were the men that F. Scott Fitzgerald described

on the opening page of *The Last Tycoon*, the Hollywood novel he was writing at the time of his death, in 1940[:] '[...] Not half a dozen men have been able to keep the whole equation of pictures in their heads.'[11]

Screenplays formed an important part of the equation, and that individual studios were indeed able to impose a marked degree of standardisation on the scripts written for their movies is one index of the producers' authority.

And yet the inter-studio standardisation of scripts didn't happen—though intra-studio standardisation did, at least up to a point. While there are some consistencies between different scripts for Warner Brothers, a comparison of the Warners scripts to those being produced contemporaneously at MGM reveals almost no agreement on format whatsoever. Apparently MGM, initially under the guidance of Irving Thalberg (who 'okayed' many of the earlier scripts), created its own format that was followed consistently by producers and writers, with only occasional variations, and which both preceded the Research Council's initiative in December 1932 and survived for decades after Thalberg's death in 1936.

The tight control exerted by MGM executives over the script is evident in the indication, on the title page of what might be considered the 'final' iteration of any given script, that it has been 'okayed' by a named producer. The degree of standardisation, meanwhile, can be gauged by extensive sampling. A survey of some two dozen MGM scripts, from *The Sin of Madelon Claudet* (the script is called *The Lullaby*, after the source play), which was 'okayed by Mr. Rapf' on 25 May 1931, through to *Meet Me in Las Vegas* (titled *Weekend at Las Vegas*, 'Okayed by Mr. J. Pasternak' and dated 27 June 1955), reveals only a very few exceptions to a standard house style that persisted unaltered throughout the classical sound period. A very short passage from *The Sin of Madelon Claudet* is sufficient to indicate the difference from the Warners scripts:

3   EXT. HOUSE   NIGHT

     As they are leaving.

              Larry
            (whispering)
There's that dog again.

            Madelon
           (whispering)
Co-co, go back. Go back.[12]

In the MGM script, the speakers' names are in lower-case. With the extreme left margin reserved for scene numbers, the dialogue text occupies the next indent, with an additional indent for slug lines and scene text, and speakers' names centred. In most of these respects bar the positioning of the scene number at the extreme left-hand margin (which was the norm across the studios), the Warners scripts are different. The Warner scripts use upper-case for speakers' names. The scene heading and scene text are justified at the first left margin (after the scene numbering), with dialogue at the following indent; in the MGM text, this order is reversed.

It was the Warner rather than MGM style of presenting the text on the page that was more widely adopted, however, which is another reason why the *Juárez* script appears to resemble the master-scene screenplays of today. Moreover, there is widespread consistency across the studios for what became the preferred method of presenting dialogue. As we saw, at the introduction of sound film-makers had hurried to find short-term solutions to incorporating audible dialogue within a form that had previously worked on the assumption that the words spoken by actors could not be directly heard, with two obvious possibilities emerging: alternation between scene text and dialogue, or an attempt to approximate their simultaneous occurrence by presenting them alongside each other in two parallel vertical columns. The former quickly became standard and is seen in all of the examples of dialogue shown above.

The use of parallel columns was still seen occasionally, however. The Laurel and Hardy vehicle *Babes in Toyland* (1934) is one of the few MGM scripts that radically varies from the studio's house style for screenplays.[13] It uses the alphabetical method of distinguishing between sequences, with five (A–E). Pages are divided into two even columns, with scene text on the left, and sound effects and dialogue on the right:

A-15

MOVING CAMERA –
GARDEN PATH – EXT:
HOUSE.

Ollie and Stan hurry along
                    path.
Suddenly:

                     STAN: (Stopping)
                               Wait a minute!

                     OLLIE: Now what's the matter?

	STAN:	I forgot my Pee-Wee stick! (He dashes out of scene towards house)
Ollie does a slow burn. At that moment he hears:		
	SOUND:	(Off-scene) Silvery tinkle of sheepbells.

Seemingly to accommodate this mode of presentation, the pages are of unusual dimensions, 8 × 13.75 inches.

The screenplay for *Lives of a Bengal Lancer* (Paramount, 1935) is identical to *Babes in Toyland* in all of these respects (alphabetised sequences, longer pages, scene and dialogue text in parallel columns). Significantly, this holds true for all seven drafts, from the first, dated 28 November 1932, to through the last, dated 22 September 1934, showing that this was a recognised working method rather than a format used to prepare final versions of particular screenplays.[14] One of the writers on *Lives of a Bengal Lancer* was John L. Balderston, who with William Hurlbut is credited with the screenplay for *Bride of Frankenstein* (Universal, 1935; the screenplay is at this stage called *The Return of Frankenstein*), which shows slight variations in the presentation of some of the elements:[15]

A-12   BYRON ... MED. CLOSE UP

                                    BYRON
                                You hear –

    CUT TO:

A-13   MARY, SHELLEY AND
         BYRON ... MED. THREE-SHOT

    Even Shelley is brought out
    of his concentration to
    smile at his friend's fancy.

                                  BYRON

                                Come, Mary – come
                                and watch the storm.

He holds out his hand to her.

Other scripts to have employed the split-page screenplay format include the prologue and epilogue pages of Paramount's *Alice in Wonderland* (1933, screenplay by Joseph L. Mankiewicz) and the 20th Century Fox war film *Hell in the Heavens* ('adaptation and screen play' by Byron Morgan and Ted Parsons, 1 August 1934).

That this mode of presentation was used for films of strikingly different genres at several studios in the period from 1933 to 1934, in screenplays authored by many different writers, suggests that it was not simply aberrant, but instead represented a recognised alternative screenplay form. It persists to the present, with modifications, in the written preparation of documentary films, and the current research of Petr Szczepanik into the screenwriting archives of the former Czechoslovakia reveals that parallel columns were a regular feature of Czech screenwriting in the 1950s, which Szczepanik ascribes to the influence of the German *Drehbuch*.[16] Perhaps the sporadic use of the form in Hollywood in the period from the introduction of sound until the mid-1930s also owes something to the large number of German filmmakers in the studios. However, it seems that after this date the format fell into disuse for narrative Hollywood films.

Nevertheless, the two different ways of presenting scene and dialogue text persisted for individual scenes requiring voice-over, or off-screen narration. *How Green Was My Valley* (20th Century Fox, 1941) uses the parallel-text method:[17]

1 CLOSE SHOT	VOICE
Huw's hands, the hands of a man about sixty, are carefully folding some shirts, ties and socks into an old blue cloth. OVER SCENE comes Huw's voice:	I am packing my belongings in the little blue cloth my mother used to tie around her hair when she did the house, and I am going from my Valley, And this time I shall never return.

The second method, of presenting scene text and voice text alternately, is illustrated in the 1944 'Final' script for *Laura*:[18]

FADE IN

1   FULL SHOT – EXT. SKY AND SUN – DAY
Veiled in mist, the sun gleams like a silver coin, giving a sense of intolerable heat. OVER SCENE comes the voice of Waldo Lydecker.

> WALDO'S VOICE (narrating)
> I shall never forget this weekend—the
> weekend Laura died...

2   FULL SHOT – (ESTABLISHING) – NEW YORK
>   The towers of the buildings are shrouded in mist. On the
>   entire length of Fifth Avenue the only vehicle is a lone bus
>   in the distance.

> WALDO'S VOICE (narrating)
> A silver sun burned through the sky like
> a huge magnifying glass... It was the
> hottest Sunday in my recollection. A heavy
> silence lay on the town. I felt as if I
> were the only human being left in New York.
> And in a sense it was true. For with
> Laura's horrible death I was alone – with
> only my crowding, poignant memories of her.

These two methods of presenting voice-over remained viable alternatives throughout the classical Hollywood sound era.

The widespread variations in the manner in which the text elements are presented during this period demonstrate that the Research Council's seemingly simple objective was not achieved, and that the studios operated in relative autonomy in matters of formatting. Since this kind of formatting was a relatively straightforward procedure that could have been implemented by central typing pools or agencies, and could have been applied to any script regardless of the budget for the film, the failure to implement a standard format suggests that differences in Hollywood practices were not confined to (for example) A-pictures or particular producers or directors.

Segmentation

As we saw in Chapter 3, the 'acts' and 'parts' of some of the early sound feature films have their origins in the introduction around 1910 of the reel, and the 1,000-foot length, as standard units of film length. Certainly there is no good evidence to suggest that film-makers in general, either then or at any time during the classical period, were thinking in terms of 'acts', or subordinating all other elements to the demand for narrative coherence. The idea that they did seems to derive largely from a retrospective re-reading of classical Hollywood cinema, beginning around 1979 with Syd Field's influential manual *Screenplay: The*

Foundations of Screenwriting, which posits the three-act structure as a key principle of narrative film in general (see Chapter 10).

David Bordwell's ongoing research into 'whether studio screenwriters of the 1930s and 1940s were consciously adhering to something like today's notion of a three-act structure' has 'found scattered evidence from memos [...] that refer to a movie's "first act" or "last act," but nothing that indicates a commitment to an overarching three-part layout'. In a 1947 story conference for *Portrait of Jennie* (1948), 'Broadway showman Jed Harris is reported as saying: "The second act–he must get the picture back because that's all he'll ever have of her.' "[19] Among published sources, Bordwell has unearthed a few retrospective references to acts in later interviews with writers and producers, and, more intriguingly, a handful of contemporaneous remarks, including a memo from Darryl F. Zanuck showing concern about 'the downbeat nature of the last act' of *Viva Zapata!* (1952), and a claim that when Preston Sturges showed photographer John F. Seitz a cut of *The Great Moment* (1944), Seitz responded: 'Why did you end the picture on the second act?'[20] But none of this amounts to a suggestion that a structure built around acts formed any significant part of a discourse around screenwriting or film-making in the Hollywood of this era.

The explicit segmentation of a script into 'sequences', however, was fairly common; an example is *Hell's Angels*, which was considered in the previous chapter. Although that film may appear anomalous, because of the circumstances of production as well as the conceptual separation of the airplane action sequences from the dramatic narrative, the designation of 'sequences' is retained in a significant minority of films in the sound period, including films that might be regarded as placing a greater priority on narrative coherence than *Hell's Angels*. *Little Caesar* (First National, 1931), for example, has 15 numbered sequences. The convention followed in *Hell's Angels* of alphabetising the sequences is more common: scenes are numbered consecutively within a sequence (if sequence A has 38 scenes, for example, the scene following A-38 will be B-1). The practice seems to have been in fairly regular use at Paramount: *Union Pacific* (1938) has seven sequences (A–G); *Double Indemnity* (1943) has five (A–E), and the writers of the latter, Billy Wilder and Charles Brackett, would continue to divide their scripts into a small number of relatively substantial sequences in their Paramount collaborations of the 1940s and 1950s. Other examples include Samson Raphaelson's scripts for Ernst Lubitsch's *Trouble in Paradise* (Paramount, 1932), with nine sequences (A–I), and *The Shop Around the Corner* (MGM, 1940), with six (A–F), although another Raphaelson script for Lubitsch, *Heaven Can Wait*

(Fox, 1943), has none.[21] In short, if a larger unit of segmentation is *specified* in a screenplay of the period, that unit will be the sequence, of which there were more than the three or four units that would allow for a correlation with 'acts'. Meanwhile, although the explicit labelling of sequences in this way is a feature of only a minority of scripts, the sequence is nevertheless clearly the larger unit of segmentation in many, if not most, screenplays of the classical era. As screenwriter John Howard Lawson remarked in 1949, the boundaries of the sequences are signalled by the FADE OUT direction at the end of one scene followed by FADE IN at the beginning of the next; '[t]here may be as many as twenty sequences, but there are rarely more than eight or nine.'[22]

As noted, the period also sees the introduction into many screenplays of quite lengthy master scenes, without further division into specified shots, as a pragmatic response to the introduction of audible dialogue into the more shot-intensive continuity script that prevailed in the silent era. However, the master scene was not followed rigorously as a unit of segmentation at any point during the classical era. One of the more elegant solutions to the admixture of scenes and shots is seen in Robert Riskin's 'Final Draft' for *Lost Horizon* (Columbia, 1936). Slug lines at the left margin, capitalised and underlined, record whether the scene is interior or exterior, and the location (though he does not include the day/night indicator). Underneath, Riskin simply numbers each shot (and separately specifies the content of any 'insert') in a continuous sequence throughout the screenplay, from 1 to 462.

For the most part, scripts until the end of the 1950s routinely specified certain shot types, with close-ups (almost invariably), and even implicit shot selection, generating a new scene number. The first four 'scenes' of *Rio Bravo* (Warner Brothers, 1959),[23] for instance, have the identical slug line: 'INT RIO BRAVO SALOON—NIGHT'. Scene 2 does not indicate a change of location, but instead implies a close-up as Dude attempts to retrieve a coin and a boot kicks the spittoon away from him. Scene 3 shows Dude looking up to see that the boot belongs to Sheriff John T. Chance, the film's hero. Scene 4 then shows the ensuing fight. All of this is continuous action within the saloon, and therefore all one scene, and in a master-scene script the second scene would commence with the cut to the street (which is scene 5 in the script).

The logic, however, is far from consistent, and at times the numbering sequence appears to be prompted less by a change of scene or shot than by the simple desire to draw attention to an important detail: the 'dramatically important piece of business' mentioned in James Seymour's memo. This is seen in *Johnny Guitar* (Republic, 1953).[24] At first glance, this has some of the attributes of the master-scene script; on closer inspection, the logic evaporates. For example, an enormously lengthy, 29-page episode in Vienna's saloon is continuous in time and location, and therefore, if it were a master-scene script, should be presented as a single scene. In fact in the script it comprises 31 scenes (19–49), occupying 29 pages, *all* carrying the slug line 'INT. VIENNA'S', some but not all of which append a specification of shot. Some of these scenes are themselves very lengthy (scene 27, 7 pages; scene 45, 11 pages), others merely a line. The scene breaks indicate close-ups, significant character entrances and exits, and the like—there is the ghost of a theatrical sensibility here—but a director or editor will of course segment the longer 'scenes' also.

The failure to remove the confusion surrounding the distinction between scenes and shots may be a symptom of a well-established working practice: since everyone was used to working in this way, it wasn't perceived as a problem. In practice, it provided for a relatively greater degree of independence in the preparation of a script than was the case with the silent continuity.

David Copperfield (MGM, 1935): the screenplay as a composite text

The scripts examined so far in this chapter suggest that ambiguities surrounding aspects of segmentation, and the failure to implement inter-studio agreements about formatting on the page, led to the creation of a wide variety of different kinds of script. There are also examples, however, of significant variations and inconsistencies within the same screenplay. A particularly striking illustration is the shooting script of *David Copperfield* (MGM, 1935), which was approved by David O. Selznick on 8 September 1934, with the 'Screen Play' credited to Howard Estabrook and the 'Adaptation' to Hugh Walpole.

It must be stressed that *David Copperfield* is an exceptional case in several ways, not least in being a pet project of Selznick, whose growing status and authority at the Metro studio at this time is exemplified by his personal commitment to this expensive, prestige project.[25] The memos and story notes show that he was continually grappling with two opposing urges: to retain certain episodes because they were well known or inherently dramatic, and to condense or entirely eliminate others in order to keep costs and running time in check. Selznick gives a lower priority to plotting and audience identification with the protagonist than to the retention of memorable scenes and a small number of secondary characters. It was only possible for him to manage this successfully because *David Copperfield* was an adaptation of a very episodic novel, one which lent itself to a process of creation in which individual scenes or sequences could relatively easily be created, revised or discarded without significant damage to the overall structure. This is less likely to be possible with a more tightly plotted narrative, and there are problems in drawing wider conclusions from *David Copperfield* about the relationship between screenplays and the narrative construction of classical Hollywood films in general.

Instead, *David Copperfield* is valuable for present purposes in two particular ways. First, the version approved by Selznick is self-evidently a composite document, comprising many different kinds of material developed by various contributors, some of whom are identified within it. Second, it was subject to a lengthy process of development that is very fully documented within the studio archives. These two factors enable us to see, with a greater degree of precision than usual, how the 'final' text was put together; and while the screenplay is atypical in many ways, it does make visible practices of collaboration and revision that were prevalent in the Hollywood of the time, but which remain relatively obscure within screenplays whose 'final' iteration is more stylistically consistent than that of *David Copperfield*.

The cover of the copy of Selznick-approved 8 September script at the British Film Institute (BFI), which has been autographed by of all of the major cast and crew, also shows that changes were made on 11 and 13 September; 6, 23 and 29 October; and 1 and 19 November.[26] It is largely identical to the personal copies of both Estabrook[27] and director George Cukor (with handwritten dedication by Selznick, a version approved by Selznick on 10 October).[28] For all of these reasons, we can think of this as the most authoritative version, although as the changes post-dating 8 September show, it continued to be modified, and there are significant differences between this document, which we might think of as the final or shooting script, and the film as released; in particular, cuts were made to the film in post-production, which especially reduced the role of Mrs Micawber.

The 169-page script contains 277 scenes or shots, the transition between many of which is a CUT. However, what is clear from the correspondence and drafts is that, from the beginning, *David Copperfield* was intended to comprise a series of sequences, each of which is marked by a major change either of location or of time. Within the script, the transitions between these larger units are invariably marked either by a FADE OUT/FADE IN or by a DISSOLVE. While these markers are at times also found within a sequence, this is usually although not invariably occasioned by the invocation of a specific cinematic device: a montage or 'IMPRESSIONISTIC EFFECT', for example. Although it would be possible to segment the story very differently, by this method we can identify some 32 discrete sequences.

Even the most cursory glance shows that these sequences comprise many different kinds of material, and that the screenplay is the product of various hands. The cover and credits pages are of some interest: the handwritten dedications on the former give the text a certain authority, while the credits are laid out in emulation of the title cards of many Hollywood films of this period. On first appearance of a major character within the screenplay itself, the name of the actor follows in parentheses; Micawber is first seen on p. 51-A, where he is said to be played by Charles Laughton, although in the event the role was played by W. C. Fields, who receives top billing on the screenplay's credits page. Also prefacing the dramatic action is a list of six locations and a note on period, including the idea that the costume designs will be based on the original Victorian illustrations by 'Phiz'. These aside, the first page begins with a FADE IN on an IMPRESSIONISTIC MOOD before a DISSOLVE to the Copperfield home and garden.

Thereafter, much of the script, especially in dialogue-intensive scenes, follows the standard MGM format illustrated in the short extract from *The Sin of Madelon Claudet* above. There are, however, extensive and striking variations:

(i) On several occasions, most or all of a page or more will comprise only scene text. Frequently in such places there are peculiarities of expression, either of narratorial commentary or of verbose description. At scene 85 a whole page—eight paragraphs—is used to describe the minimal action of boys working at the warehouse of Murdstone & Grinby, where David has been sent to work, while scene 152 again devotes a page to describing characters sitting in the Wickfield drawing-room. These are only the most extreme examples of a novelistic tendency prevalent in the descriptive mode of this screenplay, and reference to the source indicates that in such places the scene text represents a surprisingly prolix summary of the corresponding passages in Dickens, drawing extensively on the original wording.

(ii) On other occasions we find the precise opposite: remarkably detailed shot specifications, written in a paratactic style that resembles the outline or scenario forms we saw in earlier chapters. For example, as the frightened David fails to satisfy Murdstone that he has learned his lessons (scene 61), there is a 'CLOSEUP—PROCESS EXPOSURES: David as he struggles with the task—impressionistic effect—Miss Murdstone's hands and the glistening steel beads—Murdstone's cruel eyes staring mercilessly—his hands switching (sic) the cane in the air. David's face becomes smudged with finger marks—he is half in tears.' This technique of breaking up the scene text by dashes strongly suggests segmentation into shots, and is seen on many occasions throughout the screenplay; it strongly contrasts with both the more novelistic material described above, and with the conventional practice of breaking the scene down into shots with capitalised and numbered slug lines (we might expect individual close-ups to be specified for Miss Murdstone's hands, Murdstone's eyes, and David's face, for instance).

(iii) There is frequently a kind of art direction, in which the reader is referred to non-diegetic sources, including the reference to Phiz in the introductory material, as well as to photographs (of Yarmouth, for instance), which have clearly been collected during pre-production.

(iv) The screenplay explicitly states that scenes 109–27 from a previous iteration, set on the Kent and Dover roads, will be 'by Slavko Vorkapich', and that some 200 feet of footage will be required. This recalls the spaces left for the contributions of songwriters and choreographers that we saw earlier in the continuities for musicals, except that Vorkapich's shot breakdowns have been inserted, leading these scenes to appear in forms that are completely unlike the rest of the text. The Kent Road sequence, which contains a series of nine shots, defines each by means of an abbreviation followed by a few words of description, as it moves from a 'L.S.' (long shot) of a donkey cart travelling through fog, to a 'M.S.' (medium shot) of David, and finally a series of 'C.U.'s (close-ups) of David as he narrowly avoids colliding with the cart.

(v) This is followed by Vorkapich's Dover Road sequence, which is presented differently again: a page of scene text written in more conventional narrative style, detailing the visions passing through David's exhausted mind as he makes his way towards Dover. Here the types of shot (dissolves, moving shots, closeups) are specified within the scene text itself. Slightly different again is another Vorkapich sequence, scene 173, which is a montage of shots narrating the development of David's romance with Dora. The description of the rather clichéd series of images specifies how individual effects are to be achieved, via diffusion, overcorrection, a particular kind of film stock, and so on.

(vi) Less striking, but nonetheless peculiar, is the presentation of voice-over when Dan narrates the fate of Little Em'ly. The text uses the parallel-column method of situating the scene text on the left of the page and the dialogue on the right, except that on pages 145 and 147 the latter is squeezed into a remarkably narrow column just an inch and a half in width, with a slightly wider dialogue column on page 146.

The presence of these many different kinds of text in the same screenplay gives some indication of its complex compositional history, which can only be reviewed briefly here.[29] Estabrook began by summarising the entire novel, and then proposed which sequences to retain. Discussions on this matter proceeded continuously with Selznick and, to a lesser extent, with Walpole, who had initially been engaged to make the dialogue both Dickensian and speakable. The two writers initially composed drafts separately, then later iterations more collaboratively, though Estabrook was always the lead writer. In the course of grappling with problems of condensation, Estabrook proposed using Vorkapich as an expert in the kinds of montage techniques that would enable sequences to be drastically shortened, or eliminated altogether, without making the storyline incomprehensible. Similar considerations account for the decision to present the story of Little Em'ly's ruination in a visual montage with accompanying voice-over.

This accounts for most of the peculiarities of the screenplay. What is less clear is why no attempt has been made to make it more consistent in appearance or function; for example, by eliminating the prolix set descriptions, which have survived from the earlier drafts, when Estabrook was concentrating more on summarising Dickens than on preparing a script for production. What emerges from a study of the drafts is that certain scenes and sequences are being re-worked, added or omitted, while others are retained from one iteration into another. So long as the latter were functional, they were not substantially revised: one scene may contain a whole page of continuous narrative prose, while another may be carefully segmented into shots. Both could survive unaltered through to the shooting script, and the inconsistencies do not appear to have troubled the writers, the producer or the director, partly because of the continuous process of verbal and written communication between them. This tends to confirm Claus Tieber's conclusions, from his study of the production history of films such as

Grand Hotel (1932), that the screenplay needs to be considered within a wider communicational context than the simple issuing of instructions to a production team. Instead, there was a continual process of discussion, editing and refinement between several collaborators, overseen by Selznick, whose working methods drew partly on the latest iterations of the screenplay, but also on their shared knowledge and understanding of important questions related to specific aspects of the 'screen idea'.

Although the *general* consistency of the script formatting at MGM, for instance, was overseen by a team of specialists from the producer to the typing department, individual projects could deviate significantly from these norms. In some cases, this was due to the personal interest of a particular producer like Selznick. In others, the director might be given considerable latitude. Writers working on such projects might also develop scripts that deviate significantly from Seymour's insistence that '[t]he purpose of a Shooting Script is definitely NOT to make entertaining READING at the expense of concise clarity'. Our final example in this chapter is the best-known of the exceptions that prove Seymour's rule.

Citizen Kane (1941)

Citizen Kane is exceptional in many ways, but it is important to be aware of two things. The first is that the *Kane* script iterations were used for some of the standard financial and budgetary purposes, and went through some of the standard formatting processes: 'Amelia Kent reworked the 9 May script [Manckiewicz' second draft] into accepted continuity form'; this was followed by a 'breakdown script', a form which 'contains only the scene designations and their physical descriptions. It allows the architectural values of a script to be separated from its literary values and formally stated for the purposes of budgeting the production.'[30]

The second important point about the *Kane* script for present purposes is that, while it went through many drastic changes, some of its most striking elements were present from the beginning, including its astonishing opening. After a description of the 'vast gateway of grilled iron', we see

2. The Literally Incredible Domain of Charles Foster Kane

Its right flank resting for nearly forty miles on the Gulf Coast, it truly extends in all directions farther than the eye can see. Designed by nature to be almost completely bare and flat—it was, as will develop,

practically all marshland when Kane acquired and changed its face—
it is now pleasantly uneven, with its fair share of rolling hills and one
very good-sized mountain, all man-made. [...][31]

This material has survived verbatim from the first draft, which at that
point was called *American*.[32] Later in the sequence, the description of
the garden in front of the castle in scene 10 concludes: 'The dominat-
ing note is one of almost exaggerated tropical lushness, hanging limp
and despairing—Moss, moss, moss. Angkor Wat, the night the last king
died.'[33]

This writing is very different from what might be expected in a
Hollywood screenplay and contains a great deal of material that is not,
in Seymour's words, 'translatable to and capable of expression on the
screen'. Kane's 'domain', for example, is 'literally incredible' and extends
'farther than the eye can see': which means that in certain respects it
cannot be visualised. Moreover, much of what passes for description is
actually narration, that is, material in the 'comment' mode ('it was, as
will develop, practically all marshland when Kane acquired and changed
its face'). Meanwhile, the reference to Angkor Wat is a simile: the reader
is invited to make a comparison between what is shown and something
else that is not. The use of similes in a screenplay, then, is by definition
literary rather than cinematic, as noted in regard to Eisenstein's *October*
(Chapter 5).

It is as if the *Kane* script is being written in a style appropriate to the
scale of Welles' ambition, rather than as a fully functional screenplay.
Even on the assumption that the description of Xanadu originates with
Manckiewicz rather than Welles,[34] the former's knowledge that he is
working for RKO's celebrated *wunderkind* means that the text is already
showing the effects of collaboration. In short, the textual excess of
American is an index of Welles' status, regardless of the extent of his own
involvement in the creation of this particular version of the screenplay,
and the point is confirmed by the contrast between this and the relatively prosaic scene text of most contemporary screenplays. Equally, it
could be argued that the excess of the *Kane* script is a matter of genre, or,
if we do not want to see the film generically (e.g. as a drama or fictional
biopic), that the mode of writing is appropriate to its subject; it is not
difficult to see a connection between the style of the *Kane* script and the
ambitions of Kane, Welles or the film.

However, it is important to note that even in the brief quotations from
the texts mentioned earlier in this chapter, *Laura* contains several figures
of speech, including a sun that is 'veiled', towers that are 'shrouded in

mist' and one overt simile ('the sun gleams like a silver coin'). The relatively poetic scene text could be regarded as generically appropriate to
the psychological *film noir*, and the more functional scene text of *Rio
Bravo* appropriate to the Western. In these ways, what Jeff Rush and
Cynthia Baughman call the 'highly inflected screenplay' can be seen to
have a precise cinematic purpose in approximating the tone or effect of
a film (see Chapter 11).[35]

The later publication of *Kane*'s shooting script, accompanied by
Pauline Kael's ground-breaking essay on the screenplay and the relationship between Welles and Mankiewicz, had at least two consequences.
First, the intrinsic qualities of the script carried with it the possibility of
revisiting cinema history from the point of view of its written, rather
than its filmic texts, with the tantalising prospect of discovering a 'new'
form of literature. Second, the competing claims to authorship of Welles
and Mankiewicz brought the screenplay, rather than the film, into focus
as a contested site. Both of these ways of thinking about screenplays
brought with them the necessity of documenting the material texts,
rather than confining oneself to anecdotal accounts of screenwriters in
Hollywood, in which the failures of major writers like F. Scott Fitzgerald
and William Faulkner have always loomed large. The writing of these
novelists had mostly evaporated in the heat of production, leaving
behind only bitter recollections and lamentations over the death of literature in the world of film. But *Citizen Kane* was published in 1971, at
a time when the screenwriter, both in Europe and in the United States,
was coming to be regarded as, potentially at least, the 'author' of a film.

8
European Screenwriting, 1948–60

As in the aftermath of the First World War, when changes in screenwriting within other countries were influenced by the Hollywood continuity, the years immediately following the Second World War saw many European film industries considering their future anxiously in the face of American economic influence. There is a seeming allusion to this in the posters of Rita Hayworth that the protagonist Ricci posts up in *Bicycle Thieves* (1948), a film which otherwise seems quintessentially of its own time and place in post-war Italy, where the development of neo-realism had at its aesthetic and ideological core a rejection of the blueprint model of the screenplay.

In France, the Blum-Byrnes agreement in April 1946 opened the market to American imports. In an attempt to protect domestic production by concentrating on 'quality' films, in 1949 the Centre Nationale de la Cinématographie (CNC) introduced a selective system of 'bonuses for quality', awarded to established film-makers, initiating the 'tradition of quality' that would form the backdrop to Truffaut's polemical attack on contemporary French screenwriting. Less apparent at the time were the long-term effects of the anti-monopolistic Paramount case of 1948, which began the process whereby the vertically integrated Hollywood studios were eventually required to dispose of their exhibition outlets. This marked the beginning of the end of the Hollywood studio system, an industrial structure which, supported by governmental foreign policy, had projected a global reach and economic power that impacted on 'national cinemas' well beyond American shores.

Largely as a result of the Paramount decision, the Hollywood studios started to close their writing departments. As we shall see in the next chapter, this is associated with the replacement of the numbered shooting script by the master-scene screenplay, which was better tailored to the requirements of writers working relatively independently of the studio system. This desire for independence—from the shooting script, from the studio, from America and from a Hollywood that embodied all of these things—made the years following the Second World War a time of manifestos and factions in European screenwriting, surrounding such questions as the status of the shooting script, the argument that certain kinds of screenplay were literary rather than cinematic and the desire to find ways of film-making that liberated the director from the perceived shackles of the written text.

One method of moving still further away from the shooting script was to film directly from a prose story. Other than in the intermediate forms of the synopsis and the treatment, the prose scenario had not been a significant form in Hollywood production since the 1910s, but it re-emerged as an important mode of film writing in many different guises in European art-house or 'auteur' cinema of the 1950s. Within little more than ten years, an era that had begun with the seemingly unshakeable domination of the European film industry by American economic and political power would end with American cinema increasingly looking for inspiration to Europe and beyond, and in figures like Cesare Zavattini, Ingmar Bergman, Michelangelo Antonioni, François Truffaut and Jean-Luc Godard discovering film-makers whose attempts to create new forms of cinematic expression were intimately bound up with a reconceptualisation of the role and nature of the screenplay.

Italian Neo-Realism, Cesare Zavattini and Michelangelo Antonioni

Neo-realism emerged partly as a political and moral response to fascism—although this familiar argument perhaps disguises continuities between pre- and post-war cinema, and sidesteps political differences between variant forms of realism that are too complex to be unpacked in detail here.[1] The movement is in ideological, aesthetic and industrial opposition to the studio-bound 'white telephone' films of the Mussolini era, preferring instead to shoot on location with amateur actors, and demonstrating a suspicion of the script as a mechanism for creating narratives of escapist fantasy. Much like contemporaneous developments in French film theory (especially in the work of André Bazin), neo-realist cinema offers a glimpse of the possibility of an unmediated reality or truth.

At least, these are some of the views on cinema advanced by Cesare Zavattini, who like many screenwriters started his working life as a journalist. He began writing screenplays in 1934 and became best known as a theorist of neo-realism and for his work as a writer in collaboration with the director Vittorio de Sica on *Shoeshine* (1946), *Bicycle Thieves* (1948), *Miracle in Milan* (1951) and *Umberto D* (1952). For the most part, Zavattini worked within the large-scale collaborative framework that characterised film writing in Italy, and to the extent that it makes sense to speak of authorship in this context he can be seen as not so much a screenwriter but a dramaturg, working on story shape and aesthetics, rather than as a lone author writing completed screenplays. Nevertheless, he appears to have been solely responsible for the story of *Shoeshine*, and according to one of the actors who appeared in that film it 'had a perfect shooting script, a perfectly fixed, well-worked-out scenario. Only it was based on the truth'.[2]

It is what Zavattini means by 'truth' that makes him important in the history of the screenplay, to which he often appears actively hostile. Like many broadly contemporaneous writers in France, Zavattini conceived of cinema as a form of writing in itself, and his dream of a world in which cameras and film stock were as available to everyone as pens and paper was an anticipation of Alexandre Astruc's *caméra-stylo* of 1948, in which

> the cinema is quite simply in the process of becoming a means of expression, a form in which and through which an artist can express his thought, however abstract it may be, or translate his obsessions, exactly as is the case today with the essay and the novel. Better, there will no longer be screenwriters, because in such a cinema the distinction between author and director no longer makes sense. The author writes with his camera as the writer writes with a pen.[3]

Writing, by contrast, was by definition an intervention in, or distortion of, reality. This is one more or less ontological way in which the written text becomes a problem for Zavattini. A second, more specific difficulty with the screenplay text was that the narrative fiction film represented this falsification of reality in an especially intense form: 'The putting together of one situation after another in a narrative line is not so very difficult. The analysis of a situation or an action in depth is extremely difficult.'[4] To this extent, Zavattini's aesthetics are in opposition to Hollywood at least as much as to Italian cinema under Mussolini; if anything, it is the Italian left, in the form of a Marxist adherence to nineteenth-century novelistic realism, that often appears the target of his polemic.[5]

Zavattini's ideal is a precise inversion of the Hollywood continuity script and its European analogues, the Russian 'iron scenario' and the German *Drehbuch*. As we have seen repeatedly, the attempt to create a cinematic 'blueprint' inevitably confronts the pressures and serendipity of actual film production, so that the more precisely the script attempts to anticipate the film, the more noticeable will be the variations between the two. Much the same can be said of the relationship between Zavattini's ideals and his achievements: as Stefania Parigi drily remarks, 'his ideas [were] in large part contradicted by [their] practical applications', because 'his work as a scriptwriter [...] necessarily imposed compromises'.[6] Peter Bondanella, perhaps the foremost English-language historian of Italian cinema, is dismissive: unlike contemporary Italian directors, 'Zavattini emphasizes the most elementary, even banal storylines Bazin prefers, and only Zavattini stresses the need to focus upon the actual "duration" of real time', so his best-known statements contribute to a misrepresentation of Italian cinema of the period.[7] Among his 'too frequently cited' remarks, this is perhaps the best known: 'It is not enough to have the plane pass by three times; it must pass by twenty times.'[8] In his ideal cinematic world there would be no script and—it sometimes seems—almost no story.

Yet this is too simple. Zavattini was well aware of the necessary contradiction between his theoretical ideal and the nature of cinematic form, and that neo-realist film-makers were still obliged 'to compose stories invented according to tradition, and even more [...] to add to the stories some elements of what they themselves had discovered'.[9] Neo-realist films—and here he cites the familiar examples, including *Bicycle Thieves* and *Umberto D*—'were inspired by the possibility of telling everything, but, in a certain sense, they still involve translation because they tell stories and do not apply the documentary spirit simply and fully'.[10] The real basis of his critique is that cause-and-effect, linear storytelling makes the storyteller pass on by, as it were, rather than pausing to consider the deeper implications of the moment,

to 'stay' there inside it [...] For example: let us take two people who are looking for an apartment. In the past, the film-maker would have made that the starting point, using it as a simple and external pretext to base something else on. Today, one can use that simple situation of hunting for an apartment as the entire subject of the film.[11]

It is not that nothing is happening: something crucial is happening, but the narrative drive of conventional storytelling cinema has been forcing us to overlook it.

Similarly, the statement that '[i]n neo-realism, the screen writer and the writer of dialogue disappear; there will be no scenario written beforehand, and no dialogue to adapt'[12] needs to be considered not only in relation to the idea of the *camera* as a pen, but also in the context of a general argument about the nature of the film-making process that Zavattini constructs against the conception-execution model which, as we have repeatedly seen, has been a problem for many other film-makers and critics as well: 'Everything is in flux. Everything is moving. Someone makes his film: everything is continually possible and everything is full of infinite potentiality, not only during the shooting, but during the editing, the mixing, throughout the entire process as well.'[13]

The simplicity of the storylines in Zavattini's best-known films contrasts with the complex process by which the scripts themselves were developed.[14] Robert S. C. Gordon's account shows the extent to which *Bicycle Thieves*, for example, was a collaborative work. Zavattini became gripped on reading a 1946 novel by an acquaintance, Luigi Bartolini, and secured the rights after sketching out a treatment. Next, he, De Sica and another screenwriter, Sergio Amidei, worked in detail on the story; Amidei departed following a disagreement at more or less the same time as another writer, Suso Cecchi, joined the team. Four additional writers also received screen credit, 'but Zavattini always had the controlling hand. [...] *Bicycle Thieves*, Zavattini insisted, was 90 per cent his own work'.[15] Even accepting this figure, it is clear that in this collaborative environment the key factor in story development was the (formal or informal) script conference, and the '90 per cent' presumably includes the work carried out in this context.

The typescript of *Bicycle Thieves* ran to 293 pages, subdivided into over 1,100 numbered shots, and so averaging three to four shots per page.[16] The type is set in a narrow column of 30 to 35 characters per line, and is simply a numbered series of actions:

> 1137.-
> Giungono alla fermata e espettano.
> Giunge un tram stracarico.
>
> 1134.-
> Tra gomitate, spintoni, gente che
> protesta, Antonio e Bruno riesco-
> no a montare sul predellino.
>
> 1135.-
> Il ragazzo sta per cadere all'ul-
> timo momento, gli scivola un pie-

> de. Antonio lo sorregge e lo spin-
> ge dentro.
>
> 1136.-
> Bruno riesce ad entrare nel tram.
> Riesce a trovare un posticino al
> finestrino. Dai vetri del finestri-
> no vede il padre che ancora sul
> predellino dove si regge a fatica
> con un piede sul predellino e l'al-
> tro lungo il bordo della vettura.

These scenes, in which father and son take a tram, form part of 'a long, extended, alternative ending scored out by hand' on the typescript.[17]

In addition to the problem of collaboration, this presents us with a highly detailed conceptualisation of the action that seems at odds with Zavattini's suspicions about the functions of a screenplay. On the other hand, the relatively rudimentary physical presentation of the typescript—which may owe something to the conditions under which it was created—reveals none of the detailed planning functions for different members of a production team that characterise the Hollywood screenplays of this period. As Mark Shiel puts it,

> As with Zavattini's adaptation of *Bicycle Thieves* from Luigi Bartolini's novel (1946) or Visconti's adaptation of *La terra trema* from Giovanni Verga's *I Malavoglia* (1881), those scripts which did have literary sources signified a refusal of loyalty to the written word, which was seen to restrict the potential for realism. Neo-realist scripts were usually collaboratively produced by several contributors and left significant room for modification during shooting.[18]

The form of the script appears to facilitate improvisation, and it is certainly noteworthy that the episode above was deleted from a film whose ending has occasioned so much comment about the nature of storytelling. Neo-realism generally, and *Bicycle Thieves* especially, is usually viewed as presenting relatively open, unresolved endings, with a corresponding de-emphasis of the shaping narrative provided by a script. This has prompted counter-arguments that the story is, in actuality, carefully structured (e.g. around the two parallel thefts of a bicycle). Shiel understandably takes issue with the reductive view of *Bicycle Thieves* as 'a "quest" that follows a "misdeed" that upset the "initial situation" '.[19] Equally, however, it is possible to overstate the degree of 'the attenuation of classical narrative structure, active characterization and narrative closure evident in the film'.[20]

Zavattini appears multiply conflicted: as a strong-minded and independent film theorist who was working in a production context that prioritised collaboration, as a screenwriter working in an ideological and aesthetic context that questioned the function of the screenplay, and as a creator of well-structured stories who dismissed narrative fiction as a distraction from the need to engage with reality. To some extent his theoretical pronouncements represent an attempt to resolve these conflicts, although in practice there remains a contradiction between his purist conception of realism and the pragmatic demands of a storytelling mode that is readily apparent in the films themselves.

If neo-realism flourished only briefly, between about 1946 and 1953, it was still a significant inspiration on André Bazin and the younger critics of *Cahiers du Cinéma* who would proceed to forge the French New Wave. It also saw the beginning of the career of Federico Fellini, and influenced the slightly later 'internal neo-realism' of Michelangelo Antonioni. Like Zavattini, Antonioni was both a prolific writer yet suspicious of story, and anxious to preserve the creative autonomy of the filming process. For Antonioni, films are 'documents, not of a completed thought, but of a thought in the making':[21]

> Arranging scenes is a truly wearisome job. You have to describe images with provisional words which later will no longer have any use, and this in itself is unnatural. What is more, the description can only be general or even false because the images are in the mind without any concrete point of reference. You sometimes end up describing weather conditions. [. . .] Isn't it absurd? [. . .] As far as I'm concerned, it's only when I press my eye against the camera and begin to move the actors that I get an exact idea of the scene; it's only when I hear dialogue from the actor's mouth itself that I realize whether the lines are correct or not.

> Besides, if it were not so, pictures would be clumsy illustrations of a script. It often happens, but I disapprove of making movies that way.[22]

Antonioni wrote this in his introduction to a published collection of four of his shooting scripts: *Il Grido* (1957), *L'Avventura* (1959), *La Notte* (1960) and *L'Eclisse* (1962). These are essentially prose narratives interrupted by stretches of dialogue, and as Antonioni points out, there are significant variations between the films and these scripts. His unfilmed projects are often committed to paper in the form of prose stories, while his completed but unproduced screenplay *The Color of Jealousy* (1971) repeats the form of the earlier shooting scripts, but differs in placing as much emphasis on mood, character or response as on the approximation of a series of shots, in this way retaining many of the functions of a treatment:

> Matteo—that's the man's name—looks at his watch. He checks the clock on the dashboard against his wristwatch. He does this while recklessly but calmly continuing to drive on. In fact, he's a very calm sort of guy, about thirty-five, with longish hair that he sometimes runs his fingers through. But despite his self-control, it's obvious he's in a hurry and in a state of mental turmoil. His self-control comes from his tendency to be self-critical, and this quality keeps his fits of jealousy—which we shall shortly see—from becoming foolish or ridiculous.[23]

Although this kind of character description is certainly not unknown in other forms of screenwriting, seen as a body of work—screenplays, shooting scripts, critical interventions, interviews—Antonioni's writings suggest that the *auteur* film-maker needed to be liberated from the prescriptions of the conventional shooting script. It was in the work of Ingmar Bergman in Sweden, however, that the use of the prose fiction or treatment form would be most influentially and strikingly merged with screenwriting.

Ingmar Bergman and the prose fiction screenplay

Bergman's screenplays bear little resemblance to any we have seen in previous chapters. Their unique style is well summarised by Birgitta Ingemanson:

> Reading like short stories and plays, their extensive stage directions are replete with qualitative adjectives and verbs, metaphors, similes, examples of personification, interior monologues, and other noncinematic features which are not normally found in a genre noted mostly for its terse language, technical information, and line-by-line dialogue. [...] [O]nly the reading public will benefit from their information.[24]

The published screenplay for *Smiles of a Summer Night* (1955), the untypical romantic comedy that projected Bergman from a national to a global stage, illustrates these qualities well. It begins with a short scene in the office of the lawyer, Fredrik Egerman, where his employees comment on the beneficial effect of their boss's young wife on his mood. Then:

> Fredrik Egerman whistles contentedly as he walks down the street at a rapid, springy pace, occasionally greeting a passer-by. He is a well-known and highly regarded man in this small town.
>
> Now he walks into Almgren's Photo Studio and is greeted at the door by the shop owner's wife, a fat, sweet-smelling woman in a light summer gown. She curtsies politely and asks him to be seated in the outer office.[25]

Two things about this passage are immediately striking in the context of conventional understandings of screenplay form: there are no slug lines to indicate the transition from location to location, and it has a narrative mode akin to prose fiction, with the inclusion of comments that do not immediately translate into specified visual images: 'He is a well-known and highly regarded man in this small town', and the woman is 'sweet-smelling'.

Something like Bergman's present-tense, short story form, eschewing the use of slug lines to segment the script into scenes, had been used before: in the treatment stage commonplace in script development in Hollywood production, and in John Gassner and Dudley Nichols's editorial recasting of screenplays into a hybrid form combining narrative fiction and stage-play format in their 1943 collection of *Twenty Best Film Plays*.[26] These are quite different, however, from Bergman's consistent retention of the short story form within the shooting script (all four of the screenplays in the collection in which *Smiles* appears have the same format). A logical assumption would be that this form is a result of editorial intervention at the publication stage. Birgitta Steene remarks that 'the writing stage for him is not the final stage... [i]n its last, practical moment in the creative process, the Bergman script may undergo noticeable changes',[27] and as Anna Sofia Rossholm explains, 'Bergman's published scripts are rarely identical with the unpublished script versions used in the process of production, nor altogether adjusted to correspond to the released film; the published script is often a hybrid of the shooting script and the film, which in itself represents a unique version'.[28]

Nevertheless, Bergman's characteristic approach is consistent between stages. In the classical Hollywood system, script changes are ordinarily the product of negotiations and communications, written and oral, between the writer(s) and others involved in the production process, especially but not exclusively the producer. While each version of the script remains provisional, it is, as it were, the end process of one phase of production. Following the closure of the studios' writing departments in the 1950s this often became true in a strictly contractual sense, with a writer usually being commissioned to produce a certain number of drafts (frequently three), the submission of a draft representing the culmination of one stage in a contracted series. For the auteur writer-director Bergman, however, the series of drafts shows the writer working through a set of problems identified in the handwritten notebooks with which he would commence a project. During the period in which he was preparing *Persona* (1966), he spoke of a desire '[t]o be an artist for one's own sake',[29] and this is one way in which the writer-director as 'auteur' is conventionally distinguished from the Hollywood screenwriter: Bergman is in communication with himself, or at least is attempting to communicate a personal vision to others.

The form of Bergman's screenplays is arguably designed to speak to both of these addressees: the artist himself, and a small community of others tasked to bring the project to fruition. Rossholm's detailed exploration of *Persona* traces the complex processes of composition of a work that represents perhaps the most radical departure of the director's career, most obviously in deconstructing the more familiar narrative structures of his earlier films. For example, his notebook work on an ultimately unfilmed project, *The Cannibals*, furnished material for both *Persona* and *The Hour of the Wolf* (1968), which complicates the path of textual transmission. Most of Bergman's screenplays were

> written in three versions: a handwritten screenplay draft, a work script and a shooting script, later edited into the published screenplay. [...] The script versions do not differ in style or mode of writing (none of them contain technical details on camera movement, etc.) Instead, the differences between the scripts represent changes to the scenes and added or removed passages.[30]

Lorrimer's erratic Modern Film Scripts series reproduces the same text of *Wild Strawberries* as appears in the *Four Screenplays* collection that includes *Smiles*, and is prefaced with a note:

The literary script in this book is identical to that used by Ingmar Bergman when filming, except that: (1) the original script contained numbers before each sequence indicating the estimated number of shots which would be necessary for that sequence; (2) since this script was prepared before shooting began, it contains sequences and dialogue which do not appear in the final film.[31]

The structure and narrative flow of a Bergman screenplay is consequently far more 'literary' than is possible with the frequent and intrusive slug lines of more conventional forms.

It is literary in another sense also, since it engages the distinctive properties of writing in ways that do not have a direct correlative in film. One of the most remarked-upon aspects of Bergman's style is the frequent invocation of the sense of smell, as we have already seen in the extract from *Smiles*. The title of Ingemanson's article, 'The Screenplays of Ingmar Bergman: Personification and Olfactory Detail', is prompted by a 1960 article in which reviewer Hollis Alpert latches on to this peculiarity in *Wild Strawberries*.[32] Ingemanson demonstrates its appearance in no fewer than nine screenplays, and one could multiply many times her own examples, among the most striking of which are the 'musty scent of old wood and a dying house' in *Through a Glass Darkly* (1961), the 'cool fragrance of salt and seaweed, wet wood and rain-soaked juniper bushes' drifting in through an open window in *Persona* (1966), and the house full of 'whispering voices and a smell of coffee' and '[t]he scent of withering flowers . . . mixed with the cigar smoke and the smell of strangers' in *Cries and Whispers* (1972).[33]

This is only one of many ways in which the Bergman screenplay presents an overtly narrating voice. To take one of hundreds of possible illustrations, from *Smiles of a Summer Night*, 'Out of the twilight, out of nowhere, a melody is heard. It seems to have been born out of the night, out of the bouquet of the wine, out of the secret life of the walls and the objects around them'. Given the remarkably hypotactic quality of these texts, it is notable that 'there is little evidence in the films of an effort on Bergman's part to portray personification (or any other literary features) and olfactory detail cinematically'.[34] In these ways Bergman's writing exemplifies the division between the literary and the cinematic text we saw in Chapter 5 in connection with Eisenstein. One can certainly consider Bergman's scripts to be literature as much as filmic pre-texts, and to represent a meditation within the self as much as a set of instructions or communications with another. This is, in part, simply because the writer-director has a more secure sense of the intentions of the written text than does the director adapting the words of another person.

In Bergman's writing, however, there is a more particular creative sense of this relationship, in which the mode of writing is part of a holistic creative method. Rossholm remarks that 'Bergman did not consider his screenplays as autonomous literary works but as parts of a process, from initial impressions, to words, to cinematic images'.[35] Ingemanson locates the source of the 'haunting animation in Bergman's screenplays' in 'the apparent conflict between his extreme distrust of words and verbal communication on the one hand, and his nevertheless persistent need to communicate with other people on the other'—those others being, in this context, the actors and film crew, resulting in 'his unusual kind of screenplay with its extensive stage directions and abundant use of literary images'.[36]

Bergman provides a fascinating illustration of the paradox that while the function of a screenplay may lie in its anticipated transformation into a different work in another medium, for that reason it generates textual peculiarities all its own. Arguably, the more sensitive the writer to the needs of the crew, and particularly the actors, the more important it becomes to write material other than that which can be reduced to the purely visual. As Steene puts it, 'Bergman needed, at least up to the writing of *Persona* (1966), to set down his theme and vision not only in a minimal verbal way in order to clarify his cinematic intention, but also in such a fashion that the printed text achieved its own autonomy of being'.[37] As the contrast between this assessment and Rossholm's suggests, the idea of textual 'autonomy' seems to be bound up with a notion of 'literature' as a form of writing that repays attention on its own merits without reference to another sign-system such as that of cinema. Equally, however, a literary text may well provide information (e.g. pertaining to character) that is not strictly visual, but which is nonetheless valuable to an understanding of the film story. Actors often discuss matters of 'motivation' with the director, and it becomes a logical responsibility of a writer-director working with an established company, as in Bergman's case. There is no particular reason why the screenplay should not provide this information instead; indeed, commentary of this kind was routinely present in the silent continuity, as we saw in Chapter 4.

Bergman did not remain static as a writer. Steene notes a process of textual pruning, beginning with *Through a Glass Darkly* (1960) and the 'chamber film scripts', culminating in *Cries and Whispers* (1972). Thereafter, with *Scenes from a Marriage* (1973) he becomes more verbose, often including commentaries on the scenes. This practice may owe something to his work in the theatre, and coincidentally, as we shall see in the next chapter, at more or less exactly the same time Francis Ford Coppola was using comparable methods derived from theatre practitioners in compiling his 'bible' working copy of the screenplay for *The Godfather* (1972).

Both in his working processes and within the films themselves, Bergman came to exemplify, in the 1950s, the notion of the film artist. As a writer-director he epitomised the independent *auteur*, and his cinema facilitated a view of film as personal expression, pursuing a logic of symbolism or interior structure rather than that of narrative and the goal-oriented protagonist. Very problematically, this would mesh with ideas of the 'auteur' director being developed contemporaneously in France by the soon-to-become-directors writing for *Cahiers du Cinéma*. In the *nouvelle vague*, responsibility for the film would lie with the director, with a corresponding reduction in the status of the screenplay. Jean-Luc Godard, for example, may have idolised Bergman, but the 'auteurist' understanding of film-making in France arose from altogether more local concerns.

France and the 'New Wave'

The German occupation of France transformed what had previously been relatively anarchic approaches to screenwriting in that country into something more closely approximating those of the Hollywood studio system, implementing procedures which, after the war, would lead to divisions of labour and a process of script development that resembled their American equivalents. Ironically, then, 'during the sound period French scriptwriting practices moved steadily toward a more and more rigid, elaborate, and formalized set of procedures, precisely at a period when American practices were retreating from them'.[38] The demands of censorship and political control meant that by 1942 French film-makers were obliged to submit a completed *découpage* (roughly speaking, a form of shooting script) before proceeding to production. In 1944, this process was further broken down into stages of script development, requiring first the submission of a synopsis (to be assessed for quality) and later the *découpage* and the dialogues (to be assessed for 'morality').

Colin Crisp's analysis of French screenwriting manuals and magazines suggests that after the war a new division of labour arose to accommodate the approximately five stages through which script development would now proceed—though the number of these stages, the discriminations between them, and the terminology are all unstable both within the industry generally and in relation to a given project. Initially a *scénariste* would be tasked with recognising suitable material (the initial *idée de film*) and developing it into the first stage, a 10- to 20-page, present-tense prose *synopsis*, aimed at attracting the attention of a producer. The producer would then commission an *adapteur* to develop this story idea into more recognisably cinematic form, via the second stage—the *traitement* of 30 to 50 pages, analogous to its American counterpart—and the third, the *continuité*, which was akin to the master-scene script and began the cinematic process of segmenting the action into around nine to 13 sequences, with possibly 'two or three larger plot units (acts), and 40–50 "scenes," each of two to three typed pages in length: the *continuité* might therefore look somewhat like a sketchy play, with bits of dialogue indicated, of some 80–100 pages in length'. It would be packaged with a synopsis and a list of characters and settings. A third worker, the *dialoguiste*, would then add to this the dialogue, resulting in the fourth stage, the *continuité dialogue*. Finally, it was the director's responsibility to transform this material into the *découpage technique*, which inserted technical directions and 'concise sketches of the overall setup for each individual shot', to produce a text of between 125 and 200 pages.[39]

The *découpage technique* is, therefore, similar to the American 'continuity' of the silent era, as well as to the 'iron scenario' in Soviet Russia, the German *Drehbuch*, and highly detailed forms of shooting script in general. However, Crisp notes that the separation of writing stages and roles was not universal, and in many cases what developed was not so much a rigid and chronological series of iterations as an ongoing, collaborative team effort. In short, the French producer-package system facilitated a spectrum of working practices, from 'the businesslike sequentiality of divided labor to the slightly orgiastic chaos of an interactive houseparty';[40] and if that is not quite how Hollywood presented itself, the Americans, too, were often more reliant on developing screenplays via formal and informal script conferences than is apparent from the more purely industrial readings of its system, as Claus Tieber argues.[41] In any case, and making allowances for a few writers such as Jacques Prévert who could act in more than one capacity, the writing team became the norm in France, as did collaboration between the writers and a director such as Claude Autant-Lara, who worked repeatedly with the writing duo of Jean Aurenche and Pierre Bost.

This team was an especial target of François Truffaut's notorious polemic 'A Certain Tendency of the French Cinema', published in *Cahiers du Cinéma* in 1954. Truffaut argued against—and, arguably, helped to construct in the process—a French 'tradition of quality', which he considered to be dominated by *littérateurs* who were responsible for excessive 'psychological realism'.[42] Truffaut accuses Aurenche and Bost of being 'essentially literary men'[43], and of having their own thematic concerns which they impose on the material, regardless of the source text they are adapting. Against these figures, Truffaut affirms the quality of the work of 'Jean Renoir, Robert Bresson, Jean Cocteau, Jacques Becker, Abel Gance, Max Ophuls, Jacques Tati, Roger Leenhardt [. . . who] are *auteurs* who often write their dialogue and some of them themselves invent the stories they direct'[44]. What concerns him particularly is the idea that the meanings within a film can be traced not to the director but to the writer(s), and although Crisp is hostile to the 'expressive myth' that Truffaut can be accused of propounding, his own analysis confirms Truffaut's to the extent that '[o]ften the expressivity of a text can more confidently be connected to the scriptwriter than to the director, or at least to collective authorship dominated by the scriptwriter'.[45]

The structures Truffaut attacks can be traced to the division of labour outlined above, although this was not in actuality quite so inflexible in French cinema as might appear from his essay, and arguably Truffaut is laying the groundwork for a critique of Hollywood, which he did not himself pursue, rooted in the putative division between literary conception and filmic execution. Going back a little further, Truffaut's critique of the role of the screenwriter echoed long-standing concerns in French cinema following the introduction of sound. In the late 1920s and early 1930s, in common with their peers in other countries, some of the most eminent French directors, such as Abel Gance and Marcel L'Herbier, expressed anxiety about the literary effects of dialogue and the resulting reversion to studio rather than location filming. Much of the accompanying theoretical debate drew on ideas of the specifically visual nature of film, and alongside the work of theoreticians in other countries, such as Rudolf Arnhem, this helped to consolidate the view that dialogue represented the encroachment upon cinema of literature or theatre. That the sound films of directors who had come from the theatre, such as Marcel Pagnol and Sacha Guitry, were popular with audiences only compounded the crime: dialogue-intensive, commercially successful films were in opposition to 'pure cinema'.[46]

Moreover, despite the greater authorial control that was available to the French director in comparison to most of those in Hollywood, resentment of the writer was fuelled by a legal peculiarity:

Prior to 1957, French law considered the scriptwriter to be the author of a film. The law of 11 March 1957, regulating authorial rights and intellectual property, broadened the term and opened the legal way to a concept of auteur cinema. But it still seems to give priority to the written sign. Article 14 states that 'the following shall have the status of author of a cinematographic work: the author of the scenario, the author of the adaptation, the author of the spoken text, the author of the musical compositions, the director.'[47]

It was the director, by contrast, who was elevated to pre-eminence in Truffaut's cinema of 'auteurs'. However, the distinction is not straight-forward: as he notes himself, many of the directors on his list of exemplary *auteurs* also wrote their films, while in any case it was the norm in France (unlike in the United States) for a director to be closely involved in the writing stage during the construction of the *découpage technique*. It is important to note, then, that Truffaut was not opposed to screenplays *per se*, but to a particular kind and use of the screenplay, in this industry, at this time; and his representation of that industry is at the very least open to debate.

Aside from the promotion of the director as auteur, the New Wave had two broad, immediate, yet long-lasting consequences for French ideas of the screenplay, related to the two poles of what Alison Smith terms 'a hysterical relation with the concept of the screenwriter, where the role is imagined to be everything or nothing'.[48] The first was that it could, in effect, be jettisoned: 'the particularly high profile given to Jean-Luc Godard's and Jacques Rivette's improvisatory script habits led to a New Wave myth, the idea that a film could, in normal circumstances, be elab-orated from a few sketchy typewritten pages'.[49] While such approaches may have liberated the director, the consequent lack of structure to many French films—real or perceived—led to counter-demands for the re-introduction of script development within the industry, a position which in the 1980s became a matter of government policy.[50]

Ironically, Truffaut himself was generally content to work with fairly conventional screenplay forms in preparing his own films, and col-laborated extensively with others, very much in the French tradition, in writing the texts. For the first of the films that comprise the semi-autobiographical Antoine Doinel sequence, *The 400 Blows* (1959), he began with his own original treatment (in the familiar form of a present-tense prose story), but thereafter worked with Marcel Moussy, who receives credit for the dialogue and co-credit for the adaptation. For *Stolen Kisses* (1968) and *Bed and Board* (1970), he developed the story in collaboration with Claude de Givray and Bernard Revon via conferences and the resulting story notes. The screenplays that emerged from this work are, formally, fairly conventional master-scene scripts.[51] It is not entirely coincidental that, as we shall see in the next chapter, treatments and master-scene scripts became the predominant modes of creating a 'spec' or 'selling' script in the United States with the ending of the classical studio system after the 1950s, since both were appropriate means of telling a story in cinematic terms but outside the constraints of in-house production.

A second consequence of the New Wave, then (and perhaps paradoxically), was the emergence of the idea of the *screenwriter* as author. If the film is no longer to be regarded as simply the execution of an idea that had been pre-conceived in its entirety on paper, this cuts both ways: the director is liberated from the constraints of the screenplay, but so too is the screenplay liberated from having to prepare each aspect of the film precisely. It becomes a *relatively* autonomous document, and a genre in which a 'serious' writer might look to work for reasons not entirely reducible to financial reward.

This idea of the screenplay as a document worthy of attention in itself was now immediately married with another, typically French, approach: the emergence of creative partnerships between directors and writers who already had established reputations in their fields, and then came together to create some of the most striking films of the 1960s at a time when the established Hollywood model was vanishing. This development became associated with the 'Second Wave' or 'Left Bank' directors, especially Alain Resnais' collaborations with Marguerite Duras (*Hiroshima Mon Amour*, 1959) and Alain Robbe-Grillet (*Last Year at Marienbad*, 1961). Within film history, this represents perhaps the first time (other than in the work of writer-directors) that the voice of the screenwriter could be said to have an authorial weight within the film that is equal to that of the director. In transforming accepted notions of what a screenplay could be, Duras and Robbe-Grillet produced texts that can be regarded as major forms of experimental literature, not least for the simple reason that they were immediately published and thereby became part of an accepted canon of literary fiction.

They also form a significant variation on the collaborative model that had sustained French cinema since the war. Robbe-Grillet devotes much of the introduction to *Last Year at Marienbad*, which is significantly subtitled *A Ciné-Novel*, to discussing the collaborative process between a writer and director generally and himself and Resnais specifically:

> Alain Resnais and I were able to collaborate only because we had *seen* the film in the same way from the start; and not just in the same

general outlines, but exactly, in the construction of the least detail as in its total architecture. What I write might have been what was already in [his] mind; what he added during the shooting was what I might have written.[52]

This sense of an absolute fusion of roles characterises the 'ciné-novel' itself. Unlike the emerging master-scene form, which tends simply to remain silent concerning the responsibilities of other members of the production team, Robbe-Grillet's text explicitly challenges divisions of labour between writer, director, composer, editor, designer and even the creator of the title credits:

> The last two credit-pictures, instead of constituting separate shots, are gradually revealed by a sideways shift of the camera which, without stopping on the first frame when it is centred, continues its slow, regular movement, passes across a section of the wall containing only woodwork, gilding, moulding, etc., then reaches the last frame, containing the last name or names of the credits, which could begin with less important names and end with the major ones, or even mix them, especially towards the end. This last picture has a considerable margin of wall around it, as if it were seen from farther away. The camera passes across this without stopping either, then continues its movement along the wall.[53]

Here the idea of the screenplay as a blueprint for production is replaced by a notion of a film project as one that generates more than one work of art—the screenplay as literature, and the film as cinema—not least because Robbe-Grillet's text, like certain other novelistic forms, possesses a kind of omnipotence that is denied to most screenplays, which defer to others the task of creating many aspects of the fictional story world.

A related development is Chris Marker's 1962 film *La Jetée*, which is practically unique in presenting almost the entire story as a series of stills, thereby defamiliarising the sense of film as movement by drawing attention to its actual status as a succession of frames. This makes it uniquely well suited to re-presentation in book form. The cover of the published text describes the book, like *Last Year at Marienbad*, as a 'ciné-roman'.[54] It is a kind of photographic version of a graphic novel, with the minimal text below the images—which takes on something of the quality of the subtitles of a film—preserving the interplay between word and text that is the essence of the film. What finally emerges from the radical approaches to film-making in the French cinema in these few

short years from 1959 to 1962, then, is not so much the replacement of
the writer by the director as the creative interplay between written text
and visual movement, leading to the creation of strikingly new forms
of each.

Writing the introduction to a collection of his shooting scripts that
was published in 1963, Antonioni captures the historical erasure of a
particular kind of numbered shooting script:

> screenplays of ten years ago [...] were full of technical specification
> such as P.P., F.I., C.L., dolly, pan, etc. Today all that has disappeared,
> but in my opinion this isn't enough. Screenplays are on their way
> to becoming actually sheets of notes for those who, at the camera,
> will write the film themselves. The turn being taken by other arts as
> well, such as music and painting, inexorably headed towards freer
> forms, authorizes us to think so. The world is changing. [...] Today
> the movies have a different function, different rules. The Hollywood
> myth has fallen. The movie myth has fallen. Right in Hollywood,
> Marilyn Monroe commits suicide.[55]

At this moment it could seem as if Hollywood itself had died, while
European cinema had been reborn, ushered back to life by a generation
of auteurs. But it never really works that way. By the end of the 1950s
some American film-makers were looking enviously at the European art
cinema for inspiration, and finding the potential for a new model based
on the individual writer or director as 'author' of a film. This would
usher in the 'Hollywood Renaissance', accompanied by the different
kinds of film writing that would emerge from a combination of the
prose texts favoured by many European directors with a changed form
of screenplay that was relatively free of the shackles of industrial control:
the master-scene script.

9

Master-Scene Screenplays and the 'New Hollywood'

The question of when the master-scene screenplay developed as a conventional form is far from straightforward. Until the late 1940s, at least, writers would usually work within a studio's writing department under the supervision of a producer. Each iteration of the script marked a staging post in the journey of a story from the initial idea—which might have originated with anyone at the studio, or been spotted as a potential property by the studio's story department—to the completion of the screenplay. As noted in Chapter 7, this would not be composed entirely in master scenes, but instead would include suggestions for camera angles and types of shot. This made it functional as a 'shooting script', which could, if necessary, be followed by a more precise segmentation by the director.

A conceptual difference, at least, between this shooting script and a 'master scene' screenplay was, however, beginning to become more apparent at around the time of 'Paramount case' of 1948. This Supreme Court anti-trust ruling enforced 'divorcement', the separation of production and distribution from exhibition. Tom Stempel explains succinctly the consequences for screenwriters:

> The divorcement of the production and distribution sides of the business from the theater side meant the companies could no longer control guaranteed markets for their films. There was then no longer a need for the studios to have all the talent under contract, since they did not have guaranteed work for them. [...] Instead of working for studio heads, [screenwriters] now found themselves working for independent producers, directors, actors, and sometimes even themselves. The changes brought about by the Paramount decision continue into the present.[1]

By the middle of the 1950s, there were widespread closures of in-house writing and production teams. With divorcement, in place of this method of working came what Staiger terms the 'package-unit system'. The screenplay was no longer part of a process that would be handled by an in-house story department or producer, but instead was a discrete property for promotion or sale. The distinction between a 'screenplay' as a document written in its entirety in master scenes, and a 'shooting script' defined by the insertion of shooting angles and shot specifications, seems to have become more distinct at around this time.

In 1949, John Howard Lawson, who was very much a Hollywood insider, published his *Theory and Technique of Playwriting and Screenwriting*, a rare example of a screenwriting manual of the classical sound era. In attempting to address the probability 'that many readers of this book have only a vague notion concerning the written material that guides production',[2] Lawson takes as an exemplary text Abraham Polonsky's screenplay for *Body and Soul* (1947):

FADE IN

1. EXT. TRAINING CAMP—NIGHT—CRANE
    A MOVING SHOT through bright moonlight and deep shadow, articulates an edge of a building, a tree, part of the outdoor ring, a heavy sandbag slowly, but just barely, swinging in the night wind, through a wide window facing on the clearing, to CHARLEY DAVIS, asleep with moonlight nibbling on his face.

2. CLOSE SHOT—CHARLEY ASLEEP
    He is struggling with a nightmare, fear sweating on his face. Far off a train whistle in a distant river valley SOUNDS a note of melancholy hysteria, and Charley wakes up screaming.

                          CHARLEY
                (calling desperately from the dream)
            Ben...! Ben...!

    Sitting up, eyes open, he stares around the room. The nightmare still winds within his mind as he wipes the cold sweat off.

3. CLOSE SHOT—WALL
    where moonlight patterns changing branch shapes, and the sandbag swings slowly in the wind like conscience from a gibbet.[3]

It is worth noting the more literary qualities of Polonsky's scene text, including the narrative insight that Charley is still half inside the nightmare, and the unfilmable simile 'like conscience from a gibbet'. As we shall see in this chapter, such comment was by no means unusual in the early forms of master-scene screenplay that would begin to displace the numbered shooting script in the 1950s and 1960s. By the end of the 1970s, however, a dominant discourse around screenwriting was beginning to insist that authorial narration of this kind was inadmissible in screenplays (see Chapter 10). Shot specification, too, would be prohibited. In 1949, however, Lawson is still seeing the numbered script segmented by shot as the default format, and indeed he has chosen this passage precisely 'because it includes a great many technical phrases and reveals their function'.[4]

Yet the following year MGM's then head of production, Dore Schary, in his *Case History of a Movie* (1950) was speaking of the master-scene script as a clear alternative:

> *The Next Voice* happened to be divided into 172 scenes. But a shooting script which would reach the screen in exactly the same length might contain up to 500 scene numbers, if the writer and producer felt it necessary to write out each camera angle in advance. But most directors justifiably consider the handling of the camera as in their province [...] [O]ur screenplay was written in a comparatively short number of master scenes in which the action ran uninterrupted for as long as five or six pages. When Ruby Rosenberg made his initial breakdown, he grouped the scenes into eighty short sequences, each sequence linking a series of scenes which occurred in one set in one more or less continuous progression [to assist in shooting out of continuity].[5]

Two years later, Lewis Herman's *A Practical Manual of Screen Playwriting for Theater and Television Films* (1952) contains a section on 'the master-scene screen play' (two words) which, although Herman is a much less authoritative source than Schary, is also worth quoting:

> Quite often [...] the writer may not even be permitted to write a shooting script. He may be assigned to do a 'master-scene' script. He will not be required to write in camera shots and angles. What will be expected of him is simply a completed treatment. Where, in the treatment, he merely indicated that certain dialogue be spoken, now, in the master-scene script, he will write in all the dialogue. Where the treatment merely suggests, in a literary style, the action to be taken,

this time the writer will indicate the same action, but in screen-play form.⁶

After giving an illustration, Herman explains:

> That is a master scene. No camera angles have been indicated. Only a scene description, character action, and the accompanying dialogue have been attended to. [...] Working in this fashion, with master scenes, the writer will simply fill in the undetailed segments of the treatment, using as much of the treatment's material as is feasible.

Herman then posits that the writer will enter into a dialogue with the producer and others, progressively refining the script until a 'final-final screen play' emerges.⁷ Collectively, these sources, when examined alongside screenplays written in Hollywood in the 1950s, suggest that the master-scene script was coming into focus, as a viable 'shooting script' itself, at the beginning of that decade.

A 'revised shooting final, February 9, 1950' script for *Panic in the Streets*, known at this stage as *Outbreak*, closely and fairly consistently resembles the master-scene script; aside from a few numbered inserts, the segmentation, with 144 scenes in its 160 pages, is consistent by scene.⁸ As we saw in Chapter 7, however, Hollywood screenplays through to the end of the 1950s were still tending to specify shots, though less so in dialogue-intensive scenes, leading to the hybrid texts characteristic of the period. *Panic in the Streets* routinely includes the shot type in the slug line, which produces the kind of inconsistencies we saw in *42nd Street* (Chapter 6). For example, the heading for scene 28 is 'INT. MORGUE ANTEROOM – MED. SHOT', yet the scene continues for four and a half pages. Other scenes of comparable length will indicate 'FULL SHOT' in the heading. It seems unlikely that it can be envisaged that the scenes will not include any cutting, although a possibly associated peculiarity of the script is that it will routinely specify that action is happening in the foreground or background, as if we are to imagine the film to be shot consistently in deep focus, as in scene 4:

EXT. SAINTE PHILIPE STREET – FULL SHOT – NIGHT

Kochak is weaving toward CAMERA. Far in the b.g. the other three can be seen pursuing. Poldi breaks into a run and catches Kochak in f.g. There are a few whispered sentences in Armenian before Kochak again throws Poldi off and staggers on past CAMERA. Poldi stands looking after him angrily as Blackie and Fitch come up.

The master-scene screenplay does not, however, appear to be a response to the continuity script; that is, it does not seem to represent a deliberate backwards step from the more fully realised numbered continuity, although it is worth noting that by this date the Hollywood screenplay in general was making progressively less use of many elements prominent in the continuity, including shot segmentation and specification as well as parenthetical direction of speech. Instead, to the extent that it makes sense to speak in evolutionary terms, it appears more likely that the master-scene script emerged from two other, separate developments.

The first is the introduction of sound, which occasioned the writing of screenplays containing lengthy dialogue scenes without the interruption of camera directions. In this sense, we can say that master *scenes* were being written from the beginnings of sound in the late 1920s and certainly in the early 1930s, although it is less easy to identify entire scripts from this period that could be said to be in master-scene form. Going still further back, the scene as the unit of segmentation is present in the earliest extant scenarios (Chapter 2), although these directly imitate the form of theatrical play texts and do not otherwise significantly resemble the later screenplay form. Unlike the silent continuity, then, which as we have seen used three distinct modes for presenting speech (the intertitle, directly reported speech within the scene text, and vaguer indications that unspecified speech is occurring), in all of these cases writers appear to have turned to the theatrical play as a model for the presentation of spoken dialogue, and this occasioned the introduction of scenes resembling those of the later master-scene screenplay.

The second development influencing screenplay form at around this time appears to have arisen from modifications to the treatment. A published talk in 1945 by the British-Irish screenwriter Bridget Boland, who was one of the credited writers on the UK version of *Gaslight* (1940), offers a straightforward definition of 'the master scene script' as a document that 'gives the content of each scene in the film with all the settings, action and dialogue given in detail, but no camera angles or details of movement'. Importantly, however, Boland identifies the creation of the master-scene script as the next stage after the treatment: the director then has the option of using either the master-scene script or a shooting script.[9] This resembles the process of script development in France at around the same time, in the late 1940s, where the *continuité dialogue* similarly followed the treatment as a distinct stage (see Chapter 8).

In 1952, in his book *Making a Film*, the future director Lindsay Anderson presented parallel texts of two pages of the 'treatment' and 'shooting script' for the British film *Secret People*, directed by Thorold Dickinson and released that same year.[10] Here is an excerpt from the treatment:

> The cafe landing. MARIA is at the telephone. She is finishing dialling a number.
>
> | | |
> |------------|------------------------|
> | MARIA: | (in a low voice) Hullo.|
> | | Is that you, Louis? |
>
> Shot of Foley Street room – empty and left in disorder.
> Police are searching. One takes off the receiver and listens...
>
> Maria by the telephone on the cafe landing and realising that someone is on the other end of the line, repeats:
>
> | | |
> |---------|--------------------|
> | MARIA: | Is that you, Louis?|
> | LOUIS: | Hullo. |
>
> MARIA whirls round and Louis is standing behind her. He takes the receiver from her and replaces it.
>
> | | |
> |---------|------------------------------|
> | LOUIS: | Come inside. We can't talk here.|

And this is the equivalent passage in the shooting script:

> E.52   INT. ANSELMO'S CAFÉ. FIRST FLOOR LANDING. DAY (STUDIO)
>
> MARIA is at the telephone. She is finishing dialling a number.
>
> E.53   INT. LOUIS' LONDON LODGINGS. DAY (STUDIO)
>
> The Foley Street room has been left in disorder. Police are searching. One takes off the receiver and listens...
>
> E.54   INT. ANSELMO'S CAFÉ. FIRST FLOOR LANDING. DAY (STUDIO)
>
> CAMERA STARTS on C.S. of MARIA as, still by the telephone on the café landing, and realising that someone is on the other end of the line, she says:
>
> | | |
> |---------|----------------------|
> | MARIA: | |
> | | Hullo. Is that you, Louis?|
> | LOUIS' VOICE: | |
> | | Hullo. |

> MARIA whirls round, CAMERA TRACKING to M.S. LOUIS is standing behind her. He takes the receiver from her and replaces it.
>
> LOUIS:
> Come inside.

The treatment requires only the addition of scene headings to resemble very closely the master-scene screenplay of today, while the shooting script requires only the subtraction of the camera directions and numbering. In the British context it is notable that the proximity between these two forms, at least at this time, is sometimes accentuated by formatting practices. In the treatment version above, the speakers' names, instead of following the usual Hollywood convention of appearing approximately centred with dialogue below, is indented a couple of tab spaces from the left margin, with the tab setting for dialogue being placed in the middle of the page on the same line as the speaker's name. Dialogue thereby comes to occupy only the right-hand side of the page, while the descriptive scene text runs across it. This presentation, which resembles that often used for published stage plays, was in widespread use for British screenplays as well as treatments in the 1950s; Janet Green, for example, wrote several successive drafts for *Victim* (1960) in this format.[11]

More generally, the form of the master-scene script can be seen to fall somewhere between the treatment and the shooting script in terms of level of detail, segmentation and presentation of dialogue. Meanwhile, the above accounts tend to suggest that the historical emergence of the master-scene screenplay (as opposed to individual master scenes in other kinds of script) developed as a modification of the treatment, and so to have been a stage in a writing process that could lead finally to a shooting script; it does not seem to have been reverse engineered from the numbered continuity.

The beginnings of the 'New Hollywood'

Throughout the 1950s and 1960s, American scripts continued to exist on a spectrum, anywhere from a numbered shooting script to a master-scene screenplay. A good illustration of the variant possibilities is supplied by *Charade* (screenplay by Peter Stone; revised draft, 21 August 1962).[12] On the one hand, as in the master-scene script, slug lines are reserved for scene headings, and there are many scenes with much dialogue and minimal scene text; on the other hand, there is a great deal of shot specification, though unnumbered. The beginning of the second scene, for example, contains directions for an establishing shot, three close-ups, a medium shot, a two shot and a moment at which the 'camera pulls back slightly', all in half a page.

By this point, the consequences of divorcement meant that screenwriting in Hollywood was no longer a closed shop. Studios increasingly lost their identities and became absorbed within multinational conglomerates, leasing their facilities to independent producers. These changes in the studio system were accompanied by a new stage in the cross-fertilisation of the American and European film industries, as younger writers and directors, many of them the first graduates from the new American film schools, came under the sway of European art-house cinema and prevailing concepts of the cinematic 'auteur', finding their way into directing initially through the less costly method of writing screenplays. The prime example is Francis Ford Coppola.[13]

Such figures were able to write their scripts in more idiosyncratic ways than would have been possible under the old order, and this applies as much to the formal properties of their screenplays as to any thematic or generic concerns. William Goldman, for example, wrote in a wide variety of genres but consistently eliminated scene headings, relying instead on the cut from location to location within the running scene text. The 'final' of one of Goldman's best-known screenplays, *Butch Cassidy and the Sundance Kid* (1969), has no master scenes, but instead consists of 823 numbered shots.[14] For this reason, one of the screenwriting forms Goldman's work *least* resembles is the master-scene screenplay. Instead, it has much more in common with the 'outline' script of early cinema, the minimalism of Zavattini's *Bicycle Thieves* script and, most strikingly, the numbered continuity script of the silent era and the shooting script.

In his part-manual, part-memoir *Adventures in the Screen Trade*, Goldman discusses 'the first four scenes' of *Butch Cassidy*[15] and gives them titles. These correspond to the following shots in the screenplay (although the *Adventures* text differs in places): 'Butch Casing the Bank' (shots 1–14), 'Sundance Playing Cards' (15–59), 'The Ride to Hole-in-the-Wall' (60–83), 'The Kick in the Balls' (84–119). In a master-scene screenplay, the first of these scenes would have the heading 'EXT. BANK—DAY', and the action would continue without numbering of shots. Goldman instead presents it as a sequence of 14 numbered shots, each connected to the next by a CUT TO, and each with its own brief heading that indicates not (usually) the type but the content of the shot: 'ALMOST THE ENTIRE SCREEN IN BLACK SHADOW', 'A MAN',

'BUTCH', 'THE WINDOW', 'BUTCH', 'A DOOR', 'PAPER MONEY', 'A GUN', 'A WINDOW', 'THE DOOR OF A BIG SAFE', 'BUTCH', 'A BANK GUARD', 'BUTCH', 'CLOSEUP—BUTCH'. The scene text below each of these headings provides the detail and connecting narrative thread.

Bonne and Clyde (1967)

Like many of Goldman's films, *Butch Cassidy* was a reinvention of a very American genre. Despite the novelty of his writing form, there is also, in the detailed shot specification, something of the old studio tradition whereby the writing team created a shooting script. Other emerging American writers of the time were more directly influenced by European cinema, often turning to the French New Wave for inspiration about story ideas and structure, but also imbibing a spirit of independence that affected the ways in which the script was written.

In some cases, the indebtedness was direct, notably in the impetus François Truffaut gave to novice writers Robert Benton and David Newman in the development of *Bonnie and Clyde* (1967), often regarded as the first of the 'New Hollywood' films. The American duo had drawn particular inspiration from Truffaut's *Shoot the Piano Player* (1960) and *Jules et Jim* (1962), as well as from Jean-Luc Godard's *Breathless* (1959), which had been filmed in semi-improvisatory fashion, without a 'proper' shooting script, from a short treatment Truffaut had given to his *Cahiers* colleague.[16] Ironically, however, when Truffaut became involved in the development of the script for *Bonnie and Clyde*, he tried to temper the existentialist ethic the Americans had absorbed from the French New Wave by encouraging them to adapt the material to the more conventional narrative structures of a Hollywood against which Benton and Newman thought they were rebelling.[17] Nevertheless, in Lester D. Friedman's words, '*Bonnie and Clyde* ushered in a revolutionary era of American film-making where auteurs replaced contract directors',[18] and this change had important consequences for how scripts would be developed and presented.

Like the film school graduates (and indeed like most of the French New Wave directors, who began as critics), Benton and Newman were film buffs but industry outsiders: in their case, working for *Esquire* magazine. *Bonnie and Clyde* was what today would be called a 'spec' script, written up autonomously and then sent to people working in the industry in hopes of a sale. They managed to interest both Truffaut and then Warren Beatty, who paid the writers a fee to develop the material.[19] From the treatment they worked up a 129-page, undated master-scene script. Some of the differences between this and the 'Final', 134-page shooting script (dated 6 September 1966) are apparent from John G. Cawelti's reproduction of each iteration's version of the 'poem-reading' scene.[20] This shows an important change to the story: in the master-scene script Clyde responds to Bonnie's poem with indifference, prompting another fight, whereas in the shooting script version he is elated, the episode climaxing with love-making. This is in keeping with director Arthur Penn's general reorientation of the story towards a heightened sense of tragedy and confirms the movement away from the original presentation of Clyde as homosexual; instead, the overcoming of his problem with impotence becomes a key element of the story arc. Penn also lessened the comic-grotesque treatment of the antiheroes in Benton and Newman's versions.

More important for present purposes is that a formal distinction can be established between the master-scene screenplay and the shooting script. The master-scene version segments the action by scene, a new scene being occasioned by a change of location and/or time: Bonnie and Clyde in the car (scene 104), a policeman reading the poem at the police station (105) and then back to Bonnie and Clyde at the car (106). (As it happens, there has been a significant passage of time between this and scene 104, but the change of location from scene 105 would prompt the new scene number in any case.) The shooting script segments these three scenes into 14 shots, prompted by a change of shot type and/or content: the first episode at the car occupies shots 232–36, the police station shots 237–38 and the return to the car, which represents a major rewrite of the previous iteration, shots 239–44.

On the other hand, it must be emphasised that in the first scene of our example the shooting script does little more than simply follow the indications laid down in the master-scene screenplay. The slug line at the beginning of master-scene 104 ('EXT. CAR—DAY') becomes the shooting script's shot 232, the screenplay scene text's 'interior of the car' becomes shot 233 ('INT. CAR'), and each of the two close-up shots on Bonnie (234 and 236) is explicitly signalled in the earlier version. This leaves 235, but even here the shot type remains vague in the shooting script, which calls only for 'CLYDE AND BONNIE', and therefore hardly represents a more detailed breakdown than is found in the screenplay version. Similarly striking is that much of the narratorial comment of the screenplay has been carried over into the shooting script, with both versions appearing equally relaxed about incorporating within the scene text material that to today's reader might appear more appropriate within the prose-fiction form of the treatment. In each version of our sequence, we are told that Bonnie and Clyde 'have lived so much in cars that they tend to still spend much of their time in it (sic) rather than in a room', while Bonnie 'has become totally fragile, the essence of herself'.

The shooting script incorporates changes made through to 22 December. It is prefaced by a two-page cast list, including brief notes on the major characters; among other credits, Robert Towne is 'Special Consultant'. The scene text is highly detailed, with precise descriptions of the appearance of the opening title cards, for example, in addition to the many specifications of shot type. A note within the scene set in the town of Joplin (scene 100), where the first of the film's three gun battles takes place, specifies that '[t]he three major gun battles in this film of which this is the first, each have a different emotional and cinematic quality'. In addition to the incorporation of film references within the diegesis (a cinema showing *Gold Diggers of 1933*, a brief comment about Myrna Loy), and several others featuring still photography, particular film styles and eras are explicitly referenced on many occasions: the opening title cards should resemble those used in 1930s film serials; one scene is directly compared to a Sennett comedy, another to a classic Western gunfight. The self-consciousness of these reflections on visual style within the shooting script captures the writers' original desire to bring to the American screen something of the cinematic liberation and self-referentiality of the French New Wave.

There is also extensive use of the comment mode. In scene 5, for example, a parenthetical note explains Bonnie and Clyde's initial attraction, at first sight: 'Already they are in a little game instigated by Bonnie, sizing each other up, competing in a kind of playful arrogance. Before they speak, they have become co-conspirators.' Other parenthetical comments direct the delivery of almost every line in their first conversations, and specifications of this kind remain prominent throughout the text. This conspicuous use of narration within the screenplay, especially concerning motivation, presents Bonnie and, in particular, Clyde as possessing a degree of interiority that requires exploration, including by each other. It also attempts to prescribe audience reaction, as when a minor character, Eugene, mentions he is an undertaker: after this point, the narration specifies, the audience is to realise the inevitability of the gang's demise. Perhaps significantly, Towne was one of those involved in reworking the script, and was among those whose concerns about this scene resulted in a significant re-ordering of the material, with the 'undertaker' scene now preceding Bonnie's visit to her family, which therefore becomes marked by her sense of impending doom.[21]

The treatment offered one way of interesting a prospective reader; the master-scene screenplay was another, since it represented a more detailed, advanced and cinematic realisation of a treatment, concentrating on narrative, structure and dialogue while leaving room for further development by directors and others. To this extent it may be said to embrace both writers and directors as 'authors' of the film: the writer prepares a version but does not intrude on the territory of the director. Although one would not wish to push the argument too far, it is tempting to note the historical conjunction of the rise to prominence of the master-scene form and the existentialist protagonists of the 'art house' films being made on both sides of the Atlantic, of whom *Bonnie and Clyde* are exemplars: writer and hero are united in attempting to retain their identity as individuals in relation to a corporate, political or social world (Hollywood?) from which, by choice or otherwise, they are ultimately alienated.

Easy Rider (1969)

Perhaps the best example of such a film is *Easy Rider* (1969), the ultimate hippie affirmation of independence from convention. While *Easy Rider* shows that by the end of the 1960s the master-scene script could be used for the most radically unconventional movie, its production context was equally eccentric, which explains some of the peculiarities of its form.[22] The screenplay has a confused history that has never been satisfactorily resolved: credited to Peter Fonda, Dennis Hopper and the established screenwriter Terry Southern, it remains unclear how much input each of the three had, with Southern and Hopper, for example, each claiming to have written the whole of the script. Bert Schneider funded the movie almost on a whim, with little or no control over the production itself: the Mardi Gras scenes were filmed without a script, significant parts of the action and dialogue were improvised, and the producer and director of this film were also to be its stars.

This partly explains the presence of some aspects of the script that appear unconventional in light of the assumption that the master-scene screenplay separates the writing stage from that of production.[23] The *Easy Rider* screenplay is a provisional document: the very first scene, for example, refers merely to the completion of otherwise undescribed 'stunts', towards the end is a note that the Mardi Gras scenes have already been filmed, and conversely another New Orleans scene is yet to be discussed. There are several other production notes, especially in reference to the use of specific locations: for example, Trona, California and Taos, New Mexico are to represent the United States and the Mexican sides of the border, respectively. We are some way from anything resembling a 'blueprint', but on the other hand the narrative structure is clear and detailed. So, in most respects, is the formal presentation. Until about two-thirds of the way through the screenplay is in master scenes, both in formatting and in that new scene numbers are generated strictly by the introduction of a new location or montage. After scene 78 (in the diner), however, the unit of segmentation suddenly changes. From 79 to 100 (the sequence in which the travellers are attacked by the rednecks), each new number is occasioned not by a change of scene but by a change of shot (e.g. to a close-up); thereafter, the script shows little consistency in slug lines, which will at times be scene headings, and shot specifications at others. Possibly this is an indication of the chaotic nature of the writing and production stages.

Of more general significance is that master-scene screenwriting is far from immutable, and like *Bonnie and Clyde, Easy Rider* can be easily distinguished from the screenplays of today. For example, unfilmable comments intrude often, as when the narration affirms its sympathy with the contemporary counter-culture. At scene 50, a travelling montage shows us glimpses of a part of Arizona 'in the heart of "God's Country", where there exists some of the best samples of crass commercialism in the Universe'. Wyatt's famously enigmatic line 'We blew it', with its implication of a transcendental truth glimpsed but lost, has a written correlative in scene 53 as Wyatt and the Stranger look at the dying sun: 'Only Billy's disgruntled MUTTERING, as he stumbles up the path toward them, shatters some profound and crystal clarity that seemed per chance within their grasp.' A related form of narration occasionally intrudes in the form of free indirect speech, as when Billy's horror at Wyatt's decision to pick up a hitchhiker is expressed not in dialogue but as an unverbalised thought: '(Picking up a stranger?!? And us carrying all this loot! What the hell's wrong with Wyatt!?!)'

The screenplay often refers to the 'CAMERA' as a viewer of or participant within the action, very many speeches have parenthetical dialogue direction, there is a tendency to specify transitional devices such as cuts or dissolves, and while the scene text does not usually explicitly give indications of type of shot, there are many exceptions: montages are often described in detail, with frequent specification of the use of quick cuts, as for example to capture the atmosphere of the street scene as Wyatt and Billy drive along Sunset Strip; and there is some reference to pans and close-ups. On the first travelling shot of the motorbikes, the screenplay specifies that the effect should be one of romantic, balletic freedom, and suggests using a current Chrysler advertisement as a model; having established this effect, later, similar shots of the motorbikes are to be edited using this first example as a kind of template.

With the exception of montages, which can be essential for reasons of story development as opposed to editing, the dominant discourse surrounding screenwriting today tends to prohibit these forms of narration and direction. Along with *The Graduate* (1967), however, *Bonnie and Clyde* and *Easy Rider* were ushering in an era, and a mode of film-making, in which writers could develop new kinds of screenplay relatively unencumbered by the dictates of a studio. Instead, during the high point of the 'New Hollywood' in the early and mid-1970s, the script often became a site of contention between different writers; new forms of script emerged to serve the needs of writer-directors, with relatively conventional alternates being presented to executives and financiers; and individual scripts hesitated between conventional modes of presentation and the more personal, short story form of the treatment.

The 1970s

The competing accounts of the authorship of *Easy Rider* are symptomatic of changes in the perception of screenplays following the end of the classical system. Formerly, any disputes over the writing could be resolved by the producer; in any case, writers were under contract to work, according to more or less strict procedures and disciplines, towards the final creation of a shooting script over which the writer would not have any further say.

Matters were different in the New Hollywood. Robert Towne, for example, is an important figure not only because of the quality of his scripts, but because as both an original writer (notably in his disputes with director Roman Polanski over *Chinatown* [1974]) and as a 'script doctor' on films as significant as *Bonnie and Clyde* and *The Godfather* (1972), he illustrates the increasing recognition that the script is a site of contention between competing parties. Towne originally scripted a less downbeat ending to *Chinatown* in which the villain Noah Cross is killed; the ending seen on the screen is substantially Polanski's conception. Earlier instances of this phenomenon included the dispute about the authorship of *Citizen Kane* and, more generally, the suspicion that left-wing writers were planting subversive messages in films such as *High Noon* (1952, written by Carl Foreman) that might otherwise appear to be representative of conservative American values. In general, however, arguments about scripts within classical Hollywood were an everyday occurrence between contracted workers that if necessary would be resolved by management. In a post-classical Hollywood of relatively autonomous writers and directors, such disputes contribute to the rise of the notion of the writer, nearly as much as director, as *auteur*.

A second kind of conflict, concerning which version of a screenplay can be said to be authoritative, can be seen in the 'bible' text that Francis Ford Coppola constructed for the making of *The Godfather* (1972). This was a kind of private, parallel-text version of the script—a very personal kind of treatment, and one that, for Coppola, in many ways took priority over the more conventional screenplay that he debated with the studio executives. The 'bible' was a huge spiral notebook, resembling the theatrical prompt book (or 'bible') form, on each page of which Coppola pasted a page from Mario Puzo's source novel.

> This massive tome [was] biblical in proportions [...] and he did not circulate it among studio executives. It meant more to him than any formal version of the script. He began by cutting up a copy of the novel, and pasting pages down on each left-hand folio (except for pages he intended to omit from the screenplay, which were pasted in sequence with a bold, black marker pen line drawn across them). On the right-hand page he typed his detailed observations on each 'scene': what it involved, what should be avoided, what should be concentrated upon and how he would achieve this.[24]

Coppola broke the novel's story down into five acts, subdivided into a total of 50 scenes. Influenced by the theatre and film director Elia Kazan, he provided a typewritten commentary on each scene, under five headings: 'Synopsis, The Times (how to preserve the 1940s period quality), Imagery and Tone, The Core (the essence of the scene) and Pitfalls (issues to watch out for, such as pacing or clichés'.[25] For example, in the first scene—the wedding sequence, including Don Corleone's meetings with the supplicants—there are 13 separate notes on 'imagery and tone' alone. Note 'k' comments on Bonasera, which would be the first scene in the film:

> The scene with Bonasera is good and very important. It further defines the Don's power, and puts forth the essence of what it is the Don refers to as 'friendship' i.e. a pledge of loyalty. It is the gathering and manipulations of these pledges which give the Don his extraordinary power in the first place. It is very important that after Bonasera gives his pledge, that (sic) we understand he feels he is now under a grave and frightening obligation to the Godfather. Bonasera must be a super, super actor.

The 'core' of the scene is to establish the Don's power, his relationship with Michael, and 'the fusion of family and business', as well as to '[i]ntroduce all the main characters and sub-plots of the film'. Not surprisingly, among the 'pitfalls' appears a handwritten note: 'Too much exposition'.[26]

The screenplay that Coppola showed to the executives, meanwhile, passed through three completed drafts, the last of which was finished on 16 March, though it is dated 29 March.[27] In contrast to the 'bible', this is a relatively conventional master-scene screenplay, representing a 'formal version of the script' that Coppola and Puzo submitted to, and debated with, Paramount's executives.[28] Nevertheless, it has significant differences from the kind of screenplay examined in the next chapter. This is most clearly seen in the segmentation. The sequence beginning with Bonasera asking for Don Corleone's assistance, and proceeding through the wedding party, occupies the first 21 pages. The marginal numbering of each of these scenes begins with the number 1, suggesting that the writers are thinking in terms of sequences, much like the method of dividing a script into alphabetised (rather than numbered) sequences that we saw in earlier chapters. The scenes in the wedding sequence, for instance, are numbered from 1A to 1S. However, there is a total of 28 scenes within the sequence. The discrepancy is explained by the numbering of scenes according to the precise location within the house and grounds: multiple scenes within the same location are each given the same scene number. For example, the scene heading for 1D is 'INT DAY: DON'S OFFICE (SUMMER 1945)'. In this scene another supplicant, Nazorine, asks the Don for help. After the Don issues Hagen with instructions as to how to implement his proposed solution, the next scene—'1E EXT DAY: MALL (SUMMER 1945)'—takes us outside, to Francesco Nippi and Luca Brasi, whom the Don has been watching from within his office, to which we then return as the Don resumes his conversation with Hagen. However, instead of recommencing with the 'DON'S OFFICE' heading, the scene is simply numbered '1D (CONT.)', without any heading. A series of shots then cuts between the two locations: the Don and Hagen in the office, and views of Michael Corleone in the mall area where we have seen Nippi and Brasi, again resulting in the alternating numbers of '1D (CONT.)' and '1E (CONT.)'. To avoid visual confusion, throughout the script all transitions between scenes (or shots) are marked by a continuous black line across the page.

The *Godfather* screenplay thereby arranges material in three ways: by sequences (relatively continuous narrative events), scenes (grouped according to location) and shots (as the script alternates between locations). While the method of distinguishing between scenes and shots is fairly consistent throughout the screenplay, however, the sequence approach is intermittent. Perhaps one reason why Coppola preferred the 'bible' is that the rearrangement of the material in the screenplay obscures his initial, 50-scene segmentation of the story. More generally, the bible is a very personal kind of text, while the screenplay is something of a corporately engineered document, albeit one that is still idiosyncratic in a number of ways.

A third and final kind of conflict we can see in the screenplays of this period concerns a dialogue we have been tracing over the course of the last two chapters between the master-scene screenplay and the treatment. The major unit of segmentation in Paul Schrader's script for *Taxi Driver* (1976), for example, is the sequence: 'TRAVIS GETS A JOB' (scenes 1–5), the credit sequence (6–11), 'WE MEET TRAVIS' (12–31), and so on. This is an approach more commonly found in treatments than screenplays—the sequence headings read like the chapter headings of a novel—as is Schrader's very prominent use of the comment mode:

'When it rains, the boss of the City is the taxi-driver'—so goes the cabbies' maxim, proved true by this particular night's activity. Only the taxis seem to rise above the situation: they glide effortlessly through the rain and traffic, picking up whom they choose, spurning whom they choose, going where they please.

Further uptown, the crowds are neither so frantic nor so glittering. The rain also falls on the street bums and the aged poor. Junkies still stand around on rainy street corners, hookers still prowl rainy sidewalks. And the taxis service them too. All through the credits the exterior sounds are muted, as if coming from a distant room or storefront round the corner. The listener is at a safe but privileged distance.[29]

This is presented as two numbered paragraphs (9 and 10) in the screenplay itself (aside from the appearance of CREDITS and SOUNDS in upper-case in the screenplay, the published version is identical).

Each of these paragraphs could also be described as a scene, with implicit subdivision into shots. In *Taxi Driver*, however, the information we might expect to find in a scene heading is very often presented narratively within the text. The first shot, for example, is an exterior of a garage. Shot 2 is seen from inside the garage, and should therefore begin a different scene. But instead of following master-scene logic by separating the scene elements, with capitalised headings above and descriptive scene text below, Schrader presents the scene information as part of the running text: 'INSIDE GARAGE are parked row upon row of multi-colored taxis'. In these ways, *Taxi Driver* is an outstanding example of the interplay between the treatment and master-scene forms that is characteristic of the New Hollywood screenplays of this period.

American screenwriters and directors working in the aftermath of the classical studio system, then, had relative freedom to develop a script in the style of their choosing, even though compromises would often have to be made in dealing with producers. 'New Hollywood' privileged the idea of the individual film-maker in opposition to the 'system', of course, and the canonical examples of screenplays from this era therefore tend to be self-selectingly unusual. The point still holds, however, that this was a period of relative independence for screenwriters, in comparison to their predecessors working under contract in the now-defunct writing departments. Nobody was insisting that screenplays had to be written a certain way. By the end of the 1970s, however, this was about to change.

10
The Contemporary Screenplay and Screenwriting Manual

For Peter Biskind,

> [t]he thirteen years between *Bonnie and Clyde* in 1967 and *Heaven's Gate* in 1980 marked the last time it was really exciting to make movies in Hollywood, the last time people could be consistently proud of the pictures they made, the last time the community as a whole encouraged good work, the last time there was an audience that could sustain it.[1]

The kind of film the passing of which Biskind laments is one that New Hollywood writers and directors had modified from European cinema of the 1950s, characterised by a relatively aimless protagonist, or one who could not fully understand the motivations behind his or her actions, or the actions of others. From Zavattini to Godard, there is the idea that story itself is suspect, an act of bad faith that places an externally imposed structuring principle on life; and traces of this European influence, combined with the broader counter-cultural and anti-establishment movements of the 1960s, can be seen in the screenplays considered in the previous chapter, notably *Bonnie and Clyde* and *Easy Rider*. One manifestation of this resistance to narrative was the 'open' ending, in which significant questions are left unresolved, or resonating in the spectator's mind; a late example is *Being There* (1979).

By the end of the 1970s, for all the creative talent and initial commercial success of the 'New Hollywood' directors, executives saw the commercial future in the blockbuster and the event movie such as *Jaws* (1975) and *Star Wars* (1977). The contrasting fortunes of *Star Wars* and the economic catastrophe that was *Heaven's Gate* dramatically accelerated a process that had long been apparent: for all their creative achievement and critical acclaim, and despite *Easy Rider*'s remarkable return on investment, the films of the 'New Hollywood' directors and those who came in their wake had ultimately continued, rather than reversed, the commercial decline of the American film industry. The trust that executives had placed in auteurs was shown to be misplaced, economically at least.

Commercially minded producers such as Don Simpson and Jerry Bruckheimer were gaining traction in an industry that was undergoing significant transformation.[2] In 1985, the divorcement decree of 1948 was revoked, permitting the studios to return to the vertically integrated control of production, distribution and exhibition. Alongside this came both 'horizontal integration' (the incorporation of formerly independent studios within larger global conglomerates), so that a film could be marketed across several different platforms—television and video, for example—and the associated phenomenon of 'synergy', in which products such as toys and soundtracks could be marketed to promote the film, or vice versa. Ownership of multiple companies under one umbrella organisation allowed a corporation to sell its products to its own outlets.

Much critical debate surrounds whether or not, or the extent to which, these industrial and economic changes were accompanied by a transition to a 'post-classical', 'high concept' Hollywood aesthetic, characterised in part by the fragmentation of narrative and its replacement by a cinema of spectacle and soundtrack that catered to the media companies' multiple platforms. If this suggestion is correct, it has consequences for the screenplay, which in Hollywood is almost invariably a mode of storytelling. Although a full discussion of this question is beyond the scope of the present study, there is no good reason to suggest that story was *displaced* by visual spectacle or the showcasing of popular songs on the soundtrack. Instead, what is remarkable is that any putative transition to a post-classical Hollywood occurs contemporaneously with several changes within screenwriting culture, all of which have the effect of increasing the visibility of the screenplay and reinstating story—albeit, perhaps, a simplified form of story—at the centre of Hollywood discourse.[3] Three developments are particularly notable: the continued rise of the 'spec' script, Hollywood films that appeared to be indebted to reproducible story templates and the rapidly growing numbers of screenwriting manuals, of which Syd Field's *Screenplay* (1979) is widely held to have been the first and most influential. Together, these developments helped to solidify the screenplay into an object with more precisely definable characteristics than at any time since the end of the silent era.

The 'spec' script

As noted in the previous chapter, the Paramount case of 1948 led, within a few years, to the closure of writing departments in the Hollywood studios. By the end of the 1950s, writers were no longer employees on regular studio contracts but, in effect, were independent providers to independent or semi-independent producers within a system in which studios largely controlled financing and distribution. A particular producer or director might look to hire a given writer, as was Alfred Hitchcock's custom, for example; or a writer might seek to interest an insider in a particular story s/he had to sell, as happened with *Bonnie and Clyde*; or the two interests could be brought together, with a producer looking to bring together a number of different elements, of which a star might be one and a screenplay another, to attract funding from external sources. These are some of the many variant possibilities within the 'package-unit' system, which has had material effects on the nature of the screenplay text. Rather than a version of a story that has been tracked by a production team through previous iterations and is now on its way to becoming something else—a shooting script or a film—a speculatively written screenplay is a physical property, a 'selling' script, written independently of production, and circulated to multiple readerships in the hope of making a sale: if not of the screenplay, then of the writer him- or herself.

While spec scripts had existed since the end of the classical system, if not before, several additional factors converged to increase their production from the late 1970s onwards. Among the least immediately visible, but most wide-ranging, was the passing of the 1976 Copyright Act in the United States. After this came into effect in 1978, screenwriters finally achieved protection under the law for their unpublished scripts, which gave writers an element of leverage in negotiating with producers or funding providers.[4] Some ten years later, a six-month writers' strike in Hollywood from March to August 1988 further fuelled the demand for spec scripts, as did the rise of the film festival and the emergence of more powerful independent distributors such as Miramax.[5]

Another important development was the emergence of the 12-point Courier font as the default typeface for screenplays.[6] Courier had been introduced in the 1950s, but gained popularity because it was readily accessible both for typewriters and for the home computers that began to replace typewriters in the 1980s. Its widespread adoption by the computing industry was due to Courier using the same fixed width for each character; it therefore placed relatively small demands on computer memory. As a further advantage, in combination with the default master-scene format propagated by screenwriting manuals, Courier helped amateurs to follow the supposed 'one-page-per-minute' rule, and therefore to offer spec scripts that gave some indication that the writer was familiar with the idea of the script as a timing and budgeting document. Collectively, these developments caused screenplays to take on a generic physical form, characterised not only by the overall length of the document or the arrangement of the words on the page, but also by what *wasn't* there: screenplays were notable for their 'white space', which made the pages user-friendly for industry readers and film-makers who needed to skim and annotate the script for their own purposes.

The industry-wide adoption of Courier meant that aspiring screenwriters could give their work a professional sheen. Since there were no longer any in-house writing departments, the outsider could feel that in these ways, at least, s/he could compete with others on a level playing field. An additional factor in the growth of the spec script was undoubtedly the perception that not only formatting but also screen storytelling itself was something that could be relatively easily mastered by the novice. This belief was fuelled by the kinds of story that Hollywood was now making, and by the emergence of the screenwriting manual as a kind of substitute training school for aspirant novices, circumstances which also help to explain the growth of the otherwise niche market of screenplay publication.

The 'high concept' story

The precise meaning of 'high concept' is disputed, but it certainly includes an investment in visual style and spectacle, stars, and the impact of the soundtrack. It is difficult to accept, however, that the high concept film has 'little commercial investment in narrative except as a vehicle for the movie's other pleasures'[7]; rather, it has 'a simple, easily summarized narrative based on physically typed characters'.[8] If anything, it reinstates linear storytelling at the centre of Hollywood film-making after a decade in which the most lauded American films had questioned the ideological assumptions behind story itself, if by 'story' we mean the journey of a goal-oriented protagonist towards a notion of success (in love, in career, in money or in the overcoming of an adversary) validated by a dominant American philosophy of progress. In the New Hollywood, by contrast, there's no success like failure, and failure's no success at all.

It was an older kind of story to which high concept represented a return. Writing in 1982, William Goldman pointed to what he saw as a decisive shift in the kinds of film that Hollywood was making, and suggested that by that date it was almost exclusively interested in what he terms 'comic-book movies': films with melodramatically unqualified distinctions between good and evil, and which take their inspiration not from the observation of adult lives but from memories of other films, especially those associated with childhood or adolescence. While the kind of movie Goldman is thinking of appears largely synonymous with 'high concept', Goldman also identified Michael Cimino's *The Deer Hunter* (1978) as a comic-book picture, which intriguingly implies certain continuities between the artistic seriousness of the 'New Hollywood' films and contemporaneous mainstream Hollywood movies.[9] The comic-book movie par excellence is *Star Wars*, which as George Lucas acknowledged was modelled on Joseph Campbell's *The Hero with a Thousand Faces*, a book to which we shall return.[10]

Given the conjunction of propitious industrial conditions for independent writers and Hollywood's revived interest in simpler, more generic modes of storytelling than had been in favour ten years previously, it is not surprising that Goldman could remark in 1983 that '[r]ight now, with movie companies fragmented and dying and with money coming from all kinds of strange new sources, it is a golden time to write screenplays'.[11] It was also, as the success of Goldman's own *Adventures in the Screen Trade* (published the following year) would suggest, a golden time to write screenplay manuals.

The re-emergence of the screenwriting manual[12]

While noting that screenwriting manuals have proliferated during other periods when there has been a perceived crisis in story production, notably the era of 'scenario fever' during the 1910s, David Bordwell credits those that have emerged since the late 1970s with changing the conception of storytelling in three main ways.[13] First is the widespread insistence that Hollywood screenplays and films are structured in three acts. Bordwell finds little solid evidence that this was consciously used as a structuring principle in Hollywood prior to its appearance in Syd Field's *Screenplay* in 1979, other than noting that the suggestion is also found in Constance Nash and Virginia Oakey's more rudimentary and lesser-known *Screenwriter's Handbook*, published the previous year. The second emphasis Bordwell finds in the post-1978 manual lies in a particular notion of character depth, especially the idea that the protagonist should have some kind of character flaw, with the 'arc' of the character lying in the recognition and overcoming of the flaw. Third is the idea that this character undertakes a 'mythic journey', a notion derived from Campbell.

All of these are venerable ideas. The three-act structure can be traced back at least as far as Aristotle's discussion of the beginning, middle and end of a dramatic story in the *Poetics*. Aristotle's notion of *hamartia*, the fault or error in or by the tragic hero, is arguably also the ultimate source of the supposed 'tragic flaw' in the protagonist, which was a staple of Shakespearean criticism even before A. C. Bradley's *Shakespearean Tragedy* (1904), perhaps the first sustained study of fictional characters that bears comparison to the 'psychological depth' and 'backstory' familiar from today's writing manuals.[14] Campbell's *Hero with a Thousand Faces* is a relative youngster, appearing first in 1949, but the book is a study of mythic storytelling in general, and consequently the basic narrative structure itself is familiar from any number of ancient and modern tales.[15]

Also notable is that while the three concepts can be considered separately, they are interdependent, and to some extent each is an expression of the universal 'monomyth' outlined by Campbell: 'A hero ventures forth from the world of common day into a region of supernatural wonder: fabulous forces are there encountered and a decisive victory is won: the hero comes back from this mysterious adventure with the power to bestow boons on his fellow man'.[16] This archetypal story has a very clear tripartite structure—departure, initiation or adventure, and return—and although in the above formulation it describes a series of events taking place in an external world, it is equally tractable to the notion of an inner journey, with the hero doing battle with the flaw within the self that s/he overcomes at the end of the tale. This inner journey gives us the 'character arc', and very frequently manuals will recommend that it is the conjunction of the inner and outer journeys (or 'motivations') that provides the story with depth. In short, the basic structural ideas expressed in these manuals have formed a staple of Western, if not global, storytelling since long before the beginnings of cinema. It is no surprise, then, that reading films and screenplays in the light of their arguments should enable us to see similarities in narrative films of different eras, though at this level of generalisation the arguments are both indisputable and of debatable usefulness.

Bordwell is careful to qualify the idea that the manuals necessarily support his arguments in favour of the continuing centrality of narrative in the 'post-classical' era: they can only be 'a fruitful point of departure', and indeed 'few screenplay manuals inspire confidence'.[17] One reason for this is their excessive specificity. For example, not only does Field insist that screenplays have three acts ('setup', 'confrontation' and 'resolution'), but acts one and two should also have a 'plot point', which 'is an incident, or event, that hooks into the story and spins it around into another direction'. Because Field has confidence in the one-page-per-minute rule, this leads him to the remarkably precise assertion that in a screenplay for a two-hour film the first and third acts should be 30 pages each, with the middle act occupying 60 pages; the plot points, meanwhile, should occur around pages 25–27 and 85–90.[18] For Field, then, not only acts but also plot points are not matters of interpretation; they are scientifically measurable. Beliefs of this kind have proved damaging. The independent film-maker Tom DiCillo recalled taking a screenplay to the Sundance festival in 1989 only to be told that ' "Plot point A does not intersect with plot point B at the right page." I said, "I'm sorry, what is a plot point?" Everyone was saying to me, "This is not a screenplay." It was insane, destructive, and negative.'[19]

As Bordwell notes, another cause for concern is that Field, Christopher Vogler, Robert McKee and others were not themselves noted screenwriters, but instead began as studio readers or 'story analysts', whose job was to write 'coverage' or appraisals of the flood of spec scripts landing on studio desks. Rather than placing the screenplay directly within a production context, then, it would be more accurate to say, with Bordwell, that 'the screenplay manuals were guiding hopefuls to write scripts that would galvanize the frontline reader'.[20]

This invites several ways of thinking about the relationships between manuals and screenplays themselves. First, manuals are undoubtedly, to borrow Steven Maras's phrase, one of the discourses *surrounding* screenwriting, and in that capacity have also been of major interest to Staiger, Thompson and Bordwell. In this sense they certainly have a significant influence on screenwriting discourse within the academy, at least. More problematic is a second relationship, namely to what extent they represent a discourse from *within* screenwriting: that is, to what extent can they be said to represent or emanate from film industries or practitioners themselves, and what is the nature and degree of their interaction with them? We shall return to this question, but less frequently considered is a third relationship: To what extent can they be said to represent a discourse from *within screenplays* themselves? This, in turn, opens up the difficult question of what can be said to be 'inside' a screenplay text. We can approach this question by considering the manuals' representations of perhaps the two most distinctive qualities of screenplays: story structure and format.

Three acts? Revisiting classical Hollywood cinema

As noted, Bordwell has found no strong evidence that the three-act structure was in conscious use in Hollywood cinema prior to the 1970s, and neither has Claus Tieber's research into the story conferences and memos that were a crucial arena within which story ideas were disseminated. Further, Kristin Thompson has contested the notion that the three-act structure has been dominant in Hollywood even since Field's *Screenplay* book of 1979 popularised the idea. Thompson also disputes other proposals about story that routinely arise in screenwriting manuals, arguing that in most Hollywood films a protagonist usually has not one goal but 'at least two', while the rule of thumb that one page equals one minute of screen time is erroneous, because it demands the co-operation of the director.[21]

With regard to acts, Thompson finds that instead of three, the first and last of which each occupy about a quarter of screen time (as Field proposes), the norm is four acts of equal length, Field's middle act being divisible into two. Where Field sees three acts in *Terminator 2: Judgment Day* (James Cameron, 1991), for instance, Thompson sees four, plus an epilogue.[22] This phenomenon of commentators finding different numbers of acts within the same film is not confined to mainstream Hollywood; it is found with regard to 'independent' films, too. For instance, Ken Dancyger and Jeff Rush think *Stranger Than Paradise* (Jim Jarmusch, 1984) has only a single act; J. J. Murphy finds three.[23] More generally, Bordwell has proposed that there are six parts to the 'canonical' story: 'introduction of setting and characters', 'explanation of a state of affairs', 'complicating action', 'ensuing events', 'outcome' and 'ending', whereas Paul Gulino sees a 'division of feature films into eight segments'.[24]

Clearly, something is going wrong here. Part of the explanation is that much of the argument revolves around films, rather than screenplays, and the former usually lack the unambiguous meta-fictional denotations of units of action that we might hope to find in written texts. In other words, it is difficult to prove that act divisions exist *inside* films; it is rather a matter of judgement and interpretation, perhaps guided by knowledge of traditional story templates. Just as Field's three-act structure can be seen to draw on Aristotle, for example, Thompson's four acts ('setup', 'complicating action', 'development' and 'climax') have much in common with the exposition, complication, crisis and resolution of the nineteenth-century well-made play that was first popularised in France by Eugène Scribe and Victorien Sardou, and which proved influential on many of the most significant European dramatists later in the century, most notably Henrik Ibsen.[25]

The difference between the theatrical play and the screenplay in this respect is that whereas act and scene divisions are explicitly identified within the script (although not always in Shakespearean texts, for instance), this is rarely the case in screenplays. As we have seen earlier, however, there are exceptions. Gulino suggests that his eight-sequence model has historical sources, beginning with the introduction of the 1,000-foot reel length which became standard in the 1910s. The 'sequence' for the multi-reel feature films that emerged in 1913 thereby became married to the length of the reel, allowing Gulino to establish a principle of equivalence whereby one reel = one sequence = c. 10–15 minutes. By the late 1920s, screenplays were being divided 'into *sequences* identified by letter (A, B, C, etc.), a practice that lasted into the 1950s', and in Gulino's view the importation of playwrights to compose Hollywood dialogue consolidated the structure of 'an eight-sequence structure married to three acts'.[26]

There is evidence to support some of this argument, although it cannot be developed too far. Gulino concedes that the number of sequences is a matter of readerly judgement and interpretation other than in screenplays that are overtly composed in this fashion: his examples are *The Shop Around the Corner* (1940), *Double Indemnity* (1944) and *Air Force One* (1997). As we have seen, a minority of scripts of the 1920s are indeed divided into alphabetised sequences, although it is far from clear that this implied any prescribed running time. The sequences in *Hell's Angels* (1929), for example, are ultimately shaped by the nature of the material in each: spectacular flight sequences rescued from the silent version, dramatic material initially composed by Joseph Moncure March and so on. Examples of alphabetised sequences can be found in the 1950s, as in screenplays for Billy Wilder's movies; yet as the small number of sequences (four or five) in his scripts indicates, there was no reason for films of this comparatively late date to conform to a reel-based model appropriate for the shorter films of prescribed length in the pre-feature era.

Historically, a still smaller number of screenplays or scenarios have been consciously divided into acts, as opposed to sequences. As we saw in Chapter 2, *The Chicken Thief* (1904) is, as its title page proclaims,

'An Original American Comedy in a Prologue and Four Acts', the first and third of which are further subdivided into scenes. Given that the piece was submitted for copyright as a 'dramatic composition', however, it would be unwise to draw further conclusions from this overt imitation of the theatrical play-script model. More interesting is Roy L. McCardell's *The Pain Flower: A Photoplay Drama of Modern Life* (1915), released by the Equitable Motion Pictures Corporation in 1916 as *The Question*.[27] This is in many respects a conventional continuity of the time, with detailed shot specifications, and packaged with many of the usual documents, such as a synopsis, list of characters and sets, and scene breakdown. In many other respects, however, it is fashioned after the stage play, and prefaced with a note that makes the connection explicit: ' "The Pain Flower" should be enacted with restraint and naturalness by capable and experienced actors conversant with society ways, manners, attire and adjuncts—as Grace George and her company of players would mount, dress and enact such a drama for the speaking-stage.'

The explicit indication of act divisions in scenarios, continuities and screenplays, then, is in the early decades of cinema generally either an indicator of indebtedness to theatrical conventions or a response to the introduction of the multi-reel film, while those of later date indicate no commitment to three acts as a structuring principle. In short, material screenplay texts offer no support to the three-act hypothesis; although undoubtedly many are amenable to interpretation in that light, other, equally convincing methods of analysis are readily available.

Screenwriting manuals and screenplay format

More substantial is the argument that screenplays should be formatted in more or less precise ways. Maras observes that:

> The uniqueness of the screenplay itself is a complex issue. In terms of scripting practices there is little that is exclusive to the screenplay that is not present in the scene-based organisation of the scenario, the shot-by-shot format of the continuity script, 'the read' of the extended synopsis or dialogue of the playscript. Viewed in this light, the distinctiveness of the screenplay is elusive.[28]

As we have seen, the various kinds of text Maras mentions here have all been utilised and combined in distinctive ways by different screenwriters at different times, and in various industries and modes of production. Attempting to prescribe a particular form for the screenplay can therefore appear unnecessarily constricting.

Yet there is today a dominant form of screenplay, and one that certainly does not exist solely within the pages of screenwriting manuals. In 1978, Nash and Oakey could write that 'there are no absolute rules concerning the format in which a film script is typed'.[29] In 1988, another manual considered that 'within a general set of guidelines, acceptable screenplays vary somewhat'.[30] By contrast, Christopher Riley, author of today's self-proclaimed 'most accurate, complete, authoritative, and practical guide to standard script formats ever published, written by a guy who came to Hollywood to make his career as a screenwriter and instead accidentally became Hollywood's foremost authority on industry standard script formats' spells out the dangers for the novice who is reliant solely on screenwriting software such as Final Draft. In Riley's estimation, these programs do not answer the questions his book addresses: 'too many writers who think they're turning in professionally formatted scripts are in fact often turning in scripts that brand them as amateurs. [...] The fact is that a standard format exists today in Hollywood', and Riley describes it in the minutest detail.[31]

Although this is highly prescriptive, it is also essentially correct. As Joseph McBride, who is not only the author of one of the best recent manuals, but also a distinguished film historian, screenwriter and academic, puts it:

> Like any other art form, but even more so, screenwriting follows certain conventions. [...] Screenplay conventions can be broken by adept practitioners of the craft for valid creative reasons, and all good scripts have particular problems they solve in unusual ways, but if those conventions are disregarded, chaos will ensue. Someone who writes in a blissful or willful ignorance of the professional format will be immediately recognized as unprofessional, and such work will be tossed into the circular file.[32]

Most of the basic conventions of current screenplay formatting have been noted elsewhere in this book. Many are important (such as the observation of conventions for the indentation of different text elements like speakers' names, dialogue, scene text, etc.), but two aspects of the contemporary screenplay are particularly worth emphasising here because they help to position it in relation to other kinds of screenwriting.

First are the conventions that help to establish the scene as the unit of action, which is defined by continuous action in one place. A change of place generates a new scene. Basic scene headings ('slug lines') usually take a tripartite form: interior/exterior, identification of place and time of day (e.g. EXT. PARK—NIGHT). Camera angles and shot specifications should be omitted, as should parenthetical speech direction. Collectively, these conventions distinguish the master-scene screenplay from the numbered and shot-specific kinds of shooting script, and help to separate those aspects of creation that belong to the writer from those that are the province of other professionals such as the director, photographer, editor and actor. The contrast between this and the silent-era continuity is marked.

Second is the instruction that only those things that are to appear on the screen should appear within the scene text, with some possible leeway for character traits.[33] Here we may recall the three 'modes' that Sternberg distinguishes within the scene text: description, of the *mise-en-scène* and design; the report mode, which describes the sequence of actions (e.g., the movements of a character); and, finally, the 'comment' mode, which is the most significant in the analysis of screenplay texts because, as Sternberg observes, authorial commentary within the scene text is routinely discouraged: the job of the screenwriter is to visualise the action, not to comment or advise upon it.

This establishes a very clear place for the screenplay in ideas of film production. Most obviously, by eliminating technical directions such as shot specification, it separates the 'screenplay' from, and places it prior to, the 'shooting script'. This gives the 'spec' screenplay of today a different look to those master-scene screenplays considered in the previous chapter, which were written with the production process clearly in mind. Secondly, it also separates the screenplay from any anterior 'treatment' stage by eliminating the more literary, expressive qualities of the short story form. In these ways it helps to identify the screenplay as a particular kind of object, and as a relatively autonomous document, intended for particular kinds of reader, but removed from the process of production.

'Inflected' and 'uninflected' screenplays

An alternate discourse, however, sees the screenplay as being *only* about production. The second edition of Esther Luttrell's *Tools of the Screen Writing Trade* (1998) proposes that 'a screenplay is *nothing more than a set of notes to a production crew*', and suggests that an important role of the screenwriting tutor consists in 'teaching a roomful of published writers the art of translating their prose into production notes'.[34]

Yet it is doubtful whether the comment mode is ever eliminated as fully from the screenplay as the prescriptions of screenwriting manuals might suggest. The work of Jeff Rush and Cynthia Baughman implies that the discrepancy arises from a distinction between '*shooting scripts*', which 'might be read as denotative blueprints or instructions', and '*screenplays*', which 'can be understood only as a form of writing that communicates much of its meaning through the connotative nuances of language'. In their analysis, the use of modifiers and irony in 'highly inflected' screenplays, such as David Lynch's script for *Blue Velvet* (1986), for example, is essential in conveying the tone and, therefore, meaning of a shot; it is not a superfluous literary flourish, but essential to an understanding of the shot or story itself. The cumulative effect of a sequence of such moments is that '[w]e have been taught how to read' the script.[35]

Another way of approaching this discrepancy, however, would be to suggest that it arises from the ambivalent nature of a screenplay's scene text. Here the ongoing work of Ann Igelström is especially noteworthy. Igelström begins by drawing a distinction between two kinds of information in a screenplay: first, references to the '*extrafictional* world where the potential film will be produced' (directions as to kind of shot, for example)—Luttrell's 'set of notes'; and, second, 'information refer[ring] to the *fictional* story world where the story takes place' (locations, characters' names and so on).[36] Stronger still are the consequences of Igelström's distinctions between the three 'levels of narration' in a screenplay text. One of these, the 'personal fictional voice' (in most cases, that of a character), 'provides the reader with information about the fictional story world' and 'is situated in the dialogue'.[37] Of more significance in the present context is the relationship between the other two. First is the 'extrafictional voice', which 'is responsible for the fictional story world and information that refers to the extrafictional world' of production, for example by providing the information in the scene headings.[38] The extrafictional voice is often, though inaccurately, assumed to be synonymous with the author or writer of the screenplay. The second is the 'impersonal fictional voice', which is 'the narrating voice that provides the reader with information about the fictional story world (e.g. actions, characters and setting)'.[39] Igelström's example is from Tony Gilroy's published screenplay for *Michael Clayton* (2007): a character is sitting on a toilet, 'trying to fight off a panic attack using a breathing exercise she read about in an airline magazine'. The information is provided by a voice that does not appear as a character within the story world: therefore, this voice is 'impersonal'. The crucial point, and the source of the ambivalent nature of the screenplay as both a production document and a form of dramatic fiction, is that '[b]oth the extrafictional narrating voice and the impersonal fictional voice [...] exist in the scene text. It follows that it is not always easy to separate the two'.[40]

Igelström proposes that there is a spectrum: a text that included many direct indications of camera angles, for instance, would lie at one end of the spectrum, while another that eliminated any such reminders of the 'real world'—for example, in comprising only description and report, or in being written in free indirect speech—would lie at the other. This makes it very difficult to accept that the material in a screenplay refers *only* to the extrafictional world of production. A screenplay is also, in narrative cinema, a medium for storytelling, and there is always a kind of bleeding through from the extrafictional to the fictional world, and vice versa.

This tends to confirm what we have seen throughout screenplay history: that its language can rarely be reduced to the purely denotative, and that metaphors, similes and other figures of speech are part of its condition. While Claudia Sternberg's contention that 'screenwriters rarely miss the opportunity to use the mode of comment' perhaps overstates the case,[41] there is nevertheless a marked discrepancy between the familiar, theoretical argument that the scene text should present only material that can be mentally visualized as taking place on an imaginary screen, and what is actually found within screenplays themselves, in any era. Confining ourselves only to those produced in the classical Hollywood system, and to those considered in earlier chapters, we could cite *Love or Justice* (1917), *David Copperfield* (1935), *Citizen Kane* (1941), *Laura* (1944) and *Body and Soul* (1947) as texts in which Sternberg's 'comment' mode, and an interplay of Igelström's 'voices', are pronounced.

Put simply, for Sternberg comment becomes an indicator of the authorial persona. This allows her to focus not so much on how a screenplay conforms to a system but, rather, how variations within it reveal 'the individualism of the author [...] that becomes manifest in the relationship between dialogue and scene text, and the design of the modes of report, description and comment'.[42] Although Igelström's analysis suggests that this 'individualism' can be conceived differently (and needs to be, given the multiple authorship and re-writing that characterizes many forms of screenwriting), the extent to which a given writer can experiment within the scene text is often a sign of authorial style and status.

A simple illustrative example is provided by the work of Quentin Tarantino. Although his screenplays are presented in fairly conventional master-scene format, the prolix dialogue marks Tarantino as an unusual writer in a cinema and screenwriting culture that still tends to adhere to the inaccurate cliché that film is a visual medium. More significant in the present context is the nature of the scene text. For example, in *Pulp Fiction* (1994), 'The 27-year-old Butch Coolidge is dressed in boxing regalia: trunks, shoes and gloves. He lies on a table catching a few zzzzzz's before his big fight. Almost as soon as we cut to him, he wakes up with a start. Shaken by the bizarre memory, he wipes his sweaty face with his boxing glove.' Shortly afterwards, 'As Butch steps into the hallway, the crowd goes apeshit'; later, 'In the room, black boxer Floyd Ray Willis lies on a table—dead. His face looks like he went dunking for bees.'[43] Although the description largely confines itself to recording what is seen and heard, it does so using adjectives ('bizarre'), similes ('like he went dunking for bees') and a distinctive lexis ('zzzzzz's', 'apeshit') that give the text a quality of goofy irreverence, which becomes especially striking at moments of heightened anxiety or violence. In Rush and Baughman's terms, it is a 'highly inflected' text in which the 'connotative nuances of language' teach us how to 'read' a certain attitude it adopts towards the events it describes.

This is equally true of those texts that occupy the opposite end of the spectrum. A distinctive characteristic of David Mamet's writing, for example, is the extreme minimalism of the scene text, which works as far as possible to eschew comment altogether. As Mamet puts it, '[t]he job of the film director'—and by this he also means the job of the film writer—'is *to tell the story through the juxtaposition of uninflected images*—because that is the essential nature of the medium'.[44] Mamet holds to this principle so resolutely that it becomes a mark of his authorial style, revealing an adherence to a purist conception of 'uninflected' film-making, while also indicating by contrast how infrequently other screenplays in fact accord with the supposed orthodoxy of the 'uninflected' script.[45] In this way, the seemingly purely denotative script becomes richly suggestive of a particular stance towards screenwriting itself.

Ultimately, the distinction between denotative instructions and connotative expression is questionable, as is shown by a simple direction within a seemingly casual conversation in Charlie Kaufman's *Eternal Sunshine of the Spotless Mind* (2004):

CLEMENTINE

[...] I'm getting too old for this. But it keeps
me from having to develop an actual personality.
I apply my personality in a paste. You?

JOEL

Oh, I doubt that's the case.

CLEMENTINE

Well, you don't know me, so...you don't
know, do you?

JOEL

Sorry. I was just trying to be nice.

CLEMENTINE

Yeah, I got it.

There's a silence.

CLEMENTINE (CONT'D)

My name's Clementine, by the way.

JOEL

I'm Joel.[46]

'There's a silence' is, arguably, a simple instruction: there must be a pause in the delivery of the dialogue at this point. Yet clearly there is something more at work here. A post-Pinter generation can hardly be unaware that the direction of a pause or silence within dialogue is an indication that language is being used as a medium through which the struggles for power between characters are being played out. There is also something suggestive about the phrase 'there's a silence' itself. It has become a favourite device of the journalist Jon Ronson to indicate a moment at which an interviewee's mask slips, and the subject of one of his stories certainly had grounds to object that Ronson 'buried [his] attacks in clever, sneaky little phrases like, "There is a silence." '[47] In the Kaufman script, the phrase is uttered by Igelström's 'impersonal fictional voice', but that voice is still adopting a position towards the characters and their situation under the guise of providing the reader with mere production information.

The extract above is taken from the published 'shooting script' of *Eternal Sunshine of the Spotless Mind*, which suggests that the distinction between this and a 'screenplay' is a good deal murkier than might appear. Yet it is also undoubtedly the case that the vast majority of screenplays do not circulate within a production context. Instead, they are 'selling' scripts, used for purposes of development and fund-raising, and for these purposes the master-scene script has become a global form.

Development and funding

An index of the master-scene form's ubiquity can be gauged from a single illustration: the work of film development consultant Selina Ukwuoma. Ukwuoma has been a script consultant at the Berlin Film Festival since 2008, and was previously a development executive in London at Cuba Pictures, the production arm of the Curtis Brown agency, a role that involved talent scouting, script reading, pre-production and script development. The Berlin festival is a global event, with the 12 aspiring writers annually chosen being drawn from entrants from across the world; Ukwuoma alone has acted as mentor to writers from Australia, the United States, Holland, Germany, Sweden, Hungary, India, Romania, Turkey, Argentina, Serbia, Brazil, France, Colombia, Uganda and Belgium. Her colleagues throughout this period have included Gyula Gazdag, the Hungarian director, artistic director at Sundance Institute and Distinguished Professor at the University of California, Los Angeles (UCLA); the New Zealander Marten Rabarts, formerly artistic director of the Binger Filmlab in Amsterdam and now Head of Development for India's National Film Development Corporation; and Franz Rodenkirchen, a German script consultant working for the TorinoFilmLab, the Binger Filmlab in Amsterdam, and Media (the European Union's support network for audiovisual industries). Others who have worked alongside Ukwuoma at Berlin have included the dramaturgs Louise Gough, a New York-based Australian, and Ruth McCance, formerly of Scottish Screen and now based in Sweden, both of whom also work for the pan-European Sources 2 script development organisation; and Lucile Hadzihalilovic, a French producer, director, script consultant and collaborator with the French-based Argentinian director Gaspar Noé.

The remarkably diverse range of nationalities and industries represented by this list gives some indication of the global reach and inter-relation of film networks. Those mentioned have very different views on cinema, storytelling, methods for writing the screenplay and the relation between script and film. On the restricted matter of screenplay format, however, festivals such as Berlin (and Sarajevo, where Ukwuoma also works) insist that the aspiring writers chosen for tutelage refine their scripts in fairly precise accord with the master-scene template.[48] This global reach of the form is evident in other ways too, being promoted via screenwriting software such as Final Draft, or in the screenplays printed privately by the studios for the 'consideration' of members voting for best screenplay in the Academy Awards. Regardless of the kind of story these screenplays tell, they are almost invariably presented in master-scene form.

As this shows, it is possible to keep separate the two dominant ideas about the contemporary screenplay that we have considered in this chapter: that it has a more or less specific textual form, and that it is governed by a particular narrative mode. In practice, this distinction is less easy to maintain once the screenplay begins to circulate within the wider film culture. Unlike scripts generated inside the studios of the classical system, which had specific purposes within a system of production, one of the major functions of today's screenplay is as a 'selling' script. The growth in film festivals, of which the best-known probably remains Sundance, and the emergence of powerful independent distributors, of whom the most celebrated (but also, perhaps, the most commercial) is Miramax, provided opportunities of securing funding and production for film projects that otherwise would not receive the backing of major studios, or would have to go through years of development and review before finally seeing the light of day; and the screenplay plays a central role in the process of evaluation.

This does not mean that such films or screenplays are fully 'independent', however, and different film-makers have commented on the relationships between such developments and the nature of screenplay form. Writer-producer James Schamus states that

> [t]he original sin of the American independent cinema, when it shifted away from the avant-garde [in the 1980s and 1990s], was the introduction of narrative [...] because what you haven't done is seize the means of exhibition, marketing, and distribution, and so you end up having to play by the rules of the big boys.[49]

This comment implies a crudely direct equation between narrative itself and a corporate establishment, suggesting that an independent film without sin would have to be one that preserved the suspicion of story in the New Hollywood and, before that, in the French New Wave. We shall return to this argument in the final chapter. The point is more subtle, however, because 'independent' film production remains largely dependent on external sources of funding, distribution and exhibition, and for these purposes the pre-production screenplay is a crucial document. It becomes a proposal, telling the story and selling the film idea to potential backers, who in turn, should they agree to finance the project, may subsequently refer back to the screenplay as representing a kind of legal agreement or contract. When Steven Soderbergh showed the dailies of *Sex, Lies, and Videotape* (1989) to one of his backers, he was told that 'You have a commitment to shoot what's written in the script'.[50]

Such considerations impact on the nature of screenplay form, tending to consolidate the status of the 'master-scene' script. As noted, this originally emerged from the need to accommodate dialogue within the sound film, and independent and avant-garde film-makers have sometimes argued that both the form of the master-scene script and its use in attracting funding have led to a preponderance of dialogue-driven scenes. This concern was expressed in 1991 by the editors of the 'script issue' of the independent film-oriented *Millennium Film Journal*:

> For commercial films, scripts and storyboards function not only as patterns to work from: they also form an essential part of the ritual of raising funds. In the film industry, a script is initially presented as a business plan—data intended to convince a client, a potential investor, of the soundness of a story, an approach, a design, a strategy, a concept. Since investors need to evaluate one putative project against another, the form of the film script is fairly invariable, consisting of pages of dialogue interspersed with short descriptive passages. It is an unhappy fact that these same documents are later used as blueprints for production, since they result in films that tend to be quite dense in dialogue, often containing, for minutes on end, nothing but heads talking against intricate backgrounds.[51]

Such arguments help to explain the persistence of the 'blueprint' metaphor surrounding the screenplay, although it is debatable how frequently, in practice, the script that is 'initially presented as a business plan' remains unaltered through the production process, which is invariably a matter of negotiation. As we saw with *The Godfather*, the story can exist in two different forms: the selling script circulated for funding and studio purposes, and the version that the film-makers develop out of sight. Soderbergh's backer, for example, expressed surprise that the nudity he thought the screenplay promised never materialised on the screen.[52]

In some countries, the dissemination of normative ideas about screenplays have taken the form of national initiatives connecting screenplay 'development' to governmental and non-governmental sources of national film funding, recalling the 'scenario crises' of earlier eras. The danger is that identified by Kathryn Millard, whose experience in working on a film funded by the Australian Film Commission was that the script remained 'in development for approximately six years' and 'as the project progressed down the financing route there came increased pressure for the screenplay to conform to a more classic, protagonist-driven, three-act structure'.[53] Partly in consequence, Millard is today at the forefront of both creative and critical approaches that look for alternatives to such pressures towards centralisation and conformity. Nor are such alternatives difficult to find. Indeed, as we shall now see, at the very moment when globalised methods of disseminating the dominant norm of the conception-and-execution, three-act, protagonist-driven, master-scene-formatted screenplay are at their height, new digital technologies are also today pulling the screenplay in the opposite direction, towards a complete rejection of this model and even, perhaps, of the very idea of the screenplay itself.

11
Screenwriting Today and Tomorrow

This book has explored a range of different kinds of text in the attempt to show which forms of writing became normative at particular times in Western film history, why they attained that status, and what caused the adoption of new, alternate or hybrid forms that would challenge or replace those norms. A project like this entails certain assumptions, especially about the formal definition of different kinds of screenwriting. There is also a more acutely political problem, which is well articulated by Steven Maras as 'a tendency to define a particularly dominant model of industry practice as a normative form of practice that others must either follow or situate themselves against. Thus, exciting possibilities in the realm of screenwriting practice are pre-positioned in the space of "the alternative" '.[1]

Any response to this charge must acknowledge that a study of norms and variations risks the organisational, if not the willfully political, definition of other kinds of writing in this way, and that this is likely to lead to their marginalisation: for example, by grouping them together in a separate chapter. My justification for doing just this is threefold. First, Maras is able to argue for a greater 'pluralism in filmmaking and screenwriting' partly by distinguishing between 'a primarily page-based form of writing for the screen, focused on the script as a manuscript, and an extended idea of screen writing not necessarily limited to the page or a page-based format for script writing'.[2] If, however, our principal object of enquiry is indeed 'the script as a manuscript', this option is unavailable. Second, then, if we accept that most—though by no means all—writing of screenplays takes place either within, or in recognition of, 'a particularly dominant model of industry practice' (the global influence of Hollywood), this influence is likely to be traceable within the text, if only in the form of variations on the prevailing Hollywood model. In short, the textual form is inextricable from the mode of production, and it is the effects of this conjunction, and not the myriad other possible ways of writing for film, that the present study has been attempting to follow.

Thirdly, however, the mode of production is currently undergoing radical transformation, largely because of the introduction of relatively cheap methods of digital film-making. In consequence, a range of possibilities for screenwriting that were previously the preserve of the auteur writer-director or the avant-garde film-maker have become available to all. The peculiarity of the present moment is that at the same time as the global dissemination of the master-scene screenplay has caused popular conceptions of 'the screenplay' to be compacted into a single, seemingly immutable form, massive technological and industrial changes in the modes of film production have enabled an explosion of different possibilities, which call into question the very purpose and existence of the screenplay as a pre-production document. The present chapter discusses not only these new forms of writing, but also their antecedents in film writing prior to digitisation.

Improvisation

Improvisation has a long and healthy history within screenwriting, one that tends to be obscured by the ubiquity of the blueprint metaphor. In the pre-feature film era, studios such as Selig and Edison left space in their scene outlines for improvised action during location shooting, and the records of story conferences involving slightly later film-makers such as Mack Sennett show that improvisation was a feature not only of the working process, but in some cases was also visible within the scripts themselves. Even in the classical sound era, a form of improvisation can be seen in the textual gaps that leave room for material to be supplied by specialists such as a choreographer like Busby Berkeley, or a montage editor like Slavko Vorkapich. Later, improvisation proper became particularly attractive with the introduction of lighter, hand-held cameras that facilitated shooting outside the studio, as in many of the films of the French New Wave.

The latter development was a particular influence on the directorial and writing methods of John Cassavetes, beginning with *Shadows* (1959). As Ray Carney puts it, whereas Hitchcock is an exemplar of the 'blueprint' model of production (although there are significant exceptions in which a post-production stage took the film far from the screenplay, such as *The Birds*), Cassavetes represents 'a sense of creation as a process of exploration and discovery'.[3] An improvisatory quality extends to Cassavetes' scripts themselves, since 'rather than being a gradual process of refining an original, each of the revisions more commonly functioned as a series of tangents away from the previous versions. Each draft was less a refinement than a reimagining of the story'.[4] Even more than with other screenplays, this makes confident identification of *the* script for a Cassavetes film problematic. While his films bring to the screen a quality of spontaneity that is in part the result of improvisation, 'that spontaneity was (almost) always scripted and refined in take after take'.[5] Indeed, as Cassavetes remarked, the script 'was structured very carefully to set up a whole new way of thinking so that the audience could not get ahead of the film'.[6]

Moreover, the script was often in a state of incompletion and flux. In his introduction to the published text of his 1968 film *Faces*, Cassavetes states that, having 'wanted to do a film that would allow the actors the time and room to act', he worked with 'a 215-page unfinished treatment'.[7] The published version is a parallel-text edition, with the written script on the right-hand page and an editorial transcription of the film soundtrack on the left. Around half of the soundtrack pages are completely blank (in only a very few cases is the opposite the case); those containing text display marked discrepancies from the script. This slightly obscures the fact that the script itself continued to be revised: in a slightly different recollection of the process, Cassavetes estimated that originally it ran to about 270 pages, and expanded to around 320.[8] The published text tells us more about the editing of the film than about the shooting, or indeed the writing: the differences between the script and soundtrack versions are explained partly by continual reshooting and controlled improvisation, with the scenes as written being quite freely adapted in performance, and partly by the editing of the film itself, with hours of footage being omitted from the cut transcribed in the book.

The relation between script(s) and film in Cassavetes' work is superficially quite similar to that of the Greek director Theo Angelopoulos, who remarks that 'the final shooting script you will find only if you take it off the finished print of the film. If you compare that with the script I have when I start shooting, you will find there are huge discrepancies between them'.[9] Yet the working methods are quite different. Although Angelopoulos regards himself as 'basically [...] the author of my own scripts', in developing them he would work with 'another person who will play the devil's advocate, the psychoanalyst or whatever'; afterwards, another collaborator would take on the role of reader to the (always handwritten) script Angelopoulos developed.[10]

The texts themselves have none of the prolixity of Cassavetes', although Angelopoulos appears uncommitted to any one approach to writing for film:

> Sometimes my films are the exact mirror of the script; other times, the script is in the form of notes and then the filming process is very dependent on improvisation. In some cases, there is a dynamic that allows you to use improvisations, while in others you have the feeling that you have to follow exactly the written script. This depends entirely on the material you have to work with and does not depend at all on the circumstances surrounding the making of the film. [...] For example, *Landscape in the Mist* [1988] is an exact copy of the script while *The Travelling Players* [1975] began from notes. *Voyage to Cythera* [1984] is very far from the original script and *The Beekeeper* [1986] very close to it.[11]

Within this pragmatic approach, perhaps the most notable aspect of Angelopoulos' screenwriting is the discrepancy between the terseness of the prose style and the length of the corresponding scenes in the film, creating a space for improvisation, or for the film to breathe. Andrew Horton notes that the scripts bear no relation to the one-minute-per-page rule of thumb: the original script for *Ulysses' Gaze* was 69 pages long, while the film ran to almost three hours. Horton's estimate is that a page in an Angelopoulos script is equivalent to four or five minutes' screen time, '[a]nd while Hollywood has developed a very strict code of rule for format, Angelopoulos certainly does not follow them in any rigorous manner'.[12] As the director puts it, 'Everybody knows I shoot long scenes, but only my closest collaborators know that I write these short sentences, almost like Hemingway. [...] I write in prose, like a short novel. In fact, you could publish my scripts as literature. That's what I do now. Previously, I didn't "write" at all, in that sense'.[13]

A current film-maker committed to improvisation, the Hong Kong director Wong Kar-Wai, first trained as a writer; on becoming a director, he at first imagined that he would work like Hitchcock. Much as we saw with Cassavetes, however, he soon discovered that he operated at the other end of the spectrum, and this was precisely

> because I was the writer, [and so] I knew how to change [things] on set. So finally I said, "Why bother?" And also, you can't write all your images on paper, and there are so many things—the sound, the

music, the ambience, and also the actors—when you're writing all of these details in the script, the script has no tempo, it's not readable. It's very boring. So I just thought, it's not a good idea [to write out a complete script beforehand], and I just wrote down the scenes, some essential details, and the dialogue. I give the rhythm of the scenes to the actors and skip all these technical things.[14]

In practice, however, when making a film 'normally we shoot without a script, or without a real script or [even] a fake script, but we have an idea. My way of working has always started with short stories',[15] with writing and editing taking place during the shooting.

This is a radically different approach to film-making from most of those we have previously seen. On the other hand, the description of a script as 'the scenes, some essential details, and the dialogue', without 'all these technical things', sounds remarkably similar to the distinction between a master-scene screenplay and a more detailed shooting script. Similarly, working not from a screenplay but from a short story is not too far removed from the practice common in the French New Wave of shooting from a treatment, while even the creation of the script not prior to production but 'at the end of the day [...] only when the film is finished'[16] has antecedents in Soviet montage, or indeed in the widespread practice of creating a new version of a screenplay for publication. As we have noted previously, approaches to writing for film that seem radically new can often be seen as a re-thinking or re-combination of forms such as the outline or short story that have been in use ever since the beginning of screenwriting.

Although Wong Kar-Wai began refining his working methods prior to the widespread introduction of digital technology, distinct stages of pre-production, production and post-production in film-making are increasingly dissolving as a result of technological change. A previously marginal or 'alternative' mode of script writing is thereby likely to become increasingly central, and much the same can be said of improvisation. With digital cameras and editing now making location work and re-shooting a much cheaper option than was the case with celluloid, the fully realised, 'blueprint' form of screenplay is likely to become increasingly displaced by the kinds of semi-improvisatory relationship between writing and filming that has previously been most common as a method used by auteur writer-directors, or by those working outside the Hollywood system.

Independent, avant-garde and digital cinema

Because the screenplay has historically been tied to a studio or corporate method of film production, for purposes of quality and budgetary control as well as for more directly artistic reasons, the notion of independence from the script has tended to be implicated within notions of 'independent film' more generally. The concept is problematic and can be defined in many ways, not least because successful independent companies tend to become absorbed into or co-opted by larger studios, as in the case of the relationship between Pixar and Disney. The word itself often carries a political and perhaps even a moral connotation, as in Jim Jarmusch's affirmation that '[a]nyone who makes a film that is the film they want to make, and it is not defined by marketing analysis or a commercial enterprise, is independent'.[17]

We can, however, attempt to distinguish between several different kinds of 'independent' film, each of which challenges the dominant model in different ways: the 'American independent' film, which often retains a relatively conventional notion of screenwriting but implicitly offers a critique of mainstream narrative conventions; avant-garde cinema, which frequently takes an entirely different approach by foregoing narrative altogether; the kinds of independence conferred by working within media other than written texts; and the kinds of film-making enabled by the ongoing transition to digital platforms. In practice, of course, a single film may exhibit aspects of some or all of these approaches.

For J. J. Murphy, the American independent film is not wholly divorced from the commercial imperatives of Hollywood, but neither does it adhere uncritically to its aesthetic conventions; instead, it actively contests them. Contrary to the assumption that this quasi-oppositional stance is most evident in the visual or even aural style of a given film-maker—that is, in directorial style—Murphy concentrates on the mode of storytelling, finding that between the early 1980s and the mid-2000s, American independent feature films 'developed a distinct approach to film-making, centering on new conceptions of cinematic storytelling', and that 'its narrational strategy lies somewhere between classical Hollywood cinema and art cinema', 'represent[ing] a hybrid form that [...] freely incorporate[es] elements from both'. Much like Kristin Thompson's analysis of 'New Hollywood' storytelling, Murphy traces these developments back to the script, which 'is the heart of the creative originality to be found in the independent movement'.[18]

Murphy suggests that 'if someone were to follow the prescriptions found in the standard manuals, it would be virtually impossible to write a truly independent film'.[19] Inevitably, however, in the face of the proliferation of self-help guides and associated attempts to homogenise not only format but also narrative paradigms, there has arisen what might be termed the 'anti-manual manual'; and there is significant overlap between the films considered in some of these manuals and in those that form the basis of Murphy's analysis. It is a rhetorical commonplace for writers to claim an element of originality for their work, but in some cases there is a conscious attempt in these books to outline new or alternative approaches to narrative form, often in response to the success of groundbreaking films themselves.

The notion of innovation or going against the grain is overtly present in the very titles of such studies as Linda Aronson's *Scriptwriting Updated: New and Conventional Ways of Writing for the Screen* (2000), Aronson's follow-up *The 21st Century Screenplay: A Comprehensive Guide to Writing Tomorrow's Films* (2010), Josh Golding's *Maverick Screenwriting: A Manual for the Adventurous Screenwriter* (2102), and Ken Dancyger and Jeff Rush's *Alternative Scriptwriting*, which was first published in 1991 and is currently in its fifth edition, with the subtitle changing frequently, from *Writing Beyond the Rules* (1991) to *Successfully Breaking the Rules* (4th edition, 2007) and *Rewriting the Hollywood Formula* (5th, 2013). These books call attention to such formulaic conventional structures as the three-act paradigm or the arc of character development, and encourage the writer consciously to work against them—much as the illustrative films do themselves.

Prominent among the examples in these books is a selection from among a spate of films that emerged in the 1990s and early 2000s, including *Pulp Fiction* (1994, written and directed by Quentin Tarantino), *The Usual Suspects* (1995, directed by Bryan Singer, screenplay by Christopher McQuarrie), *The Game* (1997, directed by David Fincher, screenplay by John D. Brancato and Michael Ferris), *The Spanish Prisoner* (1997, David Mamet), *Run, Lola, Run* (1998, Tom Tykwer), *The Matrix* (1999, the Wachowskis), *Fight Club* (1999, directed by David Fincher, screenplay by Jim Uhls), *The Sixth Sense* (1999, M. Night Shyamalan), *Memento* (2000, written and directed by Christopher Nolan), as well as the ongoing writing career of Charlie Kaufman, including *Being John Malkovich* (1999), *Adaptation* (2002) and *Eternal Sunshine of the Spotless Mind* (2004). In light of the fraught relations we have been tracing between storytelling and certain notions of independent cinema, it is notable that the jolt such films give to the spectatorial system, as it were, is tied to narrative: they often feature disorientatingly unusual shifts in the time scheme, for instance (*Pulp Fiction*, *Memento*), or otherwise expose the story world as a fictional construct (almost all of the above). Although there is a cinematic playfulness at work in these films, in defamiliarising received notions of how cinematic stories are told they self-reflexively bring the *screenplay* as an otherwise hidden structuring mechanism uncomfortably close to the surface.[20] It should be stressed that the innovation in these screenplays themselves does not extend to matters of presentation: in most respects they are quite straightforward examples of the master-scene format (though not of narrative structure), and strictly in this sense their publication tends to validate currently dominant conventions.

A second kind of 'independent' film is more radical: experimental, avant-garde and certain forms of 'art' cinema that are, at least for the purposes of production, more or less completely divorced from major studios or other forms of financial obligation. For present purposes, a difficulty with work created in this way is that, precisely because it is divorced from mainstream and commercial cinema, it enables more or less anything to function analogously to a screenplay text. Considered strictly in this context, such projects become self-selectingly marginal to studies of the relationships between screenwriting and industry, presenting problems similar to those posed by early cinema: a 'screenplay' becomes not a definable form but any kind of document, written or otherwise, that provides purely local solutions to creative questions posed in the making of an art work in a different medium.

Precisely for this reason, of course, they possess great value in the exploration of the creative process of individual film-makers, as was illustrated by panel of four excellent papers on 'Alternative Forms of Scripting' presented at a 2013 conference in Madison, Wisconsin. J. J. Murphy examined the effects of Norman Mailer's use of improvisation, especially for *Maidstone* (1970); Line Langebek and Spencer Parsons took a detailed look at Cassavetes' work, especially *Faces*, comparing the relationship between the actors' performances and Cassavetes' continually changing script to the kinds of improvisation found in jazz; Mark Minett's archival research shows that Robert Altman's films were indeed scripted in detail, but that in *The Long Goodbye* (1973), for example, Altman permitted Elliott Gould to ad-lib Marlowe's lines as long as this did not alter the narrative spine; and John Powers presented a range of materials used by Stan Brakhage in creating such films as *Arabic 0* (1981) and *I...Dreaming* (1988), including song lyrics, storyboards, drawings, hieroglyphs and word lists.[21] Research like this positions avant-garde and independent cinema within a narrative about screenwriting that extends the scope of that term to include various kinds of 'scripting' beyond the familiar industrial text. Taken in this sense, the avant-garde does not reject screenwriting; rather, the screenplay rejects the avant-garde, the practices of which cannot be accommodated within the functions for which the conventional screenplay text has been devised.

Scripts written in connection with the avant-garde Millennium Film Workshop, which was established in 1966 by Ken Jacobs in Manhattan's Lower East Side, illustrate this very clearly. The Workshop defines itself as being 'dedicated to the exhibition, study, and practice of experimental film, video, and new media', and 'non-commercial independent film'. It 'engages ideas and issues rarely covered in mainstream media', and 'is fed by low cost access to facilities, equipment, and workshops'.[22] The *Millennium Film Journal* published in its 'Script Issue' in 1991 a range of documents produced by film-makers associated with the Workshop. These texts 'preceded or were otherwise involved in the production of film-works: materials that, in loose terms, might take the place of a script or a storyboard in a more commercial film project'.[23] All of these, in some sense, constitute the kinds of 'notes to self' that characterised writing in the early 'cameraman system'. Contrary to any putative 'blueprint' function, Ann Marie Fleming's text for *You Take Care Now* (1989) contains detailed written material, including indications of dialogue, but does not describe what will appear on the screen, instead leaving spaces marked 'picture'. Some of the other documents resemble conventional storyboards, but John Moritsugu's 'plans' for *Der Elvis* (1987) combine drawing, newspaper cut-outs and handwritten text to produce a collage that gives a clear indication of some of Moritsugu's ideas for the film (such as 'Film in black and white slo-mo à la *Eraserhead* food scene, but don't fuck it up like [David] Lynch'), without enabling any other reader to visualise the progression of the proposed film in a manner analogous to that of the conventional screenplay.

Still others indicate modes of thinking and working that anticipate the creative possibilities that would later be unleashed by digital software. Yvonne Rainer's written text for *Privilege* (1990) again resembles a familiar screenplay with handwritten annotations, but this is followed by a visual representation of how the physical cutting of the film into strips will be achieved. Lynne Sachs' documents for *The House of Science: A Museum of False Facts* (1991) combine relatively familiar forms of screenwriting (there are specifications for voice-over and on-screen narration) with sketches, storyboards and other kinds of artwork.

What is most striking today is that these experimental film-makers' approach to the cinematic pre-text, which can broadly be characterised as a combination of provisionality, mixed media and the ability to record a personal creative process, is precisely what has subsequently been enabled as an alternative to conventional screenwriting by the ongoing transformation of large areas of film production to relatively low-cost digital platforms. Instead of anything resembling a studio system with homogenised approaches to the production and formatting of screenplays, we are likely to have a largely piecemeal, fragmentary field in which almost infinite numbers of individual film projects will generate hundreds of different kinds of material that could be designated 'screenplays'. Moreover, as Kathryn Millard suggests, if we think less in terms of the 'screenplay' and more in terms of the 'prototype', then significant numbers of different kinds of pre-planning become available to the film-maker: animation, maps, graphic novels, storyboards, sounds, 'proof of concept' videos and 'digital remixing'. As she notes, 'the boundaries between writing and production are increasingly stretched in a digital era'.[24]

Meanwhile, digital software such as Redboard, and hardware such as the Simulcam, are increasingly erasing the distinction between pre-production conception and filmic execution on which, as we have seen repeatedly, many conventional assumptions about screenwriting rest. The Simulcam, a technology developed by James Cameron for the production of *Avatar* (2009), allows the director to see close estimations of how green screen scenes would look in their final state, at the moment of capture. Such aesthetic transformations would traditionally have been planned for in pre-production, through the use of concept art, inspirational sketches and storyboards, but not actually achieved until post-production. The Simulcam conflates these processes, and in doing so turns the director's on-set screen into what is effectively an interactive storyboard. At a much simpler level, software programs such as the non-proprietary, open-source CeltX provide not only conventional screenwriting programs comparable to Final Draft, but also possibilities for incorporating other media such as images, videos and storyboards. This facilitates approaches to film-making that erode familiar distinctions between phases of production, enabling revisions to the script to take place alongside the shooting and editing of the film. By such means, too, the monolithic conception of the screenplay outlined in the previous chapter is being overturned by cheap and readily available methods of production and distribution, returning film-making

230 A History of the Screenplay

and screenwriting to the cottage industries they were at the beginning of cinema.

Another striking manifestation of some of these possibilities is the Hitrecord website, which is essentially an open-source, interactive space encouraging new forms of collaboration.[25] Writers can upload their own short stories or screenplays, to be developed, storyboarded or filmed by others. This more directly creative function brings with it the dangers posed by too great an influx of material, leading to one manifestation of the contemporary problem of an over-supply of digital production combined with instant distribution. To manage the material, Hitrecord therefore also provides opportunities for users to work as curators, by sifting and editing the contributions and setting up lines of production.

The digital archive and the e-text

This curatorial function is seen also in the digitisation and archiving of screenwriting material of earlier periods. In April 2012, Warner Bros. Digital Publishing launched its 'Inside the Script' series of downloadable eBooks with four titles: *Casablanca* (1942), *An American in Paris* (1951), *North by Northwest* (1959) and *Ben-Hur* (1959). Each of the titles contains a 'shooting script', which incorporates hypertext links to stills from the film, and a variety of often previously unpublished production materials from a range of archives in Los Angeles.

At time of writing, more than a year after the initial launch, Warner Bros. has yet to create additional titles, although they are promised. As with many publishing ventures that seek to respond to developments in software technology, Warners may be holding fire until the consequences of developments in the hardware platforms become clearer. Certainly the series is upfront about the challenges presented by the still fledgling status of eBook publishing: each title in the series is prefaced with recommendations about how to use the book, depending on which devices and platforms (iBooks, Kindle) are being used to view it, and the 'word from the editors' tailored to each title notes that eBook formats (ePub, Mobipocket) present the designers with peculiar difficulties. Consequently, the screenplay texts have been customised for the platform: they are not facsimiles of the kind found on websites that purport to disseminate vintage screenplays (often illegally); nor do they in all instances preserve the formatting conventions of the texts they reproduce. Instead, partly to standardise the series and partly to accommodate the limitations of the platform, each of the texts appears in an identical Courier font. The aim is to create an audiovisually enhanced text 'that is as much like reading a script in print as possible', in full acknowledgement that the series is an experiment, and that subsequent developments in eBook technology will produce advances in future publications. Hence, perhaps, the wait-and-see nature of the series as it currently stands.

Although the current state of technology and of the market for eBooks accounts for some of the strengths and weaknesses of the series, more familiar, old-school problems in screenplay publication remain. All four texts purport to present the 'shooting script', but the problems with this concept—which, as we have seen, implies a stable, completed text of which the filming is a realisation—are not explored. The notoriously unstable production of *Casablanca* generated an equally notorious tangle of texts, and with commendable openness, the editors of the *Casablanca* e-text note that

> this shooting script didn't exist in this particular form before principal photography began in May of 1942. Because *Casablanca* was being written and rewritten as it was in production, this script version is instead a reconstruction of what the shooting script might have been. It also includes revisions that were made to the final film. In some ways, it is a hybrid and has aspects of a continuity script as well.[26]

That leaves the reader very much in the dark as to what s/he is reading. There are commercial constraints on what the 'Inside the Script' series is attempting to achieve, and the decisions taken with regard to *Casablanca* are in keeping with a conception of the series as an accompaniment to a film, in the manner of a DVD or Blu-Ray extras programme, rather than something that exploits the possibilities of the medium to present a radically new way of understanding screenplay texts.

This is disappointing, especially given the resonant introductory description of this version of *Casablanca* as a 'virtual script tour'.[27] While the supporting materials in the introductory chapters include an excellent and remarkably full, illustrated discussion of how the script was developed by different hands, the presentation remains constrained by the limitations of the print-text format of a linear, chronological account of which writer contributed what and when. This looks like a missed opportunity. The potential of the digital text with hypertext links lies instead in the possibility of revealing how a screenplay text selects from and represents a range of variant materials (preceding drafts, treatments, story memos, etc.) that can be eliminated or reinstated at will.

Links within the 'shooting script' to production stills are merely a different way of presenting an illustrated text, whereas hypertext links to variant script materials have the capacity to change the reader's perception of what a 'shooting script' really is. This would have been especially valuable in the case of *Casablanca*, because it would have performed a properly curatorial function while obviating the need for the creation of a 'shooting script' that is openly an editorial construct created for the series itself.

The potential of the digital hypertext in the field of literary studies has been demonstrated by the collaboration between T. S. Eliot's publisher Faber and Faber and the high-end digital producer Touch Press's iPad version of Eliot's 1922 poem *The Waste Land*. The app allows the user to switch freely between various audio and visual readings of the poem, or to move instantaneously from one place in the text to another. Hypertext links direct the reader to scholarly notes on lines in the poem—but not, significantly, to the drafts, which are instead presented in facsimile in a separate section. Consequently, the app is still structured in a way that preserves the stability of the author's final intentions, rather than taking the alternative route of enabling a freer exploration of how that version results from the creative dialogue surrounding the process of composition and editing by Eliot and (perhaps especially) Ezra Pound, a process that remains detectable in the fragmentary nature of the 'finished' poem.

Perhaps it is not surprising that this approach prevailed, given the involvement of Eliot's long-standing publishers, and the poem's status as a cornerstone of high modernism. But the Touch Press edition of *The Waste Land*, and Warners' Inside the Script series, are pointers to the likely future of the understanding of the screenplay, since in embryonic form they embody the twin forces guiding current screenplay research: scholarly investigation of mountainous but so far little-studied national and studio archives, and the light this is shedding on the screenplay as a 'literature in flux'[28] that in many cases achieves no final form, but instead represents a nexus of multiple possibilities generated by a plethora of writers.

Anna Sofia Rossholm's current research at the Ingmar Bergman Archive in Stockholm illustrates well the interrelation of these two developments.[29] The archive 'mainly consists of notebooks, manuscripts, production documents and letters spanning Bergman's career from the 1930s until the end of his life in 2007. Notebooks and manuscripts are digitized and made accessible through a database that gives new visibility to Bergman's working methods and the creative process'.[30] As Rossholm's exploration of this collection shows, advances in digital technology are impacting on both the creation of archives and the theoretical understanding of texts and textual editing. Drawing on John Bryant's work in describing the digital archive as a 'fluid text', she points out that

> Jacques Derrida's notion of the archive as an event in itself, an act of 'archivization that produces as much as it records the event' [...] is particularly foregrounded in the digital archive where the database and the scanned manuscripts are a form of remediation of the original drafts. [...] Compared to a book edition, the digital archive is a less authorial form of publication where alternative narratives in different manuscript versions are presented side by side without hierarchical order[.][31]

Noting the connection to the Touch Press *Waste Land*, Rossholm notes that '[s]uch an interface where writing, sound and images can be interlinked is particularly suitable for publications of screenwriting where scripts, or other forms of screenwriting pretexts, could be presented together with films or extracts of films'.[32] The Warners series is a step in this direction.

Equally pertinent, however, is that screenwriting, especially in cases of multiple authorship such as *Casablanca*, can present problems for ideas of literary authorship, the authorial persona and the authorised text that preserves the writer's final intentions. Paul Keegan, Faber's poetry editor, notes that in working on the *Waste Land* project 'I was concerned that the text be at the centre... it's still important that the poem have a chance to survive in all its strangeness', and two of Eliot's own readings of his poem are among its most striking features.[33] Yet authorship, final intentions and 'the text' itself are precisely what is at issue in screenwriting. In many film industries, notably Hollywood, the writer lacks ownership over the material and is liable to be rewritten by others, while unlike the literary poem, the screenplay is a constantly evolving text in the service of a different medium. For all of these reasons it is more provisional and evasive than a published poem like Eliot's, and for these reasons also the open, hypertextual form is ideally suited to its presentation, market and financial considerations notwithstanding.

These qualities of provisionality and openness also help to explain why 'genetic' criticism is starting to emerge as a leading methodological approach in current screenplay research. The hypertextual representation of a screenplay perhaps comes the closest we can currently imagine to what is otherwise the unrepresentable movement of what genetic criticism terms the 'avant-texte'. Like the editing procedures outlined by Jerome McGann,[34] this approach marries the familiar critical approaches of textual analysis and scholarship with a more post-theoretical understanding of texts as radically unstable products of social and textual negotiations. Genetic criticism 'examines tangible documents such as writers' notes, drafts, and proof corrections, but its real object is something much more abstract—not the existing documents but the movement of writing that must be inferred from them'.[35] This 'movement of writing' is the 'avant-texte', which is in many ways comparable to the 'screen idea' underlying the collaborative work on screenplays and other documents and practices created during work on a film project. For this reason, genetic criticism appears to complement very well ongoing archival research into existing screenplays, combining traditional scholarship into material texts with methods for examining collaboration and the anticipated realisation in another medium.[36] The still-emerging possibilities of hypertext publication promise to make this 'movement of writing' something that can be grasped more tangibly by the reader. Digitisation will take dead screenplays out of the metaphorical wastepaper basket and re-animate them, at the same time as it threatens to kill off the three-act written screenplay once and for all.

Conclusion: The Screenplay as a Modular Text

Screenplays compiled during production almost invariably reveal their provisional nature. Individual pages of revisions will ordinarily be dated in the upper left-hand corner, and the presence of multiple dates shows when the page in question was inserted, either to replace a previous iteration or as an addition to it. During the 1930s, these pages began to be colour-coded, eventually resulting in the convention whereby the first set of revision pages would be printed on blue paper, followed by pink, yellow, green and gold, reverting to white at the sixth revision.[1]

This convention is difficult to reconcile with the ubiquitous 'blueprint' metaphor, because instead of indicating a radical separation of conception and execution, it shows the screenplay in a state of change both before and during production. Indeed, in some circumstances it may continue to evolve afterwards, as in Osip Brik's recommendation that the Soviet director's screenplay should show the result of the work in compiling the montage from exposed film, or in preparing a version for publication. To the extent that the blueprint metaphor remains valid, it is principally in relation to the silent continuity from 1914 to 1929, although even in those cases there are ordinarily significant differences between what is envisaged in the written text and the release print of the film. Moreover, the continuity script frequently contains material devised during an earlier stage of composition (the scenario) that exceeds the purely industrial function implied by the blueprint metaphor.

For these reasons, Claudia Sternberg's radically different conception of the screenplay as 'literature in flux' initially appears more convincing. This trope presents the screenplay not as a stable, efficient version of a film in alternate textual form, but as a continuous and unpredictable series of stages in the production process, and this better accords with some of the empirical evidence about how screenplays were actually written both during the classical era and afterwards, with multiple writers or writing teams working on a project before and during the filming process.

However, what the dating and colour-coding conventions reveal is that not *all* of the text was in flux. On the contrary, significant sections are retained from multiple previous iterations, including, very frequently, material from quite early stages in development. A screenplay of this kind has quite literally been assembled by taking some pages from one iteration, more from a second, still others from a third, and so on, and placing them together in a provisional sequence. Moreover, something resembling this latter-day convention can be found at the very beginnings of extant screenwriting. In 1904, AM&B attempted to present their *Bulletin* copy of *The Suburbanite* as a 'dramatic composition'. Thwarted by the censor, for subsequent copyright submissions they then used the description of the action as the basis for both the *Bulletin* advertising and the scenarios themselves; the same piece of text was being flown into two different documents. Meanwhile, the scenarios themselves were constructed by combining this report-mode account of the action with a mode of scene description derived from the conventions of the contemporary theatrical play script, producing a textual form that is visibly composed of two different kinds of material.

Neither the conventional screenplay of today, then, nor the earliest surviving screenwriting texts, can comfortably be described as blueprints; neither do they show the text in a state of flux. Instead, each is a compilation of pre-existing materials that have been combined in a particular order to achieve particular effects. *Some* of these materials may continue to be re-written, but this will not ordinarily be the case with *all* of them. This suggests that the screenplay is neither a blueprint, at one end of the scale, nor 'literature in flux' at the other. Instead, it occupies a middle position: the screenplay is a *modular* text.

This is an appropriate description of most of the forms of screenwriting examined in this book. The 'outline' script composed for narrative film-making around 1907–12, prior to the advent of the multi-reel feature, facilitated an element of improvisation by providing a skeleton of action from which a director like J. Searle Dawley could deviate; for example, to accommodate location shooting. The continuity script that developed thereafter presents the strongest case for the blueprint model, but it is also very evidently comprised of distinct elements: the dramatic material of the scenario, the intertitles and the editorial work of the continuity writers. This model came under stress with the advent of sound, which Hollywood attempted to accommodate by incorporating discrete elements within the script, as in the appropriately titled 'part-talkie', or in the salvaging of material from the silent cutting continuity of *Hell's Angels*. For the remainder of the classical studio era the Hollywood script is, roughly, an amalgam of the continuity form and dialogue scenes, which often take on the appearance of those in the master-scene script. In all of these cases, the modular construction is apparent not only in the paradigmatic forms but in individual film projects, as material from previous iterations is incorporated, often verbatim, within the latest re-write.

In this way, the idea of modular screenwriting captures something of the nature of celluloid films themselves, which are produced by the juxtaposition of exposed strips of footage, some of which may then be subject to later treatment or substitution. Meanwhile, Staiger's description of the 'package-unit' system that arose in Hollywood around 1955 as one characterised by 'component packaging'[2] is equally applicable to the screenplays that service it. With the ending of in-house screenwriting at the Hollywood studios, the script becomes one element among many assembled by a producer, and one that invites re-working section-by-section by several different writers.

Yet not all forms of screenwriting can comfortably be accommodated within this model, especially those originating outside the studio system of the United States. The scripts of the Soviet-era directors were most certainly 'in flux'. Conversely, the *auteur* writer such as Carl Mayer, or the writer-director such as Ingmar Bergman, often operates in more or less explicit opposition to such an idea. In general, individual authorship is less amenable to the conception of the text as an assemblage of component parts, which can always be provided by different writers. Moreover, an *auteur* need not necessarily draw on a script that resembles the standard screenplay forms, often being able to work from his or her notes, in whatever form s/he chooses, or indeed from no script at all. In this way some of the 'independent' film-makers noted in Chapter 11 are not dissimilar to their counterparts in the 'cameraman' system that prevailed in early cinema.

In one final way, too, the material in the first and last chapters shows screenwriting coming full circle. Digital film-making carries the potential to erase the distinctions between pre-production, production and post-production: text, images, film, processing and editing can all be effected at relatively low cost, on the same computer, at the same time. There is a long way to go, and the reasons why screenwriting emerged in the first place, which were as much legal as industrial, have their counterparts today in the uses of the script as a basis on which to attract funding. Yet the return to a mode of film-making that resembles the cottage industries of early cinema has the potential to eliminate many of the divisions of labour, and the phases of production, that helped to bring the written film script into being. There will be no more need for the wastepaper basket, because the paper to go into it will no longer exist. The future of the screenplay is, perhaps, annihilation. In its end is its beginning.

Notes

Introduction

1. In Scott MacDonald, ed., *Screen Writings: Scripts and Texts by Independent Filmmakers* (Berkeley: University of California Press, 1995), p. 22.
2. In MacDonald, p. 19.
3. See in particular Steven Maras, *Screenwriting: History, Theory and Practice* (London: Wallflower, 2009), p. 82.
4. Tom Stempel, *FrameWork: A History of Screenwriting in the American Film*, 2nd ed. (New York: Continuum, 1991), p. 62.
5. Marc Norman, *What Happens Next: A History of American Screenwriting* (London: Aurum, 2008), p. 42.
6. Larry Ceplair and Steven Englund, *The Inquisition in Hollywood: Politics in the Film Community, 1930–1960* (New York: Anchor/Doubleday, 1980).
7. Lizzie Francke, *Script Girls: Women Screenwriters in Hollywood* (London: British Film Institute, 1994).
8. Richard Corliss, *Talking Pictures: Screenwriters in the American Cinema* [1974] (New York: Overlook, 1985).
9. David Bordwell, *The Way Hollywood Tells It: Story and Style in Modern Movies* (Berkeley: University of California Press, 2006); Kristin Thompson, *Storytelling in the New Hollywood: Understanding Classical Narrative Technique* (Cambridge, Mass.: Harvard University Press, 1999).
10. Maras, pp. 1–2.
11. David Bordwell, Janet Staiger and Kristin Thompson, *The Classical Hollywood Cinema: Film Style and Mode of Production to 1960* (London: Routledge, 1985); Janet Staiger, 'Blueprints for Feature Films: Hollywood's Continuity Scripts', in Tino Balio (ed.), *The American Film Industry*, rev. ed. (Madison: University of Wisconsin Press, 1985), pp. 173–92.
12. Alexander Schwarz, *Der Geschriebene Film: Drehbücher des Deutschen und Russischen Stummfilms* (Munich: Diskurs Film, 1994).
13. Colin Crisp, *The Classic French Cinema, 1930–1960* (Bloomington: Indiana University Press, 1993).
14. Kristin Thompson, 'Early Alternatives to the Hollywood Mode of Production: Implications for Europe's Avant-Gardes', in Lee Grieveson and Peter Krämer (eds), *The Silent Cinema Reader* (London: Routledge, 2004), pp. 349–67.
15. Staiger, 'Blueprints', p. 178, n. 8 and n. 9.
16. For an extensive discussion, see Maras, pp. 117–29.
17. Claudia Sternberg, *Written for the Screen: The American Motion-Picture Screenplay as Text* (Tübingen: Stauffenburg Verlag, 1997), pp. 71–76.
18. Sternberg, p. 74.
19. Torey Liepa, 'Entertaining the Public Option: The Popular Film Writing Movement and the Emergence of Writing for the American Silent Cinema',

in Jill Nelmes (ed.), *Analysing the Screenplay* (London: Routledge, 2011), pp. 15–16.

20. Maras, p. 91.

21. John Emerson and Anita Loos, *How to Write Photoplays* (New York: James A. McCann, 1920), p. 19.

22. *The New Stenographer*, scenario by J. Stuart Blackton [1911], Library of Congress, Washington, D.C.

23. Maras, p. 91.

24. Frances Marion, *How to Write and Sell Film Stories* (New York: Covici-Friede, 1937), p. 372.

25. Janet Staiger, 'Dividing Labor for Production Control: Thomas Ince and the Rise of the Studio System', *Cinema Journal* 18.2 (1979), p. 20, emphasis added.

26. B. F. Barrett, 'A Talk with C. Gardner Sullivan', *Motography* 16.23 (1916), p. 1237; quoted in Torey Liepa, 'The Devil in the Details: Thomas Ince, Intertitles, and the Institutionalization of Writing in American Cinema', in Cynthia Lucia, Roy Grundmann, and Art Simon, (eds), *The Wiley-Blackwell History of American Film*, vol. 1: *Origins to 1928* (Malden, MA: Blackwell, 2012), p. 279.

27. Ann Martin and Virginia M. Clark, ed., *What Women Wrote: Scenarios, 1912–1929* (Frederick, MD: University Publications of America, 1987), p. viii.

28. Marion, p. 374.

29. Janet Staiger, 'The Hollywood Mode of Production, 1930–60', in David Bordwell, Janet Staiger, and Kristin Thompson, *The Classical Hollywood Cinema: Film Style and Mode of Production to 1960* (London: Routledge, 1985), p. 146.

30. Maras, p. 91.

31. Ibid.

32. *Broadway* (Universal, 1929), Screen Play and Dialogue Arrangement by Edward T. Lowe, Jr., Cinema-Television Library, USC.

33. *Gold Diggers of Broadway* (WB, 1929). Undated continuity, 'Screen Play by Robert Lord', AMPAS unpublished scripts collection, MHL.

34. Maras, p. 86.

35. Steven Maras, 'In Search of "Screenplay": Terminological Traces in the Library of Congress *Catalog of Copyright Entries: Cumulative Series*, 1912–20' (2009), *Film History* 21.4, pp. 346–58.

36. Maras, *Screenwriting*, p. 6.

37. Facsimile reproduction in *The Bride of Frankenstein*, Universal Filmscripts series: Classic horror films—Vol. 2 (Absecon, NJ: MagicImage Filmbooks, 1989).

38. Jeff Rush and Cynthia Baughman, 'Language as Narrative Voice: The Poetics of the Highly Inflected Screenplay', *Journal of Film and Video* 49.3 (1997), p. 29.

39. Claus Tieber, *Schreiben für Hollywood: Das Drehbuch im Studiosystem* (Vienna: Lit Verlag GmbH, 2008).

40. For critiques of the 'blueprint' analogy, see Maras, *Screenwriting*, pp. 123–29; Steven Price, *The Screenplay: Authorship, Theory and Criticism* (Basingstoke: Palgrave, 2010), pp. 44–47; Kathryn Millard, 'After the Typewriter: The Screenplay in a Digital Era', *Journal of Screenwriting* 1.1 (2010), pp. 14–15.

41. Jean-Claude Carrière, *The Secret Language of Film*, trans. Jeremy Leggatt (London: Faber, 1995), p. 150.
42. Osip Brik, 'From the Theory and Practice of a Script Writer', trans. Diana Matias, *Screen* 15.3 (1974), p. 99.
43. Nathalie Morris, 'Unpublished Scripts in BFI Special Collections: A Few Highlights', *Journal of Screenwriting* 1.1 (2010), pp. 197–98.
44. Ian W. Macdonald and Jacob U. U. Jacob, 'Lost and Gone for Ever? The Search for Early British Screenplays', *Journal of Screenwriting* 2.2 (2011), p. 162.
45. Thompson, 'Early Alternatives', p. 350.

1 Prehistory of the Screenplay

1. Steven Maras, *Screenwriting: History, Theory and Practice* (London: Wallflower, 2009), p. 29.
2. Tom Stempel, *FrameWork: A History of Screenwriting in the American Film*, 2nd ed. (New York: Continuum, 1991), p. 5.
3. Edward Azlant, *The Theory, History, and Practice of Screenwriting, 1897–1920*, diss. (Ann Arbor, Mich.: University Microfilms International, 1980), p. 79.
4. Robert C. Allen, *Vaudeville and Film 1895–1915: A Study in Media Interaction* (New York: Arno Press, 1980), pp. 159, 212–13; cited in Tom Gunning, 'The Cinema of Attractions: Early Film, the Spectator and the Avant-Garde', in Thomas Elsaesser, ed., *Early Cinema: Space, Frame, Narrative* (London: BFI, 1990), p. 56.
5. Azlant, p. 65.
6. Ian W. Macdonald, 'Disentangling the Screen Idea', *Journal of Media Practice* 5.2 (2004), pp. 89–99.
7. Maras, pp. 171–72.
8. Quoted in Stempel, p. 7.
9. Anon., 'The Confessions of a Scenario Editor', *Photoplay* (August 1914), p. 166.
10. Cecil Hepworth, 'Those Were the Days', *Penguin Film Review* 6 (April 1948), pp. 33–39; reprinted in Harry M. Geduld, ed., *Film Makers on Film Making* (Indiana UP, 1967), pp. 26–32.
11. Stempel, p. 6.
12. Marshall Deutelbaum, 'Structural Patterning in the Lumière Film', *Wide Angle* 3:i (1979), p. 30.
13. Ibid., p. 35.
14. Georges Sadoul, 'Lumière—the Last Interview', *Sight & Sound* 17 (Summer 1948), pp. 68–70; quoted in Geduld, p. 24.
15. David Robinson, *Georges Méliès: Father of Film Fantasy* (London: BFI, 1993), p. 22.
16. Deutelbaum, p. 35.
17. Ibid.
18. Kemp R. Niver, *The First Twenty Years: A Segment of Film History* (Los Angeles: Artisan Press, 1968), p. 8.
19. Stempel, p. 3.
20. Patrick Loughney, 'From *Rip Van Winkle* to *Jesus of Nazareth*: Thoughts on the Origins of the American Screenplay', *Film History* 9.iii (1997), p. 279.

21. Ibid., p. 278.
22. Terry Ramsaye, *A Million and One Nights: A History of the Motion Picture through 1925* (New York: Simon and Schuster, 1926), p. 288.
23. Ibid., pp. 370, 366.
24. Stempel, p. 3. Loughney's research shows that Jefferson's *Rip Van Winkle* in fact has a stronger claim than either.
25. Loughney, p. 280.
26. Azlant, p. 64.
27. Noël Burch, 'Primitivism and the Avant-Gardes: A Dialectical Approach', in Philip Rosen, ed., *Narrative, Apparatus, Ideology: A Film Theory Reader* (New York: Columbia University Press, 1986), pp. 486–89.
28. Charles Musser, 'The Early Cinema of Edwin Porter', *Cinema Journal* 19.i (1979), p. 23.
29. George C. Pratt, *Spellbound in Darkness: Readings in the History and Criticism of the Silent Film*, vol. 1 (Rochester, NY: University of Rochester Press, 1966), pp. 36–37; Janet Staiger, 'Mass-Produced Photoplays: Economic and Signifying Practices in the First Years of Hollywood', *Wide Angle* 4.iii (1980), p. 18.
30. See Charles Musser, *Thomas A. Edison Papers: A Guide to Motion Picture Catalogs by American Producers and Distributors, 1894–1908: A Microfilm Edition* (Frederick, MD: University Publications of America, 1985), esp. pp. 11–15.
31. *Complete Illustrated Catalog of Moving Picture Machines, Stereopticons, Slides, Films*, Kleine Optical Company, Chicago (November 1905), pp. 256–57; reprinted in Pratt, pp. 23–24. The same outline of *A Trip to the Moon* is also printed in the Star Films catalogue (New York: 1904), p. 25.
32. *Complete Catalogue of Genuine and Original 'Star' Films (Moving Pictures) Manufactured by Geo. Méliès of Paris* (New York: undated), n.p. It is more convenient to refer to film, rather than page, numbers in this catalogue, which contains several individually paginated 'supplements'. The catalogue is formally undated, and the BFI tentatively dates it as '1907?', but the films in the supplements are 'copyright, 1904', which seems the likelier date.
33. Quoted in Robinson, p. 26; my italics.
34. Elizabeth Ezra, *Georges Méliès: The Birth of the Auteur* (Manchester: Manchester UP, 2000), pp. 13–14, 17.
35. John Frazer, *Artificially Arranged Scenes: The Films of Georges Méliès* (Boston: G.K. Hall, 1979) pp. 109, 143–44.
36. Azlant, pp. 74–75.
37. *Complete Catalogue*, p. 25.
38. *Faust and Marguerite: A New and Magnificent Cinematographic Opera in 20 Motion Tableaux*, in the *Complete Catalogue*, supplement 16, pp. 2–8. In the original, each scene is described on a separate line, as is *A Trip to the Moon*.
39. Charles Musser, *The Emergence of Cinema: The American Screen to 1907* (New York: Scribner's, 1990), p. 327. Musser presents both catalogue and *Clipper* versions in full in *Before the Nickelodeon: Edwin S. Porter and the Edison Manufacturing Company* (Berkeley: University of California Press, 1991), pp. 214–18.
40. See, for example, Martin Sopocy, 'French and British Influences in Porter's *American Fireman*', *Film History* 1.ii (1987), pp. 137–48; Musser, 'The Early

Cinema of Edwin Porter'; André Gaudreault, 'Detours in Film Narrative: The Development of Cross-Cutting', *Cinema Journal* 19.i (1979), pp. 39–59.
41. Marc Norman, *What Happens Next: A History of American Screenwriting* (London: Aurum, 2008), p. 20.
42. Ramsaye, p. 416.
43. Niver, p. 31.

2   Copyright Law, Theatre and Early Film Writing

1. For a more detailed account, see Steven Price, 'The First Screenplays? American Mutoscope and Biograph Scenarios Revisited', *Journal of Screenwriting* 2.2 (2011), pp. 195–213. Like all later scholarship in this area, mine is indebted to the work of Patrick Loughney, most widely circulated in the following articles: 'In the Beginning Was the Word: Six Pre-Griffith Motion Picture Scenarios', *Iris* 2.1 (1984), pp. 17–31; 'From *Rip Van Winkle* to *Jesus of Nazareth*: Thoughts on the Origins of the American Screenplay', *Film History* 9.3 (1997), pp. 277–89; 'Appendix: Selected Examples of Early Scenario/Screenplays in the Library of Congress', *Film History* 9.3 (1997), pp. 290–99.
2. Peter Decherney, 'Copyright Dupes: Piracy and New Media in Edison v. Lubin (1903)', *Film History* 19.2 (2007), p. 114.
3. See Decherney, and also André Gaudreault, 'The Infringement of Copyright Laws and Its Effects (1900–1906)', in Thomas Elsaesser (ed.), *Early Cinema: Space, Frame, Narrative* (London: BFI, 1990), pp. 114–22.
4. Decherney, p. 118.
5. Charles Musser, *The Emergence of Cinema: The American Screen to 1907* (New York: Scribner's, 1990), p. 375; cited in Steven Maras, 'In Search of "Screenplay": Terminological Traces in the Library of Congress *Catalog of Copyright Entries: Cumulative Series*, 1912–20', *Film History* 21.4 (2009), p. 352.
6. See Maras, p. 353. On the dating of the copyright applications, see Price, pp. 200–02.
7. Quoted in Loughney, 'Appendix', p. 292.
8. Ibid.
9. Ibid., p. 294. For reasons noted previously, however, the word 'scenario' remains problematic.
10. These scenarios are held in the Motion Picture Reading Room, Madison Building, Library of Congress, Washington, D.C., although *The Wedding* was unavailable when I visited in July 2010.
11. Kemp R. Niver (ed.), *Biograph Bulletins 1896–1908* (Los Angeles: Locare Research Group, 1971), p. 160.
12. See Price, p. 205.
13. Claudia Sternberg, *Written for the Screen: The American Motion-Picture Screenplay as Text* (Tübingen: Stauffenburg, 1997), pp. 71–76.
14. There are two exceptions, *The Chicken Thief* and *The Wedding*. For discussion of this point, see Price, pp. 201–07.
15. Loughney, 'In the Beginning', p. 30.
16. Isabelle Raynauld, 'Written Scenarios of Early French Cinema: Screenwriting Practices in the First Twenty Years', *Film History* 9.3 (1997), p. 264.

17. Ibid., p. 262.
18. Ibid., pp. 260–61.
19. Ibid., p. 258.
20. Ibid., p. 259, Raynauld's emphasis.
21. Ibid., p. 260.
22. Ibid., p. 257.
23. Ibid., p. 258.
24. Loughney, 'Appendix', p. 294.
25. *The Serenade*, scenario by William N. Selig, 1905, LoC.
26. Loughney, 'Appendix', p. 295.
27. Discussion with the author, summer 2010.
28. *From the Manger to the Cross, or Jesus of Nazareth*, scenario by Gene Gauntier, in *What Women Wrote: Scenarios, 1912–1929*, ed. Ann Martin and Virginia M. Clark (Frederick, MD: University Publications of America, 1987).
29. Ann Martin and Virginia M. Clark, 'A Guide to the Microfilm Edition of *What Women Wrote: Scenarios 1912–1929*' (Frederick, MD: University Press of America, 1987), p. 1; Loughney, 'From *Rip van Winkle*', p. 286.
30. Loughney, 'From *Rip Van Winkle*', p. 286.
31. Robert Henderson-Bland, *From Manger to Cross: The Story of the World-Famous Film of the Life of Jesus* (London: Hodder and Stoughton, 1922), p. 30.
32. Loughney, 'Appendix', pp. 298–99.
33. Martin and Clark, 'A Guide', pp. vi, 1.
34. Loughney, 'From *Rip Van Winkle*', p. 286.
35. Ibid.
36. Ibid., p. 287.
37. Ibid.
38. http://www.youtube.com/watch?v=w-y-81BMLA4, accessed 12 February 2013.
39. Torey Liepa, 'An Uneven Marketplace of Ideas: Amateur Screenwriting, the Library of Congress and the Struggle for Copyright', *Journal of Screenwriting* 2.2 (2011), pp. 185–86.
40. Henderson-Bland, p. 74.
41. Loughney, 'From *Rip Van Winkle*', pp. 282–83.
42. In David Bordwell, Janet Staiger, and Kristin Thompson, *The Classical Hollywood Cinema: Film Style and Mode of Production to 1960* (London: Routledge, 1985), pp. 121–27.

3   Outlines and Scenarios, 1904–17

1. Tom Stempel, *FrameWork: A History of Screenwriting in the American Film*, 2nd ed. (New York: Continuum, 1991), p. 8.
2. http://supreme.justia.com/cases/federal/us/222/55/, accessed 14 February 2013.
3. 'The "Ben Hur" Case', *The Bioscope*, 22 February 1912, p. 533; quoted in Torey Liepa, 'An Uneven Marketplace of Ideas: Amateur Screenwriting, the Library of Congress and the Struggle for Copyright', *Journal of Screenwriting* 2.2 (2011), p. 183.
4. Quoted in Liepa, p. 183.

5. Letter from Drury W. Cooper, on behalf of AM&B, to the Register of Copyrights, 6 December 1904, transcribed in Patrick Loughney, 'Appendix: Selected Examples of Early Scenario/Screenplays in the Library of Congress', *Film History* 9.3 (1997), p. 292.

6. For a detailed critical summary, see Steven Maras, *Screenwriting: History, Theory and Practice* (London: Wallflower, 2009), pp. 139–40.

7. Liepa, 'Uneven', p. 180.

8. Maras, pp. 140–41; Torey Liepa, 'Entertaining the Public Option: The Popular Film Writing Movement and the Emergence of Writing for the American Silent Cinema', in Jill Nelmes (ed.), *Analysing the Screenplay* (London: Routledge, 2011), esp. pp. 17–20.

9. Edward Azlant, *The Theory, History, and Practice of Screenwriting, 1897–1920*, diss. (Ann Arbor, Mich.: University Microfilms International, 1980), p. 82.

10. Epes Winthrop Sargent, *The Technique of the Photoplay*, 2nd ed. (New York: The Moving Picture World, 1913), p. 8; quoted in Janet Staiger, 'The Hollywood Mode of Production to 1930', in David Bordwell, Janet Straiger and Kristin Thompson (eds), *The Classical Hollywood Cinema: Film Style and Mode of Production to 1960* (London: Routledge, 1985), p. 118.

11. Staiger, 'The Hollywood Mode of Production to 1930', p. 117.

12. Gene Gauntier, 'Blazing the Trail', *Woman's Home Companion* 55.11 (November 1928), p. 181; quoted in Staiger, 'The Hollywood Mode of Production to 1930', p. 119.

13. Louella Parsons, *The Gay Illiterate* (Garden City, NY: Doubleday, 1944) p. 21; quoted in Stempel, p. 11.

14. Staiger, 'The Hollywood Mode of Production to 1930', p. 119.

15. Ibid., p. 126.

16. The autobiographical information about Dawley in this paragraph is drawn from the 'career information' folder, J. Searle Dawley papers, 1-f.18, MHL.

17. *Earthwork Construction Story*, scenario, 19 July 1911, J. Searle Dawley papers, 1.f-1, MHL.

18. Stempel, p. 15.

19. Ibid., p. 19.

20. The MHL has helpfully inserted a copy of the *Kinetogram* blurb into the relevant folder of each of the Dawley films.

21. Quoted in David Emrich, *Hollywood, Colorado: The Selig Polyscope Company and The Colorado Motion Picture Company* (Lakewood, Colorado: Post Modern Company, 1997), p. 14.

22. James E. McQuage, 'Making "Selig" Pictures', *Film Index* 4.47 (November 20, 1909), pp. 4–6; reprinted in Kalton C. Lahue, ed., *Motion Picture Pioneer: The Selig Polyscope Company* (Cranbury, N.J.: A.S. Barnes, 1973), pp. 57–63. The quotation is on p. 58.

23. *Across the Plains*, scenario by Chris Lane, William Selig Papers, 9-f.155, MHL.

24. *The Argonauts*, scenario, William Selig papers, 9-f.162, MHL.

25. *The Argonauts*, cutting continuity, William Selig papers, 9-f.163, MHL.

26. *The Crooked Path*, cutting continuity, William Selig papers, 10-f.204, MHL.

27. *The Cowboy's Baby*, cutting continuity, William Selig papers, 10-f.201, MHL.

28. *The Engineer's Daughter*, cutting continuity, William Selig papers, 11-f.222, MHL.

29. *Aunt Elsa's Visit* (Edison, 1913): scenario, 10 January 1913; synopsis, 31 January 1913; titles, 17 February 1913, MoMA.
30. Cari Beauchamp and Anita Mary Loos, *Anita Loos Rediscovered: Film Treatments and Fiction by Anita Loos* (Berkeley: University of California Press, 2003), p. 33.
31. Ibid., p. 33.
32. *Her Nature Dance*, Mack Sennett papers, 29-f.272, MHL.
33. *Done in Oil*, Mack Sennett papers, 16-f.148, MHL.
34. *A Clever Dummy*, Mack Sennett papers, 12-f.104, MHL.

4   The Continuity Script, 1912–29

1. See, for example, Janet Staiger, 'Blueprints for Feature Films: Hollywood's Continuity Scripts', in Tino Balio (ed.), *The American Film Industry*, rev. ed. (Madison: University of Wisconsin Press, 1985), p. 180.
2. Ibid., p. 190.
3. John Emerson and Anita Loos, *How to Write Photoplays* (New York: James A. McCann, 1920), pp. 30, 32.
4. Janet Staiger, 'The Hollywood Mode of Production, 1930–60', in David Bordwell, Janet Staiger and Kristin Thompson (eds), *The Classical Hollywood Cinema: Film Style and Mode of Production to 1960* (London: Routledge, 1985), p. 146.
5. Louis Delluc, 'Scénarii', *Comoedia* 3763 (6 April 1923), p. 4; quoted in Kristin Thompson, 'Early Alternatives to the Hollywood Mode of Production: Implications for Europe's Avant-Gardes', in Lee Grieveson and Peter Krämer, eds., *The Silent Cinema Reader* (London: Routledge, 2004), p. 352.
6. Juan Arroy, 'La Monteuse', *Cinémagazine* 5.39 (25 September 1925), p. 519; quoted in Thompson, p. 353.
7. Thompson, pp. 352–53.
8. Patrick McGilligan, *Backstory: Interviews with Screenwriters of Hollywood's Golden Age* (Berkeley: University of California Press, 1986), p. 102.
9. Janet Staiger, 'Dividing Labor for Production Control: Thomas Ince and the Rise of the Studio System', *Cinema Journal* 18 (Spring 1979), p. 19.
10. Torey Liepa, 'An Uneven Marketplace of Ideas: Amateur Screenwriting, the Library of Congress and the Struggle for Copyright', *Journal of Screenwriting* 2.2 (2011), p. 190.
11. Torey Liepa, 'The Devil in the Details: Thomas Ince, Intertitles, and the Institutionalization of Writing in American Cinema', in Cynthia Lucia, Roy Grundmann, and Art Simon, (eds) *The Wiley-Blackwell History of American Film*, vol. 1: *Origins to 1928* (Malden, MA: Blackwell, 2012), p. 271.
12. Staiger, 'Dividing Labor', p. 21.
13. Edward Azlant, *The Theory, History, and Practice of Screenwriting, 1897–1920*, diss. (University of Wisconsin–Madison) (Ann Arbor, Michigan: University Microfilms International, 1980), pp. 162–63.
14. Tom Stempel, *FrameWork: A History of Screenwriting in the American Film*, 2nd ed. (New York: Continuum, 1991), p. 42.
15. George C. Pratt reproduces the whole of what he terms the 'shooting script' of *Satan McAllister's Heir*, including the cast and location lists and cost sheet, as well as the scenario, in *Spellbound in Darkness: Readings in the History and*

Criticism of the Silent Film, vol. 1 (Rochester, NY: University of Rochester Press, 1966), pp. 135–55.

16. Stempel, p. 42.
17. B. F. Barrett, 'A Talk with C. Gardner Sullivan', *Motography* 16.23 (1916), p. 1237; quoted in Liepa, 'The Devil', p. 279.
18. Staiger, 'Dividing Labor', p. 20; Stempel, pp. 43–44.
19. Stempel, p. 44.
20. Azlant, p. 172.
21. Ibid., p. 326.
22. Liepa, 'The Devil', p. 275.
23. Ibid., pp. 283–85.
24. *The Immigrant*, scenario by Marion Fairfax, Marion Fairfax papers, 1-f.6, MHL.
25. B. F. Barrett, 'A Talk with C. Gardner Sullivan', *Motography* 16.23 (1916), pp. 1237–38; quoted in Liepa, 'The Devil', p. 279.
26. Azlant, p. 322.
27. *The Immigrant*, scenario by Marion Fairfax, Paramount scripts, MHL.
28. Cari Beauchamp, *Without Lying Down: Frances Marion and the Powerful Women of Early Hollywood* (New York: Scribner, 1997), p. 79.
29. DeWitt Bodeen, interview with Frances Marion, *Film in Review* (Feb.-Mar 1969), pp. 138–42; quoted in Marsha McCreadie, *The Women Who Write the Movies: From Frances Marion to Nora Ephron* (New York: Birch Lane, 1994), p. 28.
30. Beauchamp, p. 175.
31. *The Scarlet Letter*, treatment by Wyndham Gittens, 1 July 1925, Turner/MGM scripts, 2526-f. S-286, MHL.
32. The present account draws on the studio original: *The Scarlet Letter*, complete OK screenplay by Frances Marion, 30 December 1925, Turner/MGM scripts, 2526-f. S288, MHL. Exactly the same text is reproduced in *Motion Picture Continuities*, intro. Frances Taylor Patterson (New York: Columbia UP, 1929), except that the latter slightly alters the punctuation in places, as well as the numbering, because the original ascribes a shot number to the opening 'TITLE' ('A Sunday morning in Spring') and the published text does not.
33. Beauchamp, pp. 176–77.
34. Marsha McCreadie, *The Women Who Write the Movies: From Frances Marion to Nora Ephron* (New York: Birch Lane, 1994), p. 32.
35. *Love or Justice* (Kay-Bee, 1917), continuity (extracts), http://www.wcftr. commarts.wisc.edu/collections/featured/aitken/continuity/, accessed 7 February 2013.
36. Stempel (p.44) notes the alternative possibility that they indicate 'Ince's approval of rough cuts'.
37. Liepa, 'The Devil', p. 289.

5   The Silent Film Script in Europe

1. Ian W. Macdonald, 'Screenwriting in Britain 1895–1929', in Jill Nelmes (ed.), *Analysing the Screenplay* (London: Routledge, 2011), p. 45.
2. Quoted in Macdonald, pp. 47, 49.

3. Ian W. Macdonald and Jacob U. U. Jacob, 'Lost and Gone for Ever? The Search for Early British Screenplays', *Journal of Screenwriting* 2.2 (2011), pp. 161–77.
4. Macdonald, 'Screenwriting in Britain', p. 55.
5. Ibid., p. 54.
6. Conversation with the author.
7. Richard Abel, 'People 1890–1930: The Men and Women Who Made French Cinema', in Michael Temple and Michael Witt (eds), *The French Cinema Book* (London: British Film Institute, 2004), p. 25.
8. Quoted in Kristin Thompson, 'Early Alternatives to the Hollywood Mode of Production: Implications for Europe's Avant-Gardes', in Lee Grieveson and Peter Krämer (eds), *The Silent Cinema Reader* (London: Routledge, 2004), p. 351.
9. Colin Crisp, *The Classic French Cinema, 1930–1960* (Bloomington: Indiana University Press, 1993), pp. 285–86.
10. Quoted in Thompson, p. 354.
11. Alexander Schwarz, *Der Geschriebene Film: Drehbücher des Deutschen und Russischen Stummfilms* (Munich: Diskurs Film, 1994), pp. 43–44, 51–52.
12. Schwarz, pp. 104–07.
13. Viktor Shklovsky, 'The Film Factory (Extracts)', in Richard Taylor and Ian Christie (eds), *The Film Factory: Russian and Soviet Cinema in Documents, 1896–1939* (London: Routledge, 1988), p. 167.
14. Jürgen Kasten, 'Green Kisses and the Laughing Horror of the Big Lie: On Darkness in Film History, on Screenplays and Lost Films', in Michael Omasta, Brigitte Mayr and Christian Cargnelli (eds), *Carl Mayer Scenar[t]ist: Ein Script von Ihm War Schon ein Film: "A Script by Carl Mayer Was Already a Film"* (Vienna: Synema, 2003), pp. 97–99.
15. Hermann Kappelhoff, 'Literary Exploration of the Cinematographic Image: Carl Mayer and the Poetry of Weimar Cinema', in Omasta, p. 169.
16. Siegfied Kracauer, *From Caligari to Hitler: A Psychlogical History of the German Film* (Princeton: Princeton University Press, 1947), p. 96.
17. *Das Cabinet des Dr. Caligari: Drehbuch von Carl Mayer und Hans Janowitz zu Robert Wienes Film von 1919/20* (Berlin: Stiftung Deutsche Kinemathek, 1995).
18. David Robinson, *Das Cabinet des Dr. Caligari* (London: BFI, 1997), p. 14.
19. Kasten, p. 106.
20. Robinson, pp. 17–18; *Drehbuch*, p. 51. The translation used here is Robinson's, but his lineation, in which all the text is left-justified and continues to the right margin, differs from that of the printed German text, which lineates the text as here. Moreover, facsimiles of the original *Drehbuch* indicate that the scene text of both the typewritten and handwritten scenes was offset in the manner indicated, though this has not been preserved in the German print version.
21. Robinson, p. 19; *Drehbuch*, pp. 52–53.
22. Dietrich Scheunemann, 'Once More on Wiene's *The Cabinet of Dr. Caligari*', in Dietrich Scheunemann (ed.), *Expressionist Film: New Perspectives* (New York: Camden House, 2003), p. 144.
23. Kappelhoff, p. 177.
24. Kasten, p. 105.

25. Patrick Vonderau, ' "Two Figures Stand High up on a Cliff: Shadowy": On Carl Mayer's Screenplay *Der Gang in die Nacht*', in Omasta, p. 114.
26. Vonderau, p. 115.
27. Rolf Hempel, *Carl Mayer: Ein Autor Schreibt mit der Kamera* (Berlin: Henschelverlag, 1968), pp. 111–28.
28. Schwarz, pp. 305–06.
29. AFI SP.COL. #27, v.5. The English text is a translation of Mayer's German-language *Lied von Zwei Menschen*, held in the same archive (#27, v.4). A facsimile of Murnau's copy of Mayer's text, complete with the director's handwritten annotations, has been published in *Sunrise (Sonnenaufgang): Ein Drehbuch von Carl Mayer mit handschriftlichen Bemerkungen von Friedrich Wilhelm Murnau* (Wiesbaden: Deutschen Institut für Filmkunde, 1971).
30. Lucy Fischer, *Sunrise: A Song of Two Humans* (London: BFI, 1998), p. 12.
31. Robert C. Allen and Douglas Gomery, *Film History: Theory and Practice* (New York: Knopf, 1985), pp. 91–92.
32. Allen and Gomery, p. 102.
33. Thomas Elsaesser (ed.), *The BFI Companion to German Cinema* (London: BFI, 1999), pp. 172–73.
34. Fischer, p. 52.
35. Richard Taylor, *The Politics of the Soviet Cinema, 1917–1929* (Cambridge: Cambridge University Press, 1979), p. 9.
36. Denise J. Youngblood, *Soviet Cinema in the Silent Era, 1918–1935* (Ann Arbor: UMI Research Press, 1985), p. 13.
37. Youngblood, p. 25.
38. Viktor Pertsov, 'Literature and Cinema' [1927], in Richard Taylor and Ian Christie (eds), *The Film Factory: Russian and Soviet Cinema in Documents, 1896–1939* (London: Routledge, 1988), pp. 164–66.
39. 'Sovkino Workers' Conference Resolution: Sovkino's New Course (Extract)', in Taylor and Christie, p. 243.
40. Vsevolod Pudovkin, 'The Film Script (The Theory of the Script)', in Richard Taylor (ed.), *Vsevolod Pudovkin: Selected Essays* (London: Seagull, 2006), pp. 33–35.
41. Quoted in Youngblood, p. 68.
42. Quoted in Thompson, p. 360.
43. Thompson, p. 360.
44. Maria Belodubrovskaya, 'Plotlessness: Lessons in Soviet Screenwriting', conference paper, 6th Screenwriting Research Network conference: Screenwriting in a Global & Digital World, Madison, Wisconsin, 21 August 2013.
45. Taylor, *Vsevolod Pudovkin*, p. 301, n. 24.
46. Youngblood, pp. 133–38.
47. Sergei Eisenstein, 'The Form of the Script', in *Selected Works, vol. 1: Writings, 1922–34*, trans. and ed. Richard Taylor (London: BFI, 1988), pp. 134–35.
48. Schwarz, pp. 282–85.
49. Richard Taylor, *The Politics of the Soviet Cinema, 1917–1929* (Cambridge: Cambridge University Press, 1979), p. 34.
50. Taylor, *Politics*, p. 34.
51. See Jay Leyda and Zina Voynow, *Eisenstein at Work* (New York: Pantheon, 1982).

52. Leyda and Voynow, p. 23.
53. Quoted in *Sergei Eisenstein: Three Scripts* [*Battleship Potemkin, October* and *Alexander Nevsky*], ed. Jay Leyda, trans. Diana Matias (London: Lorrimer, 1974), p. 13. Subsequent quotations from Eisenstein's scripts are from this edition.
54. Leyda, in *Sergei Eisenstein: Three Scripts*, p. 15.
55. Ibid., p. 49.
56. Schwarz, p. 342.
57. Leyda and Voynow, pp. 38–40.

6   The Coming of Sound

1. *The Jazz Singer*, ed. Robert L. Carringer (Madison: University of Wisconsin Press, 1979).
2. Edwin Scallert, 'Vitaphone Activity in Hollywood', *Motion Picture News*, 8 July 1927, pp. 35–36; reprinted in *The Jazz Singer*, pp. 175–79.
3. *The Shopworn Angel*, Howard Estabrook papers, 10-f.132, MHL.
4. *The Shopworn Angel*, final continuity by Howard Estabrook, 6 September 1928, Paramount scripts, MHL.
5. *The Shopworn Angel*, Howard Estabrook papers, 10-f.133, MHL.
6. Mordaunt Hall, 'The Screen', *New York Times*, 1 January 1929, p. 61.
7. Edwin Schallert, 'Pathos of Love Story Stressed', *Los Angeles Times*, 14 January 1929, p. A7.
8. ' "Gag" Men May Take Hope', *Los Angeles Times*, 13 January 1929, p. C16.
9. *The Last of Mrs. Cheyney*, complete OK screenplay (silent version) by Hans Kraly, 22 February 1929, Turner/MGM scripts, 1635-f. L295, MHL.
10. *The Last of Mrs. Cheyney*, complete OK screenplay (sound version) by Hans Kraly and Claudine West, 2 March 1929, Turner/MGM scripts, 1635-f. L297, MHL. No continuity writer is credited on either the sequence synopsis or the continuity for this version; the MHL inventory credits the sound version to Kraly and West.
11. The following discussion of Hughes' plans for the film draws on Donald L. Barlett and James B. Steele, *Empire: The Life, Legend, and Madness of Howard Hughes* (New York: Norton, 1979), esp. p. 66, and Charles Higham, *Howard Hughes: The Secret Life* (New York: G.B. Putnam, 1993), esp. pp. 46–49.
12. *Hell's Angels*, dialogue script by Joseph Moncure March, undated, Howard Estabrook papers, 8-f.92, MHL.
13. *Hell's Angels*, 'final' script by Howard Estabrook, September 27, 1929, Howard Estabrook papers, 8-f.94, MHL.
14. *Hell's Angels*, continuity of silent version compiled by Douglas Biggs, August 26, 1929, Howard Estabrook papers, 8-f.91, MHL.
15. *Broadway Melody* (MGM, 1929), continuity by Sarah Y. Mason, September 11, 1928, Victor Heerman papers, 1-f.13, MHL.
16. *Gold Diggers of Broadway*, undated [1929] continuity, AMPAS unpublished scripts collection, MHL.
17. See *42nd Street*, ed. Rocco Fumento (Madison: University of Wisconsin Press, 1980), pp. 14–21.
18. *42nd Street*, p. 193.

19. *42nd Street* folder, Warner Brothers collection, USC. See also Steven Price, *The Screenplay: Authorship, Theory and Criticism* (Basingstoke: Palgrave, 2010), pp. 104–05.

7   The Hollywood Sound Screenplay to 1948

1. Janet Staiger, 'The Hollywood Mode of Production, 1930–60', in David Bordwell, Janet Staiger, and Kristin Thompson (eds), *The Classical Hollywood Cinema: Film Style and Mode of Production to 1960* (London: Routledge, 1985), p. 322.
2. 'Proceedings of the Research Council, Quarterly Meeting, December 15, 1932', *Academy of Motion Picture Arts & Sciences Technical Bulletin*, supplement 19 (23 December 1932), p. 1.
3. Staiger, 'The Hollywood Mode of Production, 1930–60', p. 323.
4. Janet Staiger, 'Blueprints for Feature Films: Hollywood's Continuity Scripts', in Tino Balio (ed.), *The American Film Industry*, rev. ed. (Madison: University of Wisconsin Press, 1985).
5. James Seymour Collection, Writers Guild of America West Records, Writers Guild Foundation Library & Archive. Thanks to Joanne Lammers for drawing this to my attention.
6. Claudia Sternberg, *Written for the Screen: The American Motion-Picture Screenplay as Text* (Tübingen: Stauffenburg, 1997), p. 209.
7. Ibid., p. 75.
8. See, for example, Tom Stempel, *FrameWork: A History of Screenwriting in the American Film*, 2nd ed. (New York: Continuum, 1991), pp. 63–69.
9. *Juárez*, ed. Paul J. Vanderwood (Madison: University of Wisconsin Press, 1983), pp. 83–84.
10. Thomas Schatz, *The Genius of the System: Hollywood Filmmaking in the Studio Era* (New York: Pantheon, 1989), p. 5.
11. Ibid., pp. 7–8.
12. *The Sin of Madelon Claudet* (MGM, 1931), dialogue continuity by Charles MacArthur, Motion Picture Scripts Core Collection, MHL.
13. *Babes in Toyland* (MGM, 1934), screenplay by Frank Butler and Nick Grinde, 'Final Script', 28 July 1934, Motion Picture Scripts Core Collection, MHL.
14. *The Lives of a Bengal Lancer* (Paramount, 1935), Paramount Scripts collection, MHL.
15. *The Bride of Frankenstein* (Universal, 1935), Universal Filmscripts series: Classic Horror Films, Vol. 2, Absecon, NJ: MagicImage Filmbooks, 1989, p. A-4.
16. Petr Szczepanik, 'Micropolitics of Screenplay Development: A Political History', conference paper, Screenwriting in a Global & Digital World, Madison, Wisconsin, 21 August 2013.
17. *How Green Was My Valley* (20th Century Fox, 1941), screenplay by Philip Dunne, '2nd revised Final', 18 April 1941, p. 1.
18. *Laura* (20th Century Fox, 1944), 'Shooting Final, April 18, 1944', 'Screenplay by Jay Dratler, With revisions in this version by Ring Lardner Jr., Samuel Hoffenstein and Betty Reinhardt', BFI S18036, p. 1.
19. "Portrait of Jenny Story Conference", 29 April 1947, David O. Selznick papers, Harry Ransom Research Center, Austin, Texas, p. 2, cited in http://

www.davidbordwell.net/blog/2012/12/17/a-dose-of-dos-trade-secrets-from-selznick/, accessed 12 September 2013.

20. Rudy Behlmer, *Memo from Darryl F. Zanuck: The Golden Years at Twentieth Century-Fox* (New York: Grove, 1993), pp. 173–74; James Curtis, *Between Flops: A Biography of Preston Sturges* (New York: Harcourt, Brace, 1982), p. 173. Both cited in an email from David Bordwell to the author, 21 August 2013.
21. Samson Raphaelson, *Three Screen Comedies by Samson Raphaelson: Trouble in Paradise, the Shop Around the Corner, Heaven Can Wait* (Madison: University of Wisconsin Press, 1983).
22. John Howard Lawson, *Theory and Technique of Playwriting and Screenwriting* (New York: G.P. Putnam's, 1949), p. 370.
23. *Rio Bravo* (WB, 1959), final draft screenplay by Jules Furthman and Leigh Brackett, 26 February 1958, BFI S6285.
24. *Johnny Guitar* (Republic, 1954), screenplay by Philip Yordan, 8 October 1953, Motion Picture Scripts Core Collection, MHL.
25. Schatz, pp. 167–68.
26. *David Copperfield* (MGM, 1935), screen play by Howard Estabrook, adaptation by Hugh Walpole, 8 September 1934, BFI S5237.
27. Howard Estabrook papers, f-58, MHL.
28. George Cukor collection, f-96, MHL.
29. *David Copperfield*, f. D-208 to f. D-223, Turner/MGM scripts, MHL, and Howard Estabrook papers, *David Copperfield*, f-57, MHL.
30. Robert L. Carringer, *The Making of* Citizen Kane, rev. ed. (Berkeley: University of California Press, 1996), p. 26.
31. *The Citizen Kane Book* (London: Secker & Warburg, 1971), p. 91.
32. A facsimile of the first page is reproduced in Carringer, p. 20.
33. *The Citizen Kane Book*, p. 95.
34. On the disputed extent of Welles' involvement in the first draft of *American*, see Carringer, p. 18.
35. Jeff Rush and Cynthia Baughman, 'Language as Narrative Voice: The Poetics of the Highly Inflected Screenplay', *Journal of Film and Video* 49.3 (1997), pp. 28–37

8   European Screenwriting, 1948–60

1. See Mark Shiel, *Italian Neorealism: Rebuilding the Cinematic City* (London: Wallflower, 2006), pp. 26–29, and Peter Bondanella, *A History of Italian Cinema* (New York: Continuum, 2009), pp. 25–26.
2. Quoted in P. Adams Sitney, *Vital Crises in Italian Cinema* (Austin: University of Texas Press, 1985), p. 87.
3. Michael Temple and Michael Witt, eds., *The French Cinema Book* (London: British Film Institute, 2004), p. 177.
4. Cesare Zavattini, 'A Thesis on Neo-Realism' [1952–54], in David Overbey, ed. and trans., *Springtime in Italy: A Reader on Neo-Realism* (London: Talisman, 1978), p. 74.
5. Stefania Parigi, *Cinema—Italy*, trans. Sam Rohdie (Manchester: Manchester University Press, 2009), p. 15.
6. Ibid., p. 19.

7. Bondanella, p. 62.
8. Zavattini, p. 70.
9. Ibid., p. 72.
10. Ibid., p. 73.
11. Ibid., p. 71.
12. Ibid., p. 76.
13. Ibid.
14. These have not been well served by publication, since in most cases the available 'screenplays' are in fact transcriptions of the films. The version of *Bicycle Thieves* in *L'Avant-Scène Cinema* 76 (December 1967) is a description of the film; that in the 'Associazione Amici' text is a technical breakdown of the film, shot by shot. Similarly, the version of *Umberto D* in *L'Avant-Scène du Cinema* (April 1980) is a 'Découpage integral après montage et dialogue in extenso'.
15. Robert S. C. Gordon, *Bicycle Thieves* (London: British Film Institute, 2008), pp. 22–25.
16. A facsimile of p. 289 in Gordon's monograph closes on shot 1,136 (Gordon, p. 35).
17. Gordon, p. 35.
18. Shiel, p. 12.
19. Jacques Aumont et al., *Aesthetics of Film* (Austin: University of Texas Press, 1999), p. 111; quoted in Shiel, p. 55.
20. Shiel, p. 55.
21. Michelangelo Antonioni, *The Architecture of Vision: Writings and Interviews on Cinema*, ed. Carlo di Carlo and Giorgio Tinazzi, trans. Andrew Taylor (New York: Marsilio, 1996), p. 58.
22. Michelangelo Antonioni, 'Introduction', *Screenplays of Michelangelo Antonioni [Il Grido, L'Avventura, La Notte, L'Eclisse]*, trans. Roger J. Moore (New York: Orion, 1963), pp. xiv–xviii.
23. Michelangelo Antonioni, *Unfinished Business: Screenplays, Scenarios and Ideas*, ed. Carlo di Carlo and Giorgio Tinazzi, trans. Andrew Taylor (New York: Marsilio, 1998), pp. 118–19.
24. Birgitta Ingemanson, 'The Screenplays of Ingmar Bergman: Personification and Olfactory Detail', *Literature/Film Quarterly* 12.1 (1984), p. 26.
25. Ingmar Bergman, *Four Screenplays of Ingmar Bergman*, trans. Lars Malmström and David Kushner (New York: Simon and Schuster, 1960), p. 6.
26. John Gassner and Dudley Nichols, eds., *Twenty Best Film Plays* (New York: Crown, 1943). See Steven Price, *The Screenplay: Authorship, Theory and Criticism* (Basingstoke: Palgrave, 2010), pp. 27–28.
27. Birgitta Steene, *Ingmar Bergman: A Reference Guide* (Amsterdam: Amsterdam University Press, 2005), p. 53.
28. Anna Sofia Rossholm, 'Tracing the Voice of the Auteur: *Persona* and the Ingmar Bergman Archive', *Journal of Screenwriting* 4.2 (2013), p. 138.
29. Ingmar Bergman, 'The Snakeskin', in *Persona and Shame*, trans. Keith Bradfield (London: Calder & Boyars, 1972), p. 15.
30. Rossholm, p. 143.
31. Ingmar Bergman, *Wild Strawberries*, trans. Lars Malmström and David Kushner (London: Lorrimer, 1970), p. 7.
32. Ingemanson, p. 32, n. 2.

33. Ibid., p. 28.
34. Bergman, *Four Screenplays*, p. 70; Ingemanson, p. 29.
35. Rossholm, p. 138.
36. Ingemanson, p. 30.
37. Birgitta Steene, *Ingmar Bergman: A Reference Guide* (Amsterdam: Amsterdam University Press, 2005), p. 53.
38. Colin Crisp, *The Classic French Cinema, 1930–1960* (Bloomington: Indiana University Press, 1993), p. 301.
39. Ibid., pp. 301–03.
40. Ibid., pp. 306–07.
41. Claus Tieber, *Schreiben für Hollywood: Das Drehbuch im Studiosystem* (Vienna: Lit Verlag GmbH, 2008).
42. François Truffaut, 'A Certain Tendency of the French Cinema', in Bill Nichols (ed.), *Movies and Methods: An Anthology* (Berkeley: University of California Press, 1976), p. 224.
43. Ibid., p. 229.
44. Ibid., p. 233.
45. Crisp, p. 317.
46. Temple and Witt, p. 94; Crisp, pp. 286–93.
47. Alison Smith, 'People 1960–2004: The Other Auteurs: Producers, Cinematographers and Scriptwriters', in Michael Temple and Michael Witt (eds), *The French Cinema Book* (London: British Film Institute, 2004), p. 204.
48. Ibid.
49. Ibid.
50. Susan Hayward, 'State, Culture and the Cinema: Jack Lang's Strategies for the French Film Industry 1981–93', *Screen* 34.4 (1993), p. 384.
51. François Truffaut, *The Adventures of Antoine Doinel: Four Autobiographical Screenplays* (New York: Simon & Schuster, 1971).
52. Alain Robbe-Grillet, *Last Year at Marienbad: A Ciné-Novel*, trans. Richard Howard (London: Calder, 1961), p. 6.
53. Ibid., p. 16.
54. Chris Marker, *La Jetée* (New York: Zone, 1992).
55. Antonioni, 'Introduction', p. xviii.

9   Master-Scene Screenplays & the 'New Hollywood'

1. Tom Stempel, *FrameWork: A History of Screenwriting in the American Film*, 2nd ed. (New York: Continuum, 1991), p. 156.
2. John Howard Lawson, *Theory and Technique of Playwriting and Screenwriting* (New York: G.P. Putnam's, 1949), p. 367.
3. Quoted in Lawson, pp. 368–69.
4. Ibid., p. 370.
5. Dore Schary [and Charles Palmer], *Case History of a Movie* (New York: Random House, 1950), pp. 59–60.
6. Lewis Herman, *A Practical Manual of Screen Playwriting for Theater and Television Films* [1952] (Cleveland: Forum, 1963), p. 169.
7. Ibid., pp. 170–71.

8. *Outbreak (Panic in the Streets)*, screenplay by Richard Murphy, revised shooting final, 9 February 1950, Motion Picture Scripts Core Collection, MHL.

9. Bridget Boland, *Screen Writing* (London: British Film Institute, 1945). I am grateful to Ian Macdonald for drawing this to my attention.

10. Lindsay Anderson, *Making a Film* (New York: Garland, 1977 [1952]).

11. I am grateful to Jill Nelmes for confirming this point.

12. *Charade* (Stanley Donen Film, 1963), screenplay by Peter Stone, revised draft, 21 August 1962, Motion Picture Scripts Core Collection, MHL.

13. Stempel, pp. 197–207.

14. William Goldman, *Butch Cassidy and the Sundance Kid*, final, 15 July 1968, BFI S18546.

15. William Goldman, *Adventures in the Screen Trade: A Personal View of Hollywood and Screenwriting* [1984] (London: Futura, 1985), pp. 199–205.

16. *Breathless: Jean-Luc Godard, Director*, ed. Dudley Andrew (New Brunswick, N. J.: Rutgers University Press, 1987), p. 27.

17. Matthew Bernstein, 'Perfecting the New Gangster: Writing *Bonnie and Clyde*', *Film Quarterly* 53.4 (2000), pp. 16–31.

18. Lester D. Friedman, *Bonnie and Clyde* (London: British Film Institute, 2000), p. 27.

19. Peter Biskind, *Easy Riders, Raging Bulls: How the Sex 'n' Drugs 'n' Rock 'n' Roll Generation Saved Hollywood* (London: Bloomsbury, 1999), pp. 26–28.

20. John G. Cawelti (ed.), *Focus on Bonnie and Clyde* (Englewood Cliffs, N. J.: Prentice-Hall, 1973), pp. 158–65. Cawelti prints additional excerpts from the shooting script—the first 16 scenes, and the gun battle at Joplin (beginning part-way through scene 100 and continuing through scene 105)—on pp. 151–57. Confusingly, however, Cawelti's otherwise very helpful account of the differences between the film and the 'original script' (pp. 138–45) uses that term to refer variously to both the undated master-scene script and the 6 September shooting script, without always clearly indicating which. Reference to the full shooting script, however, eliminates the confusion: *Bonnie and Clyde*, screenplay by David Newman and Robert Benton, 'Final', 6 September 1966, BFI S4215. This is a copy of the shooting script referred to by Cawelti.

21. Cawelti, p. 142; Arthur Penn, 'Making Waves: The Directing of *Bonnie and Clyde*', in Lester D. Friedman, ed., *Arthur Penn's Bonnie and Clyde* (Cambridge: Cambridge University Press, 1999), pp. 23–24.

22. For the *Easy Rider* production, see Biskind, pp. 61–75.

23. *Easy Rider*, screenplay by Peter Fonda, Dennis Hopper and Terry Southern, Donn Cambern papers, f. 9, MHL; BFI S2715.

24. Peter Cowie, *The Godfather Book* (London: Faber, 1997), p. 28.

25. Jenny M. Jones, *The Annotated Godfather: The Complete Screenplay* (New York: Black Dog & Leventhal, 2007), p. 20.

26. Reproduced in Jones, p. 20.

27. *The Godfather*, screenplay by Mario Puzo and Francis Ford Coppola, third draft, 29 March 1971, BFI 18610.

28. Cowie, pp. 26–27.

29. Paul Schrader, *Taxi Driver* (London: Faber, 1990), p. 4.

10 The Contemporary Screenplay and Screenwriting Manual

1. Peter Biskind, *Easy Riders, Raging Bulls: How the Sex 'n' Drugs 'n' Rock 'n' Roll Generation Saved Hollywood* (London: Bloomsbury, 1999), p. 17.
2. For a range of perspectives on these developments, see the essays in Steve Neale and Murray Smith (eds) *Contemporary Hollywood Cinema* (London: Routledge, 1998).
3. The most sustained study of these matters that is of direct relevance to story structure and the writing manual is Kristin Thompson, *Storytelling in the New Hollywood: Understanding Classical Narrative Technique* (Cambridge, Mass.: Harvard University Press, 1999).
4. Torey Liepa, 'An Uneven Marketplace of Ideas: Amateur Screenwriting, the Library of Congress and the Struggle for Copyright', *Journal of Screenwriting* 2.2 (2011), pp. 180–81.
5. Peter Biskind, *Down and Dirty Pictures: Miramax, Sundance and the Rise of Independent Film* (London: Bloomsbury, 2005).
6. See Kathryn Millard, 'After the Typewriter: The Screenplay in a Digital Era', *Journal of Screenwriting* 1.1 (2010), pp. 15–17.
7. Richard Maltby, ' "Nobody Knows Everything": Post-Classical Historiographies and Consolidated Entertainment', in Neale and Smith, p. 39.
8. Murray Smith, 'Theses on the Philosophy of Hollywood History', in Neale and Smith, p. 12.
9. William Goldman, *Adventures in the Screen Trade: A Personal View of Hollywood and Screenwriting* [1984] (London: Futura, 1985), pp. 151–58.
10. On Lucas's indebtedness to Campbell, see David Bordwell, *The Way Hollywood Tells It: Story and Style in Modern Movies* (Berkeley: University of California Press, 2006), p. 33.
11. William Goldman, 'The Screenwriter', in Jason E. Squire, ed., *The Movie Business Book*, London: Columbus, p. 52; cited in Steven Maras, *Screenwriting: History, Theory and Practice* (London: Wallflower, 2009), p. 79.
12. Some of the most useful or influential manuals consulted for the following discussion are Syd Field, *Screenplay: The Foundations of Screenwriting* (New York: Dell, 1979); Robert McKee, *Story: Substance, Structure, Style, and the Principles of Screenwriting* (London: Methuen, 1998); Lew Hunter, *Screenwriting* (London: Robert Hale, 1994); Michael Hauge, *Writing Screenplays That Sell* (Harmondsworth: Elm Tree, 1989).
13. Bordwell, pp. 28–35.
14. Manuals that explicitly relate Aristotle to screenwriting include Lance Lee, *A Poetics for Screenwriters* (Austin: University of Texas Press, 2001), and Ari Hiltunen, *Aristotle in Hollywood* (Bristol: Intellect Press, 2002).
15. The most influential and explicit appropriation of Campbell is Christopher Vogler, *The Writer's Journey: Mythic Structure for Storytellers and Screenwriters*, 2nd ed. (London: Pan, 1998); also see Stuart Voytilla, *Myth and the Movies: Discovering the Mythic Structure of 50 Unforgettable Films* (Studio City, CA: Michael Wiese Productions, 1999).
16. Joseph Campbell, *The Hero with a Thousand Faces* (Princeton: Princeton UP, 1949), p. 30.
17. Bordwell, p. 28.

18. Field, pp. 8–9.
19. Quoted in Biskind, *Down and Dirty Pictures*, p. 76.
20. Bordwell, p. 28.
21. Thompson, pp. 14, 367.
22. Ibid, pp. 40–42.
23. J. J. Murphy, *Me and You and Memento and Fargo: How Independent Screenplays Work* (New York: Continuum, 2007), p. 17.
24. Paul Joseph Gulino, *Screenwriting: The Sequence Approach* (New York: Continuum, 2004), p. 4.
25. For a full account of the influence of the four-act structure on modern drama, see Austin E. Quigley, *The Modern Stage and Other Worlds* (London: Methuen, 1985).
26. Gulino, pp. 3–4.
27. Roy L. McCardell, *The Pain Flower: A Photoplay Drama of Modern Life* (1915), Warner Brothers archive, USC.
28. Maras, p. 6.
29. Constance Nash and Virginia Oakey, *The Screenwriter's Handbook: What to Write, How to Write It, Where to Sell It* (New York: Barnes and Noble, 1978), p. 44.
30. Hauge, p. 112.
31. Christopher Riley, *The Hollywood Standard: The Complete and Authoritative Guide to Script Format and Style*, 2nd ed. (Studio City, CA: Michael Wiese, 2009), pp. xv–xvi.
32. Joseph McBride, *Writing in Pictures: Screenwriting Made (Mostly) Painless* (New York: Vintage, 2012), pp. 179–80.
33. Hunter, p. 129; Hauge, p. 127.
34. Esther Luttrell, *Tools of the Screen Writing Trade*, rev. ed. (Mt. Dora, Fla.: Broadcast Club of America, 1998), pp. 10, 141; emphasis in the original.
35. Jeff Rush and Cynthia Baughman, 'Language as Narrative Voice: The Poetics of the Highly Inflected Screenplay', *Journal of Film and Video* 49.3 (1997), p. 28.
36. Ann Igelström, 'Communication and the Various Voices of the Screenplay Text', *Journal of Screenwriting* 4.1 (2013), p. 46.
37. Ibid., p. 50.
38. Ibid., p. 48.
39. Ibid., p. 50.
40. Ibid., p. 51.
41. Claudia Sternberg, *Written for the Screen: The American Motion-Picture Screenplay as Text* (Tübingen: Stauffenburg, 1997), p. 84.
42. Sternberg, p. 74.
43. Quentin Tarantino, *Pulp Fiction* (London: Faber, 1994), pp. 86–90.
44. David Mamet, *A Whore's Profession: Notes and Essays* (London: Faber, 1994), p. 383, emphasis in the original.
45. See Steven Price, 'Character in the Screenplay Text', in Jill Nelmes (ed.), *Analysing the Screenplay* (London: Routledge, 2011), pp. 201–16.
46. Charlie Kaufman, *Eternal Sunshine of the Spotless Mind: The Shooting Script* (London: Nick Hern, 2004), p. 8.

47. Jon Ronson, *Lost at Sea: The Jon Ronson Mysteries* (London: Picador, 2012), p. 323.
47. Biskind, *Down and Dirty Pictures*, p. 31.
48. Conversation with the author.
49. Quoted in Biskind, *Down and Dirty Pictures*, p. 21.
50. Ibid., p. 31.
51. *Millennium Film Journal* 25 (Summer 1991), p. 5.
52. Quoted in Biskind, *Down and Dirty Pictures*, p. 76.
53. Kathryn Millard, 'After the Typewriter: The Screenplay in a Digital Era', *Journal of Screenwriting* 1.1 (2010), pp. 11–12.

11   Screenwriting Today and Tomorrow

1. Steven Maras, *Screenwriting: History, Theory and Practice* (London: Wallflower, 2009), p. 171.
2. Ibid.
3. Ray Carney, *The Films of John Cassavetes: Pragmatism, Modernism, and the Movies* (Cambridge: Cambridge University Press, 1994), p. 187.
4. Carney, p. 137.
5. Tom Charity, *John Cassavetes: Lifeworks* (London: Omnibus, 2001), p. xi.
6. Quoted in Raymond Carney, *American Dreaming: The Films of John Cassavetes and the American Experience* (Berkeley: University of California Press, 1985), p. 111.
7. John Cassavetes, *Faces* (New York: Signet, 1970), p. 8.
8. Carney, *American Dreaming*, p. 92.
9. Quoted in Dan Fainaru (ed.), *Theo Angelopoulos: Interviews* (Jackson: University Press of Mississippi, 2001), p. 142.
10. Ibid., pp. 141–42.
11. Ibid., p. 74.
12. Andrew Horton, *The Films of Theo Angelopoulos: A Cinema of Contemplation* (Princeton, N.J.: Princeton UP, 1997), p. 183.
13. Quoted in Fainaru, p. 103.
14. Peter Brunette, *Wong Kar-Wai* (Urbana: University of Illinois Press, 2005), p. 126.
15. Ibid., p. 124.
16. Ibid., p. 125.
17. Quoted in J. J. Murphy, *Me and You and Memento and Fargo: How Independent Screenplays Work* (New York: Continuum, 2007), p. 4.
18. Murphy, pp. 6, 16.
19. Murphy, p. vii.
20. Steven Price, *The Screenplay: Authorship, Theory and Criticism* (Basingstoke: Palgrave, 2010), pp. 22–23.
21. J. J. Murphy, 'Cinema as Provocation: Norman Mailer's Assault on the Screenplay'; Line Langebek and Spencer Parsons, 'Cassavetes' Screenwriting Practice: Improvising the Emotions'; Mark Minett, 'Altman Unscripted?'; John Powers, 'A Pony Not to Be Ridden: Screenwriting and the Avant-Garde Cinema', conference papers, Screenwriting in a Global & Digital World, University of Wisconsin-Madison, 22 August 2013.

22. http://millenniumfilm.org/about/, accessed on 22 February 2013.
23. *Millennium Film Journal* 25 (Summer 1991), p. 5. The following texts considered in this section appear partially or wholly in this issue of *MFJ*: Ann Marie Fleming, *You Take Care Now* (1989), pp. 10–11; John Moritsugu, *Der Elvis* (1987), pp. 37–41; Yvonne Rainer, *Privilege* (1990), pp. 50–55; Lynne Sachs, *The House of Science: A Museum of False Facts* (1991), pp. 58–61.
24. Kathryn Millard, 'The Screenplay as Prototype', in Jill Nelmes (ed.), *Analysing the Screenplay* (London: Routledge, 2011), p. 156.
25. http://www.hitrecord.org/, accessed 19 May 2013.
26. *Casablanca: Inside the Script* (Burbank, CA: Warner Bros. Digital Publishing, 2012), p. 17.
27. Ibid., p. 19.
28. Claudia Sternberg, *Written for the Screen: The American Motion-Picture Screenplay as Text* (Tübingen: Stauffenburg, 1997), p. 28.
29. See also Maaret Koskinen, 'Out of the Past: *Saraband* and the Ingmar Bergman Archive', in Maaret Koskinen, ed., *Ingmar Bergman Revisited*, (London: Wallflower, 2008), pp. 19–34.
30. Anna Sofia Rossholm, 'Tracing the Voice of the Auteur: *Persona* and the Ingmar Bergman Archive', *Journal of Screenwriting* 4.2 (2013), p. 135.
31. Ibid., p. 136.
32. Ibid., p. 137.
33. http://www.guardian.co.uk/culture/video/2011/jun/07/ipad-apple-the-wasteland-apps-video, accessed on 6 February 2013.
34. For a discussion of McGann in relation to screenwriting, see Price, pp. 100–02.
35. Daniel Ferrer and Michael Groden, 'Introduction: A Genesis of French Genetic Criticism', in Jed Deppman, Daniel Ferrer and Michael Groden (eds), *Genetic Criticism: Texts and Avant-texts* (Philadelphia: University of Pennsylvania Press, 2004), p. 2.
36. See Steven Price, 'The Screenplay: An Accelerated Critical History', *Journal of Screenwriting* 4.1 (2013), pp. 94–95.

Conclusion: The Screenplay as a Modular Text

1. Judith H. Haag and Hillis R. Cole Jr., ed., *The Complete Guide to Standard Script Formats, Part 1: The Screenplay* (Los Angeles: CMC, 1980), pp. 111–14.
2. Janet Staiger, 'The Hollywood Mode of Production, 1930–60', in David Bordwell, Janet Staiger and Kristin Thompson (eds), *The Classical Hollywood Cinema: Film Style and Mode of Production to 1960* (London: Routledge, 1985), p. 330.

Bibliography

Abbreviations

BFI: Reuben Library, British Film Institute, London.
LoC: Motion Picture Reading Room, Madison Building, Library of Congress, Washington, D.C.
MHL: Margaret Herrick Library, Academy of Motion Picture Arts and Sciences, Los Angeles.
MoMA: Film Study Center, Museum of Modern Art, New York.
USC: University of Southern California, Los Angeles.

Primary

42nd Street (WB, 1933), ed. Rocco Fumento, Madison: University of Wisconsin Press, 1980. This reprints the 'final' continuity credited to Rian James and James Seymour. See also the cutter's copy of the 'final—master' continuity, 22 September 1932, Warner Brothers archive, USC.

Across the Plains (Selig Polyscrope Co., 1910), scenario by Chris Lane, William Selig Papers, 9-f.155, MHL; handwritten cutting continuity by Otis Turner, William Selig Papers, 9-f.156, MHL.

Anita Loos Rediscovered: Film Treatments and Fiction by Anita Loos, ed. Cari Beauchamp and Anita Mary Loos, Berkeley: University of California Press, 2003.

Antonioni, Michelangelo, *Screenplays of Michelangelo Antonioni*, trans. Roger J. Moore, New York: Orion, 1963.

Antonioni, Michelangelo, *Unfinished Business: Screenplays, Scenarios and Ideas*, ed. Carlo di Carlo and Giorgio Tinazzi, trans. Andrew Taylor, New York: Marsilio, 1998.

Argonauts, The (General Film Co., 1911), scenario, William Selig papers, 9-f.162, MHL; cutting continuity, William Selig papers, 9-f.163, MHL.

Aunt Elsa's Visit (Edison, 1913), scenario, 10 January 1913; synopsis, 31 January 1913; titles, 17 February 1913, MoMA.

Babes in Toyland (MGM, 1934), screenplay by Frank Butler and Nick Grinde, 'Final Script', 28 July 1934, Motion Picture Scripts Core Collection, MHL.

Bergman, Ingmar, *Four Screenplays of Ingmar Bergman*, trans. Lars Malmström and David Kushner, New York: Simon & Schuster, 1960.

Bergman, Ingmar, Persona *and* Shame, trans. Keith Bradfield, London: Calder & Boyars, 1972.

Bergman, Ingmar, *Wild Strawberries*, trans. Lars Malmström and David Kushner, London: Lorrimer, 1970.

Bonnie and Clyde, screenplay by David Newman and Robert Benton, 'Final', 6 September 1966, BFI S4215.

Bride of Frankenstein, The (Universal, 1935), Universal Filmscripts series: Classic horror films—Vol. 2, Absecon, NJ: MagicImage Filmbooks, 1989.

Broadway (Universal, 1929), Screen Play and Dialogue Arrangement by Edward T. Lowe, Jr., Cinema-Television Library, USC.

Broadway Melody (MGM, 1929), continuity by Sarah Y. Mason, 11 September 1928, Victor Heerman papers, 1-f.13, MHL.

Butch Cassidy and the Sundance Kid, screenplay by William Goldman, final, 15 July 1968, BFI S18546.

Cabinet des Dr. Caligari, Das: Drehbuch von Carl Mayer und Hans Janowitz zu Robert Wienes Film von 1919/20, Berlin: Stiftung Deutsche Kinemathek, 1995.

Casablanca: Inside the Script, Burbank, CA: Warner Bros. Digital Publishing, 2012.

Charade (Stanley Donen Film, 1963), screenplay by Peter Stone revised draft, 21 August 1962, Motion Picture Scripts Core Collection, MHL.

Chicken Thief, The, scenario by Frank J. Marion and Wallace McCutcheon, 1904, LoC.

Chinatown, by Robert Towne, 3rd draft, 9 October 1973, BFI S17788; published in Robert Towne, Chinatown *and* The Last Detail, London: Faber, 1998.

Citizen Kane: The Shooting Script, by Herman J. Mankiewicz and Orson Welles, in *The Citizen Kane Book*, London: Secker & Warburg, 1971.

Clever Dummy, A (Triangle, 1917), Mack Sennett papers, 12.f-104, MHL.

Cowboy's Baby, The (Selig Polyscope Co., 1908), cutting continuity, William Selig papers, 10-f.201, MHL.

Crooked Path, The (Selig Polyscope, 1909), cutting continuity, William Selig papers, 10-f.204, MHL.

David Copperfield (MGM, 1935), Turner/MGM scripts, f. D-208 to f. D-223, MHL; Howard Estabrook papers, f-57, MHL; screenplay by Howard Estabrook, adaptation by Hugh Walpole, 8 September 1934, BFI S5237.

Done in Oil (Triangle, 1917), Mack Sennett papers, 16.f-148, MHL.

Earthwork Construction Story, scenario, 19 July 1911, J. Searle Dawley papers, 1.f-1, MHL.

Easy Rider, screenplay by Peter Fonda, Dennis Hopper, and Terry Southern, Donn Cambern papers, f. 9, MHL; BFI S2715.

Engineer's Daughter, The (Selig Polyscope, 1909), cutting continuity, William Selig papers, 11-f.222, MHL.

Eternal Sunshine of the Spotless Mind: The Shooting Script, screenplay by Charlie Kaufman, London: Nick Hern, 2004.

Faces [1968], treatment by John Cassavetes, New York: Signet, 1970.

From the Manger to the Cross, or Jesus of Nazareth, scenario by Gene Gauntier, in *What Women Wrote: Scenarios, 1912–1929*, ed. Ann Martin and Virginia M. Clark, Frederick, MD: University Publications of America, 1987.

Godfather, The, screenplay by Mario Puzo and Francis Ford Coppola, third draft, 29 March 1971, BFI 18610.

Gold Diggers of Broadway (WB, 1929), undated continuity, 'Screen Play by Robert Lord', AMPAS unpublished scripts collection, MHL.

Hell's Angels (Caddo, 1930): continuity of silent version compiled by Douglas Biggs, 26 August 1929, 8-f.91; dialogue script by Joseph Moncure March, undated, 8-f.92; final script by Howard Estabrook, 27 September 1929, 8-f.94; all Howard Estabrook papers, MHL.

Her Nature Dance (Triangle, 1917), Mack Sennett papers, 29.f-272, MHL.

How Green Was My Valley (20th Century Fox, 1941), screenplay by Philip Dunne, '2nd revised Final', 18 April 1941, BFI S16392.

Immigrant, The (Paramount, 1915), scenario by Marion Fairfax, Marion Fairfax papers, 1-f.6, MHL; Paramount scripts, MHL.

Jazz Singer, The [Warner Brothers, 1927], Adaptation and Continuity by Alfred A. Cohn, ed. Robert L. Carringer, Madison: University of Wisconsin Press, 1979.

Jetée, La, by Chris Marker, New York: Zone, 1992.

Johnny Guitar (Republic, 1954), screenplay by Philip Yordan, 8 October 1953, Motion Picture Scripts Core Collection, MHL.

Juárez (WB, 1939), by John Huston, Aeneas MacKenzie and Wolfgang Reinhardt, ed. Paul J. Vanderwood, Madison: University of Wisconsin Press, 1983.

Last of Mrs. Cheyney, The, complete OK screenplay (silent version) by Hans Kraly, 22 February 1929, Turner/MGM scripts, 1635-f. L295, MHL; complete OK screenplay (sound version) by Hans Kraly and Claudine West, 2 March 1929, Turner/MGM scripts, 1635-f. L297, MHL.

Last Year at Marienbad: A Ciné-Novel, by Alain Robbe-Grillet, trans. Richard Howard, London: Calder, 1961.

Laura (20th Century Fox, 1944), 'Shooting Final, April 18, 1944', screenplay by Jay Dratler, with revisions by Ring Lardner Jr., Samuel Hoffenstein and Betty Reinhardt. BFI S18036.

Little Caesar (WB, 1931), ed. Gerald Peary, Madison: University of Wisconsin Press, 1981.

Lives of a Bengal Lancer (Paramount, 1935), drafts from 28 November 1932 to 22 September 1934, Paramount Scripts collection, MHL.

Lost Horizon (Columbia, 1936), screenplay by Robert Riskin, 'Final Draft March 23, 1936', AMPAS unpublished scripts collection, MHL.

Love or Justice (Kay-Bee, 1917), continuity (extracts), http://www.wcftr.commarts. wisc.edu/collections/featured/aitken/continuity/, accessed 7 February 2013.

New Stenographer, The, scenario by J. Stuart Blackton (Vitagraph, 1911), LoC.

Nihilists, The, unpublished scenario by Frank J. Marion and Wallace McCutcheon, (AM&B, 1905), LoC.

Outbreak (Panic in the Streets), screenplay by Richard Murphy, revised shooting final, 9 February 1950, Motion Picture Scripts Core Collection, MHL.

Pain Flower, The: A Photoplay Drama of Modern Life, scenario by Roy L. McCardell (1915), Warner Brothers archive, USC.

Pulp Fiction, screenplay by Quentin Tarantino, London: Faber, 1994.

Ride with Billy, A [c. 1915?], by Anita Loos, in Cari Beauchamp and Anita Mary Loos, eds, *Anita Loos Rediscovered: Film Treatments and Fiction by Anita Loos*, Berkeley: University of California Press, 2003, pp. 33–35.

Rio Bravo (WB, 1959), final draft screenplay by Jules Furthman and Leigh Brackett, 26 February 1958, BFI S6285.

Scarlet Letter, The, complete OK screenplay by Frances Marion, 30 December 1925, Turner/MGM scripts, 2526-f. S288, MHL; treatment by Wyndham Gittens, 1 July 1925, Turner/MGM scripts, 2526-f. S-286, MHL.

Screen Writings: Scripts and Texts by Independent Filmmakers, ed. Scott MacDonald, Berkeley: University of California Press, 1995.

Serenade, The, unpublished scenario by William N. Selig, 1905, LoC.

Sergei Eisenstein: Three Scripts [*Battleship Potemkin, October* and *Alexander Nevsky*], ed. Jay Leyda, trans. Diana Matias, London: Lorrimer, 1974.

Shopworn Angel, The (Paramount, 1928]), final screenplay, adaptation and continuity by Howard Estabrook, 6 September 1928, with revisions to 8 September
1928, Howard Estabrook papers, 10-f.132, MHL; Paramount scripts, MHL; script
revisions, Howard Estabrook papers, 10-f.133, MHL.

Sin of Madelon Claudet, The (MGM, 1931), dialogue continuity by Charles
MacArthur, Motion Picture Scripts Core Collection, MHL.

Sunrise, photoplay by Carl Mayer, Special Collections, Louis B. Mayer Library,
American Film Institute, Los Angeles, no. 27, v.5. The English text is a translation of Mayer's German-language *Lied von Zwei Menschen*, held in the same
archive (no. 27, v.4). A facsimile of Murnau's copy of Mayer's German text,
complete with the director's handwritten annotations, has been published
as *Sunrise (Sonnenaufgang): Ein Drehbuch von Carl Mayer mit handschriftlichen
Bemerkungen von Friedrich Wilhelm Murnau*, Wiesbaden: Deutschen Institut für
Filmkunde, 1971.

Taxi Driver, by Paul Schrader, 29 April 1975, BFI S18179; published in slightly
modified form as Paul Schrader, *Taxi Driver*, London: Faber, 1990.

*Three Screen Comedies by Samson Raphaelson: Trouble in Paradise, the Shop Around
the Corner, Heaven Can Wait*, Wisconsin/Warner Brothers Screenplay Series,
Madison: University of Wisconsin Press, 1983.

Tom, Tom, the Piper's Son, scenario by Frank J. Marion and Wallace McCutcheon,
1905, LoC.

Truffaut, François, *The Adventures of Antoine Doinel: Four Autobiographical
Screenplays*, New York: Simon & Schuster, 1971.

Wanted: A Dog, scenario by Frank J. Marion and Wallace McCutcheon, 1905, LoC.

What Women Wrote: Scenarios, 1912–1929, ed. Ann Martin and Virginia M. Clark,
Frederick, MD: University Publications of America, 1987.

Secondary

Abel, Richard, 'People 1890–1930: The Men and Women Who Made French Cinema', in Michael Temple and Michael Witt (eds), *The French Cinema Book*,
London: British Film Institute, 2004, pp. 18–33.

Allen, Robert C., and Douglas Gomery, *Film History: Theory and Practice*, New York:
Knopf, 1985.

Anderson, Lindsay, *Making a Film*, New York: Garland, 1977 [1952].

Andrew, Dudley, ed., *Breathless: Jean-Luc Godard, Director*, New Brunswick, N.J.:
Rutgers University Press, 1987.

Anon., 'The Confessions of a Scenario Editor', *Photoplay* (August 1914), p. 166.

Antonioni, Michelangelo, 'Introduction', *Screenplays of Michelangelo Antonioni [Il
Grido, L'Avventura, La Notte, L'Eclisse]*, trans. Roger J. Moore, New York: Orion,
1963.

Antonioni, Michelangelo, *The Architecture of Vision: Writings and Interviews on Cinema*, ed. Carlo di Carlo and Giorgio Tinazzi, trans. Andrew Taylor, New York:
Marsilio, 1996.

Aronson, Linda, *The 21st Century Screenplay: A Comprehensive Guide to Writing
Tomorrow's Films*, Los Angeles: Silman-James, 2010.

Azlant, Edward, *The Theory, History, and Practice of Screenwriting, 1897–1920*, diss.,
Ann Arbor, Mich.: University Microfilms International, 1980.

Barlett, Donald L., and James B. Steele, *Empire: The Life, Legend, and Madness of Howard Hughes*, New York: Norton, 1979.

Beauchamp, Cari, *Without Lying Down: Frances Marion and the Powerful Women of Early Hollywood*, New York: Scribner, 1997.

Belodubrovskaya, Maria, 'Plotlessness: Lessons in Soviet Screenwriting', conference paper, 6th Screenwriting Research Network conference: Screenwriting in a Global & Digital World, Madison, Wisconsin, 21 August 2013.

Bernstein, Matthew, 'Perfecting the New Gangster: Writing *Bonnie and Clyde*', *Film Quarterly* 53.4 (2000), pp. 16–31.

Biskind, Peter, *Easy Riders, Raging Bulls: How the Sex 'n' Drugs 'n' Rock 'n' Roll Generation Saved Hollywood*, London: Bloomsbury, 1999.

Biskind, Peter, *Down and Dirty Pictures: Miramax, Sundance and the Rise of Independent Film*, London: Bloomsbury, 2005.

Boland, Bridget, *Screen Writing*, London: British Film Institute, 1945.

Bondanella, Peter, *A History of Italian Cinema*, New York: Continuum, 2009.

Bordwell, David, Janet Staiger, and Kristin Thompson, *The Classical Hollywood Cinema: Film Style and Mode of Production to 1960*, London: Routledge, 1985.

Bordwell, David, *The Way Hollywood Tells It: Story and Style in Modern Movies*, Berkeley: University of California Press, 2006.

Brik, Osip, 'From the Theory and Practice of a Script Writer', trans. Diana Matias, *Screen* 15.3 (1974), pp. 95–103.

Brunette, Peter, *Wong Kar-Wai* (Urbana: University of Illinois Press, 2005).

Burch, Noël, 'Primitivism and the Avant-Gardes: A Dialectical Approach', in Philip Rosen, ed., *Narrative, Apparatus, Ideology: A Film Theory Reader*, New York: Columbia University Press, 1986, pp. 483–506.

Campbell, Joseph, *The Hero with a Thousand Faces*, Princeton: Princeton University Press, 1949.

Carney, Raymond, *American Dreaming: The Films of John Cassavetes and the American Experience* (Berkeley: University of California Press, 1985).

Carney, Ray[mond], *The Films of John Cassavetes: Pragmatism, Modernism, and the Movies*, Cambridge: Cambridge University Press, 1994.

Carrière, Jean-Claude, *The Secret Language of Film*, trans. Jeremy Leggatt, London: Faber, 1995.

Carringer, Robert L., *The Making of Citizen Kane*, rev. ed., Berkeley: University of California Press, 1996.

Cawelti, John G. (ed.), *Focus on Bonnie and Clyde*, Englewood Cliffs, N.J.: Prentice-Hall, 1973.

Ceplair, Larry, and Steven Englund, *The Inquisition in Hollywood: Politics in the Film Community, 1930–1960*, NY: Anchor/Doubleday, 1980.

Charity, Tom, *John Cassavetes: Lifeworks*, London: Omnibus, 2001.

Complete Catalogue of Genuine and Original "Star" Films (Moving Pictures) Manufactured by Geo. Méliès of Paris, New York: undated [1904?].

Corliss, Richard, *Talking Pictures: Screenwriters in the American Cinema* [1974] New York: Overlook, 1985.

Cowie, Peter, *The Godfather Book*, London: Faber, 1997.

Crisp, Colin, *The Classic French Cinema, 1930–1960*, Bloomington: Indiana University Press, 1993.

Decherney, Peter, 'Copyright Dupes: Piracy and New Media in Edison v. Lubin (1903)', *Film History* 19.2 (2007), pp. 109–24.

Deutelbaum, Marshall, 'Structural Patterning in the Lumière Film', *Wide Angle* 3.1 (1979), pp. 29–37.

Eisenstein, Sergei, 'The Form of the Script', in *Selected Works, vol. 1: Writings, 1922–34*, trans. and ed. Richard Taylor, London: BFI, 1988, pp. 134–35.

Elsaesser, Thomas, ed., *Early Cinema: Space, Frame, Narrative*, London: BFI, 1990.

Elsaesser, Thomas, ed., *The BFI Companion to German Cinema*, London: BFI, 1999.

Emerson, John, and Anita Loos, *How to Write Photoplays*, New York: James A. McCann, 1920.

Emrich, David, *Hollywood, Colorado: The Selig Polyscope Company and The Colorado Motion Picture Company*, Lakewood, Colorado: Post Modern Company, 1997.

Ezra, Elizabeth, *Georges Méliès: The Birth of the Auteur*, Manchester: Manchester UP, 2000.

Fainaru, Dan (ed.), *Theo Angelopoulos: Interviews*, Jackson: University Press of Mississippi, 2001.

Ferrer, Daniel, and Michael Groden, 'Introduction: A Genesis of French Genetic Criticism', in Jed Deppman, Daniel Ferrer and Michael Groden (eds), *Genetic Criticism: Texts and Avant-texts*, Philadelphia: University of Pennsylvania Press, 2004, pp. 1–16.

Field, Syd, *Screenplay: The Foundations of Screenwriting*, New York: Dell, 1979.

Fischer, Lucy, *Sunrise: A Song of Two Humans*, London: BFI, 1998.

Francke, Lizzie, *Script Girls: Women Screenwriters in Hollywood*, London: BFI, 1994.

Frazer, John, *Artificially Arranged Scenes: The Films of Georges Méliès*, Boston: G.K. Hall, 1979.

Friedman, Lester D., *Bonnie and Clyde*, London: British Film Institute, 2000.

Gassner, John, and Dudley Nichols, eds., *Twenty Best Film Plays*, New York: Crown, 1943.

Gaudreault, André, 'Detours in Film Narrative: The Development of Cross-Cutting', *Cinema Journal* 19.1 (1979), pp. 39–59.

Gaudreault, André, 'The Infringement of Copyright Laws and Its Effects (1900–1906)', in Thomas Elsaesser (ed.), *Early Cinema: Space, Frame, Narrative*, London: BFI, 1990, pp. 114–22.

Geduld, Harry M. ed., *Film Makers on Film Making*, Bloomington: Indiana UP, 1967.

Goldman, William, *Adventures in the Screen Trade: A Personal View of Hollywood and Screenwriting* [1984], London: Futura, 1985.

Gordon, Robert S. C., *Bicycle Thieves*, London: British Film Institute, 2008.

Gulino, Paul Joseph, *Screenwriting: The Sequence Approach*, New York: Continuum, 2004.

Gunning, Tom, 'The Cinema of Attractions: Early Film, the Spectator and the Avant-Garde, *Wide Angle* 8.3–4 (1986), reprinted in Thomas Elsaesser, ed., *Early Cinema: Space, Frame, Narrative*, London: BFI, 1990, pp. 56–62.

Haag, Judith H., and Hillis R. Cole Jr., eds, *The Complete Guide to Standard Script Formats, Part 1: The Screenplay*, Los Angeles: CMC, 1980.

Hauge, Michael, *Writing Screenplays That Sell*, Harmondsworth: Elm Tree, 1989.

Hayward, Susan, 'State, Culture and the Cinema: Jack Lang's Strategies for the French Film Industry 1981–93', *Screen* 34.4 (1993), pp. 380–91.

Hempel, Rolf, *Carl Mayer: Ein Autor Schreibt mit der Kamera*, Berlin: Henschelverlag, 1968.

Henderson-Bland, Robert, *From Manger to Cross: The Story of the World-Famous Film of the Life of Jesus*, London: Hodder and Stoughton, 1922.

Herman, Lewis, *A Practical Manual of Screen Playwriting for Theater and Television Films* [1952], Cleveland: Forum, 1963.

Higham, Charles, *Howard Hughes: The Secret Life*, New York: G.B. Putnam, 1993.

Hiltunen, Ari, *Aristotle in Hollywood*, Bristol: Intellect, 2002.

Horton, Andrew, *The Films of Theo Angelopoulos: A Cinema of Contemplation*, Princeton, N.J.: Princeton University Press, 1997.

Hunter, Lew, *Screenwriting*, London: Robert Hale, 1994.

Igelström, Ann, 'Communication and the Various Voices of the Screenplay Text', *Journal of Screenwriting* 4.1 (2013), pp. 43–56.

Ingemanson, Birgitta, 'The Screenplays of Ingmar Bergman: Personification and Olfactory Detail', *Literature/Film Quarterly* 12.1 (1984), pp. 26–33.

Jones, Jenny M., *The Annotated Godfather: The Complete Screenplay*, New York: Black Dog & Leventhal, 2007.

Kappelhoff, Hermann, 'Literary Exploration of the Cinematographic Image: Carl Mayer and the Poetry of Weimar Cinema', in Michael Omasta, Brigitte Mayr and Christian Cargnelli, eds, *Carl Mayer Scenar[t]ist: Ein Script von Ihm War Schon ein Film: "A Script by Carl Mayer Was Already a Film"*, Vienna: Synema, 2003, pp. 169–84.

Kasten, Jürgen, 'Green Kisses and the Laughing Horror of the Big Lie: On Darkness in Film History, on Screenplays and Lost Films', in Michael Omasta, Brigitte Mayr and Christian Cargnelli, eds, *Carl Mayer Scenar[t]ist: Ein Script von Ihm War Schon ein Film: "A Script by Carl Mayer Was Already a Film"*, Vienna: Synema, 2003, pp. 97–110.

Koskinen, Maaret, 'Out of the Past: *Saraband* and the Ingmar Bergman Archive', in Maaret Koskinen, ed., *Ingmar Bergman Revisited*, London: Wallflower, 2008, pp. 19–34.

Kracauer, Siegfied, *From Caligari to Hitler: A Psychological History of the German Film*, Princeton: Princeton University Press, 1947.

Lahue, Kalton C. ed., *Motion Picture Pioneer: The Selig Polyscope Company*, Cranbury, N.J.: A.S. Barnes, 1973.

Langebek, Line, and Spencer Parsons, 'Cassavetes' Screenwriting Practice: Improvising the Emotions', conference paper, Screenwriting in a Global & Digital World, University of Wisconsin-Madison, 22 August 2013.

Lawson, John Howard, *Theory and Technique of Playwriting and Screenwriting*, New York: G.P. Putnam's, 1949.

Lee, Lance, *A Poetics for Screenwriters*, Austin: University of Texas Press, 2001.

Leyda, Jay, and Zina Voynow, *Eisenstein at Work*, New York: Pantheon, 1982.

Liepa, Torey, 'An Uneven Marketplace of Ideas: Amateur Screenwriting, the Library of Congress and the Struggle for Copyright', *Journal of Screenwriting* 2.2 (2011), pp. 179–93.

Liepa, Torey, 'Entertaining the Public Option: The Popular Film Writing Movement and the Emergence of Writing for the American Silent Cinema', in Jill Nelmes (ed.), *Analysing the Screenplay*, London: Routledge, 2011, pp. 7–23.

Liepa, Torey, 'The Devil in the Details: Thomas Ince, Intertitles, and the Institutionalization of Writing in American Cinema', in Cynthia Lucia, Roy Grundmann, and Art Simon, eds, *The Wiley-Blackwell History of American Film*, vol. 1: *Origins to 1928* Malden, MA: Blackwell, 2012, pp. 271–92.

Loughney, Patrick, 'In the Beginning Was the Word: Six Pre-Griffith Motion Picture Scenarios', *Iris* 2.1 (1984), pp. 17–31.

Loughney, Patrick, 'From *Rip Van Winkle* to *Jesus of Nazareth*: Thoughts on the Origins of the American Screenplay', *Film History* 9.3 (1997), pp. 277–89.

Loughney, Patrick, 'Appendix: Selected Examples of Early Scenario/Screenplays in the Library of Congress', *Film History* 9.3 (1997), pp. 290–99.

Luttrell, Esther, *Tools of the Screen Writing Trade*, rev. ed., Mt. Dora, Fla.: Broadcast Club of America, 1998.

Macdonald, Ian W., 'Finding the Needle: How Readers See Screen Ideas', *Journal of Media Practice* 4.3 (2003), pp. 27–39.

Macdonald, Ian W., 'Disentangling the Screen Idea', *Journal of Media Practice* 5.2 (2004), pp. 89–99.

Macdonald, Ian W., 'Screenwriting in Britain 1895–1929', in Jill Nelmes (ed.), *Analysing the Screenplay*, London: Routledge, 2011, pp. 44–67.

Macdonald, Ian W., and Jacob U. U. Jacob, 'Lost and Gone for Ever? The Search for Early British Screenplays', *Journal of Screenwriting* 2.2 (2011), pp. 161–77.

Maltby, Richard, ' "Nobody Knows Everything": Post-Classical Historiographies and Consolidated Entertainment', in Steve Neale and Murray Smith, eds, *Contemporary Hollywood Cinema*, London: Routledge, 1988, pp. 21–44.

Mamet, David, *A Whore's Profession: Notes and Essays*, London: Faber, 1994.

Maras, Steven, *Screenwriting: History, Theory and Practice*, London: Wallflower, 2009.

Maras, Steven, 'In Search of "Screenplay": Terminological Traces in the Library of Congress *Catalog of Copyright Entries: Cumulative Series*, 1912–20', *Film History* 21.4 (2009), pp. 346–58.

Marion, Frances, *How to Write and Sell Film Stories*, New York: Covici-Friede, 1937.

Martin, Ann, and Virginia M. Clark, 'A Guide to the Microfilm Edition of *What Women Wrote: Scenarios 1912–1929*', Frederick, MD: University Press of America, 1987.

McBride, Joseph, *Writing in Pictures: Screenwriting Made (Mostly) Painless*, New York: Vintage, 2012.

McCreadie, Marsha, *The Women Who Write the Movies: From Frances Marion to Nora Ephron*, New York: Birch Lane, 1994.

McGilligan, Patrick, *Backstory: Interviews with Screenwriters of Hollywood's Golden Age*, Berkeley: University of California Press, 1986.

McKee, Robert, *Story: Substance, Structure, Style, and the Principles of Screenwriting*, London: Methuen, 1998.

Millard, Kathryn, 'After the Typewriter: The Screenplay in a Digital Era', *Journal of Screenwriting* 1.1 (2010), pp. 11–25.

Millard, Kathryn, 'The Screenplay as Prototype', in Jill Nelmes (ed.), *Analysing the Screenplay*, London: Routledge, 2011, pp. 142–57.

Millennium Film Journal 25, Summer 1991.

Minett, Mark, 'Altman Unscripted?', conference paper, Screenwriting in a Global & Digital World, University of Wisconsin-Madison, 22 August 2013.

Morris, Nathalie, 'Unpublished Scripts in BFI Special Collections: A Few Highlights', *Journal of Screenwriting* 1.1 (2010), pp. 197–202.

Murphy, J. J., *Me and You and Memento and Fargo: How Independent Screenplays Work*, New York: Continuum, 2007.

Murphy, J. J., 'Cinema as Provocation: Norman Mailer's Assault on the Screenplay', conference paper, Screenwriting in a Global & Digital World, University of Wisconsin-Madison, 22 August 2013.

Musser, Charles, 'The Early Cinema of Edwin Porter', *Cinema Journal* 19.1 (1979), pp. 138.

Musser, Charles, *Thomas A. Edison Papers: A Guide to Motion Picture Catalogs by American Producers and Distributors, 1894–1908: A Microfilm Edition*, Frederick, MD: University Publications of America, 1985.

Musser, Charles, *The Emergence of Cinema: The American Screen to 1907*, New York: Scribner's, 1990.

Musser, Charles, *Before the Nickelodeon: Edwin S. Porter and the Edison Manufacturing Company*, Berkeley: University of California Press, 1991.

Nash, Constance, and Virginia Oakey, *The Screenwriter's Handbook: What to Write, How to Write It, Where to Sell It*, New York: Barnes and Noble, 1978.

Neale, Steve, and Murray Smith, eds, *Contemporary Hollywood Cinema*, London: Routledge, 1988.

Nelmes, Jill (ed.), *Analysing the Screenplay*, London: Routledge, 2011.

Niver, Kemp R., *The First Twenty Years: A Segment of Film History*, Los Angeles: Artisan, 1968.

Niver, Kemp R. (ed.), *Biograph Bulletins 1896–1908*, Los Angeles: Locare Research Group, 1971.

Norman, Marc, *What Happens Next: A History of American Screenwriting*, London: Aurum, 2008.

Omasta, Michael, Brigitte Mayr and Christian Cargnelli, eds, *Carl Mayer Scenar[t]ist: Ein Script von Ihm War Schon ein Film: "A Script by Carl Mayer Was Already a Film"*, Vienna: Synema, 2003.

Parigi, Stefania, *Cinema—Italy*, trans. Sam Rohdie, Manchester: Manchester University Press, 2009.

Penn, Arthur, 'Making Waves: The Directing of *Bonnie and Clyde*', in Lester D. Friedman, ed., *Arthur Penn's Bonnie and Clyde*, Cambridge: Cambridge University Press, 1999, pp. 11–31.

Powers, John, 'A Pony Not to Be Ridden: Screenwriting and the Avant-Garde Cinema', conference paper, Screenwriting in a Global & Digital World, University of Wisconsin-Madison, 22 August 2013.

Pratt, George C., *Spellbound in Darkness: Readings in the History and Criticism of the Silent Film*, vol. 1 Rochester, NY: University of Rochester Press, 1966.

Price, Steven, *The Screenplay: Authorship, Theory and Criticism*, Basingstoke: Palgrave, 2010.

Price, Steven, 'The First Screenplays? American Mutoscope and Biograph Scenarios Revisited', *Journal of Screenwriting* 2.2 (2011), pp. 195–213.

Price, Steven, 'Character in the Screenplay Text', in Jill Nelmes (ed.), *Analysing the Screenplay*, London: Routledge, 2011, pp. 201–16.

Price, Steven, 'The Screenplay: An Accelerated Critical History', *Journal of Screenwriting* 4.1 (2013), pp. 87–97.

Proceedings of the Research Council, Quarterly Meeting, 15 December 1932', *Academy of Motion Picture Arts & Sciences Technical Bulletin*, Supplement 19, 23 December 1932.

Pudovkin, Vsevolod, 'The Film Script (The Theory of the Script)', in Richard Taylor (ed.), *Vsevolod Pudovkin: Selected Essays* (London: Seagull, 2006), pp. 32–64.

Quigley, Austin E., *The Modern Stage and Other Worlds*, London: Methuen, 1985.

Ramsaye, Terry, *A Million and One Nights: A History of the Motion Picture through 1925*, New York: Simon & Schuster, 1926.

Raynauld, Isabelle, 'Written Scenarios of Early French Cinema: Screenwriting Practices in the First Twenty Years', *Film History* 9.3 (1997), pp. 257–68.

Riley, Christopher, *The Hollywood Standard: The Complete and Authoritative Guide to Script Format and Style*, 2nd ed., Studio City, CA: Michael Wiese, 2009.

Robinson, David, *Georges Méliès: Father of Film Fantasy*, London: BFI, 1993.

Robinson, David, *Das Cabinet des Dr. Caligari*, London: BFI, 1997.

Rossholm, Anna Sofia, 'Tracing the Voice of the Auteur: *Persona* and the Ingmar Bergman Archive', *Journal of Screenwriting* 4.2 (2013), pp. 135–48.

Rush, Jeff, and Cynthia Baughman, 'Language as Narrative Voice: The Poetics of the Highly Inflected Screenplay', *Journal of Film and Video* 49.3 (1997), pp. 28–37.

Schary, Dore [and Charles Palmer], *Case History of a Movie*, New York: Random House, 1950.

Scheunemann, Dietrich, 'Once More on Wiene's *The Cabinet of Dr. Caligari*', in Dietrich Scheunemann, ed., *Expressionist Film: New Perspectives*, New York: Camden House, 2003, pp. 125–56.

Schwarz, Alexander, *Der Geschriebene Film: Drehbücher des Deutschen und Russischen Stummfilms*, Munich: Diskurs Film, 1994.

Seymour, James, 'Shooting Script Format', 26 March 1944, James Seymour Collection, Writers Guild of America West Records, Writers Guild Foundation Library and Archive.

Sitney, P. Adams, *Vital Crises in Italian Cinema*, Austin: University of Texas Press, 1985.

Smith, Alison, 'People 1960–2004: The Other Auteurs: Producers, Cinematographers and Scriptwriters', in Michael Temple and Michael Witt, eds, *The French Cinema Book*, London: British Film Institute, 2004, pp. 194–208.

Smith, Murray, 'Theses on the Philosophy of Hollywood History', in Steve Neale and Murray Smith, eds, *Contemporary Hollywood Cinema*, London: Routledge, 1988, pp. 3–20.

Sopocy, Martin, 'French and British Influences in Porter's *American Fireman*', *Film History* 1.2 (1987), pp. 137–48.

Staiger, Janet, 'Dividing Labor for Production Control: Thomas Ince and the Rise of the Studio System', *Cinema Journal* 18.2 (1979), pp. 16–25.

Staiger, Janet, 'Mass-Produced Photoplays: Economic and Signifying Practices in the First Years of Hollywood', *Wide Angle* 4.3 (1980), pp. 12–27.

Staiger, Janet, 'Blueprints for Feature Films: Hollywood's Continuity Scripts', in Tino Balio (ed.), *The American Film Industry*, rev. ed. Madison: University of Wisconsin Press, 1985, pp. 173–92.

Staiger, Janet, 'The Hollywood Mode of Production to 1930', in David Bordwell, Janet Staiger and Kristin Thompson, *The Classical Hollywood Cinema: Film Style and Mode of Production to 1960*, London: Routledge, 1985, pp. 85–153.

Staiger, Janet, 'The Hollywood Mode of Production, 1930–60', in David Bordwell, Janet Staiger and Kristin Thompson, *The Classical Hollywood Cinema: Film Style and Mode of Production to 1960*, London: Routledge, 1985, pp. 309–37.

Steene, Birgitta, *Ingmar Bergman: A Reference Guide*, Amsterdam: Amsterdam University Press, 2005.

Stempel, Tom, *FrameWork: A History of Screenwriting in the American Film*, 2nd ed., New York: Continuum, 1991.

Sternberg, Claudia, *Written for the Screen: The American Motion-Picture Screenplay as Text*, Tübingen: Stauffenburg, 1997.

Szczepanik, Petr, 'Micropolitics of Screenplay Development: A Political History', conference paper, Screenwriting in a Global & Digital World, University of Madison-Wisconsin, 21 August 2013.

Taylor, Richard, *The Politics of the Soviet Cinema, 1917–1929*, Cambridge: Cambridge University Press, 1979.

Taylor, Richard (ed.), *Vsevolod Pudovkin: Selected Essays*, London: Seagull, 2006.

Taylor, Richard, and Ian Christie (eds), *The Film Factory: Russian and Soviet Cinema in Documents, 1896–1939*, London: Routledge, 1988.

Temple, Michael, and Michael Witt (eds), *The French Cinema Book*, London: British Film Institute, 2004.

Thompson, Kristin, *Storytelling in the New Hollywood: Understanding Classical Narrative Technique*, Cambridge, Mass.: Harvard University Press, 1999.

Thompson, Kristin, 'Early Alternatives to the Hollywood Mode of Production: Implications for Europe's Avant-Gardes', in Lee Grieveson and Peter Krämer, eds, *The Silent Cinema Reader*, London: Routledge, 2004, pp. 349–67.

Tieber, Claus, *Schreiben für Hollywood: Das Drehbuch im Studiosystem*, Vienna: Lit Verlag GmbH, 2008.

Truffaut, François, 'A Certain Tendency of the French Cinema', in Bill Nichols (ed.), *Movies and Methods: An Anthology*, Berkeley: University of California Press, 1976, pp. 224–37.

Vogler, Christopher, *The Writer's Journey: Mythic Structure for Storytellers and Screenwriters*, 2nd ed., London: Pan, 1998.

Vonderau, Patrick, ' "Two Figures Stand High up on a Cliff: Shadowy": On Carl Mayer's Screenplay *Der Gang in die Nacht*', in Michael Omasta, Brigitte Mayr and Christian Cargnelli, eds, *Carl Mayer Scenar[t]ist: Ein Script von Ihm War Schon ein Film: "A Script by Carl Mayer Was Already a Film"*, Vienna: Synema, 2003, pp. 111–22.

Voytilla, Stuart, *Myth and the Movies: Discovering the Mythic Structure of 50 Unforgettable Films*, Studio City, CA: Michael Wiese Productions, 1999.

Youngblood, Denise J., *Soviet Cinema in the Silent Era, 1918–1935*, Ann Arbor: UMI Research Press, 1985.

Zavattini, Cesare, 'A Thesis on Neo-Realism' [1952–54], in David Overbey, ed. and trans., *Springtime in Italy: A Reader on Neo-Realism*, London: Talisman, 1978, pp. 67–78.

Index

87688152R00162

Made in the USA
San Bernardino, CA
06 September 2018